WM 60 MAT

2014

Approved Mental Health Prac

Approved Mental Health Practice

Essential Themes for Students and Practitioners

Edited by

Sarah Matthews

Philip O'Hare

Jill Hemmington

First published 2014 by
PALGRAVE MACMILLAN

Palgrave Macmillan in the UK is an imprint of Macmillan Publishers Limited, registered in England, company number 785998, of Houndmills, Basingstoke, Hampshire RG21 6XS.

Palgrave Macmillan in the US is a division of St Martin's Press LLC, 175 Fifth Avenue, New York, NY 10010.

Palgrave Macmillan is the global academic imprint of the above companies and has companies and representatives throughout the world.

Palgrave® and Macmillan® are registered trademarks in the United States, the United Kingdom, Europe and other countries.

ISBN 978–1–137–00013–2

This book is printed on paper suitable for recycling and made from fully managed and sustained forest sources. Logging, pulping and manufacturing processes are expected to conform to the environmental regulations of the country of origin.

A catalogue record for this book is available from the British Library.

A catalog record for this book is available from the Library of Congress.

Printed in China

Contents

Abbreviations

AC	Approved Clinician
ADASS	Association of Directors of Adult Social Services
AMHP	Approved Mental Health Professional
AMP	Approved Medical Practitioner
ASW	Approved Social Worker
BASW	British Association of Social Workers
BDP	Borderline Personality Disorder
BMA	British Medical Association
BSL	British Sign Language
CCW	Care Council Wales
CIA	Critical Incident Analysis
CPA	Care Programme Approach
CPN	Community Psychiatric Nurse
CQC	Care Quality Commission
CRHT	Crisis Resolution and Home Treatment
CSIP	Care Services Improvement Partnership
CTO	Compulsory Treatment Order
DCA	Department of Constitutional Affairs
DDA	Disability Discrimination Act
DEFRA	Department of the Environment, Food and Rural Affairs
DH	Department of Health
DHSSPS	Department of Health, Social Services and Public Safety (Northern Ireland)
DOLS	Deprivation of Liberty Safeguards
DSM	Diagnostic and Statistical Manual
EBP	Evidence-Based Practice
ECHR	European Court of Human Rights
GSCC	General Social Care Council
GP	General Practitioner
HRA	Human Rights Act
HSCIC	Health and Social Care Information Centre
HCPC	Health and Care Professions Council
IMHA	Independent Mental Health Advocate
ISL	Irish Sign Language
LGA	Local Government Association

LRA	Least Restrictive Alternative
MCA	Mental Capacity Act
MHA	Mental Health Act
MHAC	Mental Health Act Commission
MHCT	Mental Health (Care and Treatment) Scotland Act
MHO	Mental Health Officer
MHT	Mental Health Tribunals
MIND	National Association of Mental Health
MP	Member of Parliament
MWC	Mental Welfare Commission
MWO	Mental Welfare Officer
NHS	National Health Service
NIMHE	National Institute for Mental Health England
NMC	Nursing and Midwifery Council
NMHDU	National Mental Health Development Unit
NR	Nearest Relative
NWW	New Ways of Working
OT	Occupational Therapist
PCF	Professional Capabilities Framework
PCT	Primary Care Trust
PTSD	Post Traumatic Stress Disorder
RC	Responsible Clinicians
RCN	Royal College of Nursing
RCP	Royal College of Psychiatrists
RCT	Randomized Control Trial
RMO	Responsible Medical Officer
SCIE	Social Care Institute of Excellence
SSI	Social Services Inspectorate
SSSC	Scottish Social Services Care Council
TCSW	The College of Social Work
TINA	There is no alternative
UK	United Kingdom
USA	United States of America
WAG	Welsh Assembly Government
WNMC	Welsh Nursing and Midwifery Council

Contributors

Daisy Bogg is a qualified and HCPC registered social worker and practicing AMHP and is co-chair of the Social Perspectives Network (SPN) for mental health. She is currently undertaking PhD research at the University of York exploring AMHP attitudes towards coexisting mental health and substance misuse issues and is the author of a number of social work text books, including *Values and Ethics in Mental Health*.

Gavin Davidson is a Lecturer in Social Work in the School of Sociology, Social Policy and Social Work, Queen's University Belfast. Before moving to Queen's in 2008 he worked in adult mental health services as a social worker, team leader and Approved Social Worker. His main areas of research have been in mental health including: the use of compulsory powers; the interface between mental health and child protection services; and the associations between childhood adversity and later mental health. He is the social work representative on the Department of Health, Social Services and Public Safety's Reference Group for the Mental Capacity (Health, Welfare and Finance) Bill.

Roger Davis is an Open University in Scotland staff tutor in the faculty of Health and Social Care. He has a professional background in social work practice, mental health work and for the last 15 years in social work education. He presently chairs modules in social work practice and social work law in Scotland, co-editor of the Scottish social work law module Reader and contributor to other UK social work publications.

Jean Gordon is a researcher, trainer and writer in mental health, law and social work education. She has worked as a social worker and MHO in a range of hospital, community mental health and supported employment settings in Scotland. Recent work has included co-editing a book (with Roger Davis), *Social Work and the Law in Scotland*, and developing a freely available Open University online course about personalization and self-directed support in Scotland.

Jill Hemmington is a Senior Lecturer and Programme Leader for the Approved Mental Health Professional programme at the University of Central Lancashire. She is also a practicing AMHP and is undertaking research as part of a PhD exploring decision making and professional wisdom within AMHP practice. Jill also teaches mental health as part of the post- and undergraduate Social Work programmes at UCLan. Jill's professional background is in Mental Health Social Work and management within a multi-disciplinary community mental health team setting.

Sarah Matthews is a qualified, registered social worker. She has worked extensively in Adult Social Services, primarily within mental health, practising as an Approved Social Worker and senior manager in an inner city multi-disciplinary setting. Sarah spent 9 years as an Area Commissioner for the Mental Health Act Commission. Currently, Sarah heads the Social Work Degree programme for the Open University in the North West of England and in Yorkshire and has edited a number of social work text books including *Professional Development in Social Work; Complex Issues in Practice*. She is undertaking a part time PhD in Social Work at the University of Manchester investigating the role and experiences of the Approved Mental Health Professional.

Anthea Murr, a registered social worker, is a lecturer at Wolverhampton University with interests in mental health and practice education. Anthea began her career in the voluntary sector in inner city advice centres. After qualifying she practiced in community mental health teams in rural areas prior to taking work at Wolverhampton University in 2001.

Philip O'Hare is a Principal Lecturer in the School of Social Work at the University of Central Lancashire. He teaches across several courses on the theme of mental health social care, law and policy. He was previously a mental health social worker and Approved Social Worker with Liverpool City Council. His main areas of research include international perspectives on compulsion and working across professional boundaries in mental health care.

David Pilgrim is Professor of Health and Social Policy at the University of Liverpool. He has worked at the boundary between clinical psychology and medical sociology for the past 20 years and has produced over 60 articles in peer reviewed journals, based upon his research into mental health policy and practice. *A Sociology of Mental Health and Illness* (3rd edition), co-authored with Anne Rogers, won the British Medical Association's medical book of the year award for 2006. His other books include *Key Concepts in Mental Health* (3rd edition to appear in 2014) Currently he is writing a book on critical realism and mental health.

Julie Ridley is a Reader in Social Policy and Practice at the University of Central Lancashire. Prior to joining UCLan she has held a number of research, information technology and development posts in local government and in the independent sector. Julie's research work has been mainly in the broad area of health and community care. Her work has focused on disability issues, particularly policy and practice developments in learning disability and mental health. More recently she has managed studies for the Scottish Government of early implementation of new mental health legislation and worked on projects evaluating Self-Directed Support (SDS) test sites, Supported Employment and the effectiveness of ethnic matching in adoption services. She is currently lead for a national implementation project for the Department of Health translating the IMHA research findings into practice.

Helen Spandler is a Reader in Mental Health in the School of Social Work at the University of Central Lancashire. She has published widely on critical and alternative approaches to mental health care. She is on the editorial collective of *Asylum*: the magazine for democratic psychiatry (www. asylumonline.net).

Tim Spencer-Lane is a lawyer in the public law team at the Law Commission and was in charge of the review of adult social care. The Commission's final report on adult social care was published in 2011 and formed the basis of the Care Bill 2013 which was introduced into Parliament in 2013. He is currently working on a review of health and social care professional regulation which is due to report in 2014. Tim previously worked as the policy adviser to the Law Society on mental health and disability law, and is also an associate lecturer with the Open University.

Amanda Taylor is a senior lecturer at the University of Central Lancashire. Her professional background is as a registered social work practitioner with an interest in mental health, deafness and the impact of the lived experience on life stage development and functionality. Amanda practiced in mental health and specialist provision for Deaf adults and children in Northern Ireland before moving to the UK mainland four years ago to pursue her academic career. She teaches across a range of subjects on post- and undergraduate social work and social care courses.

Tamsin Waterhouse, a registered social worker, is a teaching fellow at the University of Birmingham with interests in mental health and practice education. Since qualifying Tamsin has worked in a community mental health team in a rural county and as a trainer. She has many years' experience as an Approved Social Worker (and more latterly an Approved Mental Health Professional). She has been a Best Interest Assessor since 2009. She joined the University in 2012 where she teaches on a range of programmes.

Introduction

Sarah Matthews, Philip O'Hare and Jill Hemmington

This book sets out to explore a range of issues as they affect the particular statutory responsibility of approved mental health practice. As editors, we agonized over how best to refer to this responsibility; it is undertaken in a range of countries and under a variety of Mental Health Acts; it involves statutory duties which differ, albeit slightly, and it also attracts different titles. We finally settled on the phrase *approved mental health practice*, which for us best captured the essence of 'the doing'. Additionally, we know that the responsibility can be undertaken by a range of qualified professionals and, therefore, we decided to use the term *approved mental health practitioner* to refer to 'the doer'. We acknowledge that our chosen terminology is closely matched with the role title, Approved Mental Health Professional (AMHP), as it is currently known in England and Wales, and that while this might be the biggest readership, the proximity could have two consequences; first that the book will be perceived as being relevant only to this group – it is not – and, second, that individual authors and in turn the reader might conflate both, giving rise to confusion and irritation. We trust that our explanation and editorial stringency assuages both.

Why then did we put ourselves through the agony? Approved mental health practice has undergone, or is undergoing, review in each nation of the United Kingdom, with differing outcomes. In Scotland approved mental health practice remains an exclusive responsibility of social workers, who are given the title Mental Health Officer (MHO). For England and Wales, the responsibility embraces a broader range of professionals namely Social Workers, Mental Health Nurses, Psychologists and Occupational Therapists with the working title of Approved Mental Health Professional (AMHP). The review of mental health legislation in Northern Ireland is ongoing, but it is anticipated that approved mental health practice will remain within the social work domain where it currently has the job title of Approved Social Worker (ASW). Throughout this book we will refer to the acronyms MHO, AMHP, or ASW only when the discussion is jurisdiction specific. In all nations in the United Kingdom, the main responsibility nonetheless remains the same; to undertake an assessment of a person with a mental disorder, taking into account social circumstances, and to consider the need for an

1

application for formal admission to a psychiatric hospital. Approved mental health practice as we refer to it here is also undertaken internationally; the discussion herein does in our opinion also apply, and is a theme to which later editions will return.

Drawing from the strength of a collaborative interest group from the Open University, a national provider of the Social Work Degree and the University of Central Lancashire (an AMHP programme provider in the North West of England) the book is timely. There is currently no other textbook that provides a critical assessment of the elements of approved mental health practice. Each approved mental health practitioner has to undergo a formal process of learning and assessment before they are approved. Much of this education, in our experience, covers knowledge and application of the law comprehensively. There are also a number of well-respected textbooks that support these elements. We contend that the education around other requirements, including the social perspective, independence, values and principles is less developed or is, at the very least, inconsistent. Moreover, no recognized textbook exists that challenges the reader to reflect critically upon these elements of approved mental health practice. It is our intention to provide such a text. Moreover, as we also firmly believe that research needs to be embedded into practice, we also want to open the reader's eyes as to how this might be achieved.

The replacement of the General Social Care Council in England with new regulators, the Health and Care Professions Council (HCPC) now requires a new framework against which the education of approved mental health practitioners should be judged; a framework which has to encompass not just the Professional Capabilities Framework for Social Work, but also satisfy the continuing professional development frameworks of all eligible professionals. The HCPC published formal criteria for approving and monitoring AMHP programmes in September 2013 (Health and Care Professions Council, 2013). The key message reinforces the quality of training in providing safe and effective AMHPs within a framework of autonomous decision making. This book therefore, arrives at a significant time for AMHP training providers in England as they review their programmes.

It is our belief that the issues discussed within this book are relevant to all who undertake approved mental health practice regardless of professional, national or legal background, as it is defined herein. We wanted to bring together chapters written from a variety of perspectives each of which seek not to provide answers to the 'doing' but, rather, to reflect critically upon and question it. This, then, is not a practical guide. It is, rather, a collection of chapters designed to challenge the reader's perceptions of the criticality and capability of approved mental health practice and, by being reflective, evidence based and ethical, to become better approved mental health practitioners.

Structure of the book

In the interests of cohesion, each chapter has a similar format. First, we introduce each chapter with an 'editors' voice' to set the scene. The individual authors then argue their respective case drawing on theory, research and practice where, and if, appropriate. The editors conclude each chapter by posing a number of reflective questions which we hope will facilitate further examination and analysis. These questions we suggest are crucial to the debate as to what constitutes effective approved mental health practice. It is our intention, in so doing, to engage the reader in an active dialogue, whether as a learner, a practitioner, an educator, manager or policy maker.

Chapter 1, by Sarah Matthews, discusses the theory and research about approved mental health practice and brings them together in a way not previously available. Here the social perspective is fundamental. The author discusses what this means and whether its application is effective. A correlating theme is that of independence. The author challenges the reader to reflect again upon what this means and also questions its effectiveness. Both are brought into sharp focus by the challenge that opening up the responsibility to other professionals might bring. The section closes with a précis of the research into approved mental health practice that has taken place since the 1980s. It will be seen that to begin with activity was low, but this gradually increased. Simultaneously, education of approved mental health practitioners became more formalized and as a result more effective. Paradoxically, at the same time practitioners reported increased levels of stress. Currently available research appears to echo this. There are high levels of activity and also continued high levels of reported stress among practitioners. In this opening chapter the reader is asked to reflect upon what it is like to experience being an approved mental health practitioner and to pick up on underpinning themes that are considered throughout the book.

Chapters 2 and 3 pull together the legislative context across all regions of the United Kingdom. Written by Tim Spencer-Lane, who was present throughout much of the determinations in England and Wales, Chapter 2 sets out to provide a flavour of the protracted period of consultation and review of mental health legislation at that time. Here the reader is introduced to the tension that exists in all approved mental health practice between individual rights to liberty and physical integrity and the duty to protect vulnerable people and the public from harm. As editors we contend that all approved mental health practitioners have to embody this tension. Chapter 2 highlights that, despite initial calls for a root and branch review, ultimately, the legislation in England and Wales was merely amended; a lost opportunity and a disappointment for all who had hitherto advocated the need for an overhaul. One of the more significant changes discussed, particularly pertinent to this book is the replacement of the Approved Social

Worker with the newly reconfigured role of the Approved Mental Health Professional and with it the extension of the role to other professional groups. The impact of divergence across the nations of the United Kingdom is a crucial theme for this book as highlighted in Chapter 1 and carried through this and subsequent chapters. Lastly this chapter outlines the controversies that accompanied the legislative amendments, contrasting these with other legislative changes of the time which it is suggested were brought about, by contrast, in the spirit of collaboration and goodwill.

No text book on approved mental health practice in the United Kingdom can ignore intranational perspectives and this is a central theme to this book. Chapter 3, by Jean Gordon and Roger Davis, builds on the legislative context of Chapter 2 to widen the debate to changes that have occurred in Scotland or about to occur in Northern Ireland. A discussion is held about the similarities and differences in each nation of the United Kingdom including the different outcomes of the reform of legislation, which has resulted in maintaining the role as a social work one in some nations while opening it up to other professionals in others. Finally the authors call for further research into approved mental health practice.

In Chapter 4, David Pilgrim brings to a close the opening chapters of the book by asking the reader to consider a number of questions as a reminder to all approved mental health practitioners to revisit their sanctioned role. Consider, he suggests, what is actually meant by mental health law and mental health policy? How do practitioners come to be doing what they are doing and thinking what they think? This is for us a fundamental mind-set for this text.

Despite the review of mental health legislation in the United Kingdom, the responsibilities of approved mental health practitioners have remained mainly unaltered. There are, however, a number of critical issues for education and practice that arise from the shift in focus away from the sole domain of social work and from the impact of devolved legislation. There is apprehension that these changes threaten some fundamental aspects of approved mental health practice.

In Chapter 5 Helen Spandler, begins this debate by asking the reader to consider the nature of psychiatric diagnostic criteria in relation to how this impacts on the course and outcomes of approved mental health practice. She provides a critique of the standard medical model approach to managing psychiatric illness and the prescription of medication as a cure and challenges future approved mental health practitioners to evaluate a range of different treatment models and interventions in order to develop practice that reflects current evidence and theoretical analysis of recovery.

We know that many service users have significant problems in their lives and, when there is a superimposed mental illness, it becomes difficult to determine what the 'problem' is, or indeed *whose* problem it is. In Chapter 6

Daisy Bogg, discusses the ethics and values of approved mental health practice and in particular how ethical considerations underpin it; considerations include compulsory detention and treatment, informed consent and capacity, and treatment refusal. The focus throughout is how an approved mental health practitioner reflects on value-based decision making in the context of compulsory mental health assessments. This chapter provides a broad analysis of structural and organizational ethics with a practice focus on the impact of these on decision making. It complements Chapter 7, which focuses on an inter-cultural-communication- and inter-personal-skills-based approach to assessing diversity.

Assessing in diverse communities is fundamental to all approved mental health practice. There is considerable evidence that service users from some communities are disadvantaged within the mental health system and particularly at the point of contact with approved mental health practitioners (Hatfield, 2008). Difficult dialogues about gender, sexuality, race, ethnicity and other cultural differences are exacerbated when approved mental health practitioners do not recognize or reflect on them or are developmentally unprepared to handle them. Approved mental health practitioners in training must 'negotiate the disposition they have acquired from family and community with the new dispositions they are supposed to acquire' (Makoe, 2006, p. 374) and experienced practitioners must continue to reflect on 'difference' and diversity. Chapter 7 discusses the impact of all of this on the assessment process. Amanda Taylor and Jill Hemmington use deafness as a concept and a model to demonstrate core, transferable skills in assessing, understanding and engaging with human beings. The reader is encouraged to reflect upon how they understand a person within the context of their own culture. The chapter reflects on the ethical and cultural dynamics of the relationship between practitioner and service user, and appraises the requisite skills to work competently with 'difference', the barriers to this and the significance of the practitioner's awareness and attitude.

Arguably, approved mental health practice in rural localities is underrepresented in the literature and, in turn, poorly understood in theory and in practice. Likewise, much research refers to urban areas as if they are homogenous and findings are applied as if they are transferable to all settings. Thus, Chapter 8 reflects upon different environments and their impact on approved mental health practice. Anthea Murr and Tamsin Waterhouse explore working as an approved mental health practitioner in rural environments and discuss if there are particular skills and knowledge that practitioners use in each. The authors provide examples from practice and evidence from the literature to underpin their discussion.

Chapter 9 analyses an extensive research project that recorded service users' and carers' experiences of compulsory care and treatment in Scotland. It is important that practitioners are able to hear and reflect on service users' and carers' experiences of approved mental health practice. The chapter presents the findings and conclusions of the project including the 'voice' of service users, who have important messages and learning material for all practitioners working in approved mental health practice.

A further crucial aspect of approved mental health practice is that of the influence of the Nearest Relative. In Chapter 10, Philip O'Hare and Gavin Davidson consider the role of Nearest Relative and relate it to the issue of authority in decision making, as well as the role of the approved mental health practitioner in attempting to preserve fairness and justice.

Chapter 11 explores the evidence and knowledge base that underpins approved mental health practice. Here Philip O'Hare argues that evidence at most offers support to decisions rather than determining interventions and actions. He warns against an elevation of Evidence-Based Practice to a concept that offers certainty. 'Evidence' in this sense lends *support* to decisions rather than determining interventions and actions, and it is suggested that the practitioner's values and professional autonomy should be given equal weighting. Building on this, Chapter 12 closes the main text with reference to the inherent 'uncertainty' within approved mental health practice and how an understanding of chaos or complexity theories can go some way to allowing the approved mental health practitioner to approach the work confidently and creatively.

Our concluding section asks the reader to reflect upon the changing nature of approved mental health practice and evaluates some of the issues that are raised throughout the book. It is clear that there is much more to approved mental health practice than a technical application of the law. Moreover, approved mental health practice does not happen in an organizational or political vacuum; practitioners have to be mindful of various changes and be able to work in a multilayered, non-linear manner. Embracing and balancing these multiple realities and uncertainties will, we suggest, depict effective approved mental health practice.

There are no certainties, and all professionals will approach the work from their own viewpoint (professionally and personally). 'Best practice' in this sense rests on an aspiration to make judgements that are lawful, but also ones that are ethical and filtered through the respective Codes of Practice. The skills borne out of the capacity for critical thinking and critical reflection are, for the editors, crucial and we trust that this book has enabled its readers to engage in just these.

1

Underpinning Themes, Theories and Research

Sarah Matthews

Editors' Voice

The remit of the opening chapter is to introduce the reader to the core underpinning themes, theories and research of approved mental health practice. As is the case throughout the book, readers are asked to reflect upon what it means to be an approved mental health practitioner. Here the author focuses on areas which as editors we feel are the foundation of approved mental health practice; the social perspective and independence. We were also mindful of the sociological and psychological influences that underpin the responsibility, whether consciously or not, and these are also introduced. No book on approved mental health practice can ignore the political context; the responsibility is sanctioned in legislation and based upon decisions that reflect a wider political environment. Devolved nations add to this complexity. The chapter, therefore, asks the reader to consider the impact of political decisions, in particular the opening up of the responsibility of approved mental health practice beyond social work. Mirroring a policy of the redistribution of mental health roles in England and Wales, this change was also based on research reporting the negative impact of approved mental health practice on social workers including high levels of stress and a 'disappearing' workforce. The chapter, therefore, asks the reader to reflect upon the influence of research. These themes, theories and research add to the uncertainty common to approved mental health practice and are revisited throughout the book.

There is no doubt that the responsibility of approved mental health practice courts debate. Empirical research also reinforces what is, in effect, an underlying uncertainty. This chapter will précis the main themes, theories and research of approved mental health practice, which have hitherto neither been gathered together, nor fully explored. This, along with the relative paucity of research into responsibility is a flaw, and one which was identified as such by policy makers during the reviews of mental health legislation. This chapter contends that, to be effective, all approved mental health practitioners, regardless of their legal, national or professional background should engage not only in the requirement to apply the law effectively but also in critical reflection of the underpinning themes, theories and research identified here. This chapter therefore provides a foundation upon which the remainder of the book rests.

Themes

The social perspective

Understanding and engaging in the social perspective is generally agreed by all interested commentators to be the cornerstone of approved mental health practice and the primary model for understanding mental disorder, or providing a non-medical viewpoint. In essence, the social perspective refers to the focus on the social determinants of mental 'ill health'. These determinants are taken into consideration by approved mental health practitioners in order to highlight a different perspective, usually as a balance to the medical one, and in order to pursue alternatives to formal detention. This consideration is primarily achieved in practice by an overt assessment of social circumstance and is referred to as the approved mental health practitioners' social lens. The social perspective is a thread that permeates all formal manifestations of approved mental health practice. Preservation of this perspective is indicated in research studies (Hatfield, 2008) and its retention remains a current concern (Bogg, 2012) In addition regulations include it as a key competence and Codes of Practice also spell this out: in England the role of Approved Mental Health Professionals is to 'bring a social perspective to bear on their decision' (Department of Health, 2008, p. 36). In Scotland medical and social factors are central: there has to be a 'consideration of as much available and relevant information on the patient's medical and social circumstances' (Scottish Executive, 2005c, p. 28).

Perhaps most readily associated with social work, understanding and engaging with the social perspective is the crux of the deliberation about which profession, if any, is best able to conduct effective approved mental health practice. Nathan and Webber (2010, p. 16) view the primary function of mental health social workers as ensuring 'the long held tradition of promoting psychosocial perspectives' or 'an alternative to psychiatric hegemony'. Nonetheless, as we shall see in Chapter 2, some social work roles in mental health have been opened up to allied professionals. The review of mental health legislation in England and Wales, known as the Richardson review (outlined in detail in Chapter 2), recommended such an outcome for approved mental health practice based on the reported difficulty in retention and a disappearing workforce. The Richardson review was persuaded that the skills of Approved Social Workers were available across the mental health workforce. The redistribution of the role can, therefore, also be seen as a consequence of 'new ways of working in mental health' (Department of Health, 2007a); a progression of a policy whose rationale is to assign roles on the basis of competency rather than professional status.

The impact of opening up the responsibility of approved mental health practice in England and Wales has been greeted as both an opportunity and a threat and is primarily discussed within nursing and social work literature. Some mental health nurses were keen to embrace the responsibility as a 'sensible extension to their repertoire' (Allen, 2002). Others, such as Hurley and Linsley (2006) maintain that mental health nurses already engage in restrictive care and can easily transfer skills and knowledge from the hospital environment. To equate restrictive care with approved mental health practice is a contentious assertion, intimating as it does, a pre-emptive outcome. Nonetheless, it cannot be ignored that nurses do already work with detained patients. The responsibility of approved mental health practice, when first proposed, was, on the other hand, also perceived by nurses as potentially negative, compared with what was perceived as their therapeutic relationship with a patient; a concern that was highlighted in the Royal College of Nursing's response to the draft Mental Health bill (Royal College of Nursing, in Allen 2002). Empirical research does not wholly support this fear. Hurley and Linsley (2006) conclude that being involved in coercion could be both positive and negative; echoing earlier work which found that 'being there', through bad times as well as good, could actually strengthen any therapeutic rapport (Bowers et al., 2003, p. 965). Early indications also show that some nurses who are undertaking the responsibility are optimistic about its impact on their relationship with service users (Laing, 2012, p. 237). Further evidence is required however before any meaningful conclusion can be reached about the way in which nurses 'do' approved mental health practice, and the impact whether positive or negative this has.

From the standpoint of social workers, opening up the responsibility was initially viewed by some as a threat, and in particular, as a 'watering down' of the social perspective. In other words, the social perspective was perceived to be social work's prerogative and that without exclusivity its influence would diminish. Some even feared the end of the social work profession in mental health. There is no evidence yet to suggest that any such outcome has been realized. On the contrary, the social perspective remains embedded in the approval frameworks. The debate about the future of social work in mental health continues to occupy current commentators. Nathan and Webber (2010, p. 16) have defined the three distinct stances. The first of these they describe as traditionalist, or those who argue that social work needs to retain its distinct identity and return to its local authority location. For them this traditionalist viewpoint reverts to 'ghettoisation of mental health social work as a professional backwater' (Nathan and Webber, 2010, p. 16). Moreover, they suggest, it leaves the Health Trusts in an even stronger position to promote a bio-medical model without challenge. The second stance Nathan and Webber describe as genericist, or those who suggest that retaining distinctions between professions has no purpose. Genericists predict that there will be a mental health professional able to undertake all roles; a standpoint which mirrors contemporary policy in relation to new ways of working in metal health. But, for Nathan and Webber generic roles would mean an end of a professional base in mental health social work. The 'best' future for mental health social work they contend is eclectic, or integrated; that is they anticipate a merging of roles between social work and heath, while maintaining professional diversity (Nathan and Webber, 2010, pp. 16–17).

The future of social work in approved mental health practice where the role has been distributed is likewise occupying commentators; will practitioners be able to retain a professional diversity despite a merging of the responsibility? This question currently remains unanswered. The current evidence is that social workers make up the biggest proportion of Approved Mental Health Professionals being trained in England and Wales (General Social Care Council, 2012). Interestingly, no psychologist has yet trained while occupational therapists are also few in numbers; according to these latest statistics there are just eight occupational therapists, a figure representing just 1 per cent of the total (General Social Care Council, 2012). Initial findings into sites involved in the early implementation of new roles in mental health, including that of the Approved Mental Health Professionals, provide some insight into the reasons for uptake, or indeed lack of it! The primary reason for uptake was reported to be the need to respond to a shortage of social work applicants. Other factors such as senior management support and staff (nurses) attitudes were also highlighted. Aside from lack of interest where recruitment was not a problem, factors which mitigated against uptake included difference in remuneration and difficulties covering absence when training was being undertaken (National Institute of Mental Health England, 2009). It is not yet known whether current proportions will become the norm nor is it fully understood what the possible impact might be.

The extent to which consideration of the social perspective influences outcomes in approved mental health practice remains open to further exploration. The unspoken assumption here of course is that social workers are somehow naturally professionally 'versed' in the social perspective of mental health. This assertion also attracts dialogue in the literature. In basic social work education, the attention given to social perspectives of mental health is said in some quarters to be at best inadequate, or too simplistic. Moreover, this is in contrast to the education received by nurses, who, even at the basic level, have a specialist branch in mental health. Far from being trailblazers for the social perspective, social workers might instead be viewed as 'sorting out the practical problems around the edges while doctors (and nurses) undertake the core business; of diagnosis, treatment and management' (Tew and Anderson, 2004, p. 232). On the other hand, social workers have a basic education which is underpinned by social sciences, including an appreciation of the impact of social factors. In addition, Laing argues that the social perspective does not feature in the initial training of nurses and that such an omission will need to be addressed if they are to succeed in 'fully harnessing' approved mental health practice (Laing, 2012, p. 236). Finally, professional skills including the assessment of the impact of social factors are undoubtedly specific to social work education and it is upon this which the training for approved mental health practitioners is based.

The perspective that social work brings to approved mental health practice is challenged in other ways. Commentators are beginning to question that if a profession, such as social work, claims to have a knowledge base and in turn a desire to bring a different perspective to the medical norm, then there should be greater evidence of refusal to apply for admission (Campbell, 2010). In short, requests for an application for detention should be 'turned down' more often than the available statistics about the outcome of assessments currently suggest; numbers of detentions are reported to have 'hit record levels' with an increase of 5 per cent since 2010 (Health and Social Care Information Centre, 2011). Campbell (2010) also wonders why, if social workers as approved mental health practitioners recognize the potential for discrimination in the use of compulsory powers, are the attributes of those detained under mental health legislation ironically mirroring those of the socially disadvantaged. Extensive work carried out by Hatfield and colleagues during the 1990s and 2000s, a time when social workers were exclusively carrying out this responsibility clearly show this to be the case (Hatfield, 2008; Hatfield and Antcliffe, 2001; Hatfield and Robinshaw, 1994). Do social workers as approved mental health practitioners, then, struggle to promote a model that views the manifestations of mental health in any way other than the dominant and, some argue, pathological one?

The focus on the social perspective has also been seen as a paradox, suggesting, as it does, that the responsibility enables an approved mental health practitioner to consider a 'least restrictive alternative' based, not just on the assessment of social circumstances, but on active diversion to alternatives. Some authors argue that such an expectation is unrealistic as such alternatives do not really exist (Prior, 1992). Prior was of course writing at the beginning of the 1990s, at a time when community mental health services were developing. Since then alternative services, primarily in the form of crisis intervention and resolution services have developed, and as one might expect the use of them has increased. Ironically, such services are now viewed as gatekeepers to approved mental health practice, referring a person for assessment only when, in their opinion, detention is needed, thereby negating any outcome other than the required administrative legal function.

Independence

An underpinning theory of approved mental health practice is that it should be enacted independently. There are two aspects to this independence; of the influence of medical views and of the influence of the employing agency. As is the case with the social perspective, the notion of the maintenance of independence in decision making is required (General Social Care Council, 2010; Matthews, 2011). Early commentators, when reflecting upon this attribute, referred to independence as a 'creative tension' between the social worker and the doctor (Bingley in Brown, 2002). Others contend that independence from medical opinion is both a sign of effectiveness and a necessary check, 'the involvement of mental health social workers in the use of compulsory powers is an indispensable component of quality mental health services' in particular because this maintains 'an independent voice outside of medical hegemony' (Manktelow et al., 2002). The concern that such independence might be lost is the second most debated threat of the opening up of the responsibility to others. The British Association of Social Work in its response to the consultation on the proposals to reform the Mental Health Act in England and Wales feared that the inclusion of other non-social work professionals to conduct approved mental health practice would result in insufficient independence from medical influence (British Association of Social Workers, 2005).

Let us examine such claims of independence and question whether this 'creative tension' is merely rhetoric. Independence has, it is argued, never existed. Rather, approved mental health practitioners, mostly agree with medical opinion and sign an application for admission. Research carried out into decision making supports this view. Based on an inspection of the Approved Social Worker service in 10 local authorities, one report concluded that disagreements (between medics and social workers) were reputedly rare, with negotiation rather than conflict being the norm (Social Services Inspectorate, 2001). Roberts et al. (2002, p. 81) also report 'concordance rather than conflict' although do not view this evidence as grounds for saying that independent decision making is not retained. In their words 'there will be situations where one profession will act as a brake for another in respect of compulsion' (Roberts et al., 2002 p. 81; Peay, 2003).

Others conclude that approved mental health practitioners are primarily administrators who 'merely transport'. Hargreaves in clarifying what he refers to as the several strands of approved mental health practice suggests that this concept is a simplistic one and that other strands including 'crisis manager' and 'social assessor' are present. However, none of these he argues requires independence but rather this is negated by the overarching policy that in contemporary mental health work no major decision should be taken without prior consultation with other professionals (Hargreaves, 2000, p. 143). Even in relation to his 'protecting rights' strand, Hargreaves contends that this is essentially an administrative function shared with a Mental Health Act Officer' (2000, p. 143). He believes that only an external body can be truly independent. Commenting on the outcome of the review of mental health legislation in England and Wales, he condemns the decision as prioritizing collective decision making over quasi-judicial principle and also questions who will actually continue to undertake the responsibility. He argues that the outcome misses the opportunity for 'true' independence but that possibly different professionals will be doing the same job (Hargreaves, 2007).

Does Hargreaves's view pander to those who perceive the responsibility as 'simply' a bureaucratic task? Arguably this view is also retrograde and based on an assumption that the responsibility is a purely legal one. It may also be the case that more robust investigation might uncover instances where avoidance of compulsion is more prevalent than the evidence which is cited would suggest. Walton, for example, when checking the approved mental health activity of team local to her found that 18 per cent of patients for whom two doctors had already recommended compulsory admission were being dealt with in an alternative way by the approved mental health practitioners, in this case Approved Social Workers (Walton, 2000). Might we then be looking in the wrong place for the evidence? High admission numbers may not mean that there are not also high 'diversion' numbers. Independence in decision-making, while central, is contested.

When considering which profession is best placed to ensure independence, the debate continues. The future participation of mental health nursing in approved mental health practice is viewed with some apprehension, primarily based on this perceived inability to make independent decisions. Hurley and Linsley regard the opportunities for engaging in approved mental health practice as a challenge to the 'legislative passivity' of mental health nursing (2007, p. 535). It is however also suggested by them that mental health nurses risk being taken to, rather than embracing new roles, as to engage in such might be an 'evolutionary change too far' (Hurley and Linsley, 2007, p. 536). This is an interesting viewpoint pertinent to the discussion here. Does mental health nursing need to adapt and undertake new perspectives? In particular should it do so in order to be able to make decisions in approved mental health practice independent of medical influence? Hurley and Linsley contend that nurse's caring skills equate to those of social workers and therefore this should be possible (Hurley and Linsley, 2007, p. 536).

Turning to the second element associated with the theme of independence, that of independence of the employing authority. The concern is whether professions aligned closely to each other and accountable to the same employer can be expected to make decisions that differ. A difference in decision outcome might involve a challenge by someone who had been deferential to a previously dominant other. Opening up the role to other professions, and thereby opening up this possible dilemma, is however not an entirely new employment situation. For instance many Approved Social Workers in England and Wales were employed by Mental Health Trusts, albeit seconded back to Local Authorities when undertaking approved mental health practice. Nonetheless there remains a qualitative difference here; it remains to be seen whether the 'creative tension' between social worker and doctor can replicate itself between a nurse and a doctor, or any of the other allied health professionals. Far from being new, neither is this situation contemporary. Formerly, practitioners when acting as Mental Welfare Officers declared any possible conflicts and asked others to temporarily deputize. Is this a practice that can be repeated? Structural and organizational tensions will play their part in any such possibility and its limitations are already documented; the tensions which either of these creates might continue to affect and limit the operation (Ulas and Connor, 1999).

This chapter contends that the social perspective and independence are underpinning themes crucial to any critical understanding of approved mental health practice. As is seen, however, the discussions raise as many questions as they provide answers. A review of different aspects of the literature also reveals a number of sociological and psychological theories that underpin approved mental health practice. This chapter now considers some of the main ones and questions to what extent they impact on practice. Throughout, the question is raised whether practice as underpinned by such theory is specific to any one profession. This question is yet to be answered by any empirical research.

Theories

Emotional labour

Emotional labour is a widely held concept in the literature on professions, including the so called 'caring ones' and it is no surprise that the concept is also applied here. Hochschild (1983), an early proponent, defines emotional labour as a process of adopting an 'on-stage self', that is, that a worker adopts a 'forced' persona as a strategy for coping with the difficult circumstances that they might be required to handle in the course of their formal employment. The concept has been applied to mental health social work generally (Keeping, 2008, pp. 71–2), and to approved mental health practices in particular (Gregor, 2010, p. 432). Here both authors agree that emotional labour pertains to the management of relationships between service user and practitioner. For Gregor, this concept especially helps to describe the worker's management of the stressful aspects of a compulsory role by creating a distance, or an 'on-stage' self; an aspect of the responsibility she refers to as unconscious.

Working with emotions is again an attribute not exclusively aligned with social work. Its part has been examined in relation to a number of caring professions. Of particular relevance here is nursing. Henderson (2001) discusses the relevance of emotional engagement and detachment in pursuit of excellence in practice. She states that there is a link between a caring professional and emotional labour arguing that nurses 'care for their clients by calming them and appearing reassuring and positive' (Henderson, 2001, p. 130). James, meanwhile, attempts to 'establish emotional labour as a key factor in domestic and workplace care work' (James, 1992, p. 489). Both authors agree that caring professions, in this instance nurses, engage in emotional labour. There is no doubt that engagement in emotional labour is required; 'nurses need to embrace emotional and relational themes inherent within active mental health law participation' (Hurley and Linsley, 2007, p. 536). How then does this impact on the discussion here? Arguably, approved mental health practitioners need to be aware of and engage in emotional labour. Moreover, this engagement can, and should, apply across social work and other professional caring backgrounds.

Containment

Closely associated with the theory of emotional engagement is containment. First introduced in the 1960s, Bion's (1962) contention, that a mother processes difficult feelings for her child and returns them in a more manageable format, is now applied to approved mental health practice. The mother, it is suggested, contains others' distress without appearing to be affected by it herself and it is this which an approved mental health practitioner might also accomplish. Aside from the obvious gender issues containment provokes about the impact and role of a particular parent, this is, for Gregor, an 'occupational hazard for an approved mental health practitioner', and the second of her unconscious aspects (2010, p. 432). The notion of containment in approved mental health practice has also been discussed by other authors. Dwyer concurs with Gregor's assertion of the 'appropriateness of containment as a way of encapsulating the process involved' (2011, p. 8).

Such alignments are of course not new. Writing about approved mental health practice in the late 1990s, Thompson (1997) suggests that such psychotherapeutic understanding was both crucial and could also, he argued, form part of the intervention. Approved mental health practice here is viewed not just as a bureaucratic process underpinned by a certain perspective and independence, but also a form of intervention, here a therapeutic one. Bower, writing on psychoanalytical themes for social work practice, also concludes that Bion's (1962) theory of containment is immensely valuable, both 'as a model of the management of emotional states' and as a way of understanding how 'a thoughtful and emotionally receptive stance...can have therapeutic value' (Bower, 2002). But, are these elements, unconscious or otherwise, exclusive to one profession? Or is containment also applicable across the professions. The literature to date does not give us cause to support or refute either viewpoint.

Dirty work

To conclude where this section began, on a sociological note, a theory which is also applied to approved mental health practice is that of 'dirty work'. In the early 1970s, Hughes contended that all occupations contain dirty work. In short dirty work describes the notion that people are compelled to play a role in work about which they ought to be a little ashamed, morally (in Emerson and Pollner, 1976, p. 343). Hughes went on to suggest that, commonly, dirty work involves the development of collective pretensions, or dignifying rationalizations (in Emerson and Pollner, 1976, p. 243). In other words, a profession embraces unpleasant tasks as a means of establishing its credibility or undertakes such tasks as a necessary, albeit difficult, element. Emerson and Pollner (1976) applied this theory to an emergency community psychiatric setting by observing emergency psychiatric teams, primarily nurses. They noticed that team members did indeed consider some of their work as dirty, and that this had two dimensions; the work which they believed involved no therapeutic value and the work which involved coercion. The inability to do something *for* a client therapeutically and the necessity of having to do something *to* him in a coercive sense were both perceived as dirty (Emerson and Pollner, 1975, p. 246). Such a dilemma might also be a core one, certainly for the moral compass of approved mental health practitioners, and is an issue which this book returns to in later chapters. Do approved mental health practitioners rationalize their work in such ways as to dignify it, or have collective pretensions as a way of explaining it? Either way, to view approved mental health practice as dirty seems unduly pessimistic and does not fully take account of the empirical research which has to date underpinned approved mental health practice. It is to this we now turn.

Research

The relative lack of empirical studies to explore the responsibility of approved mental health practice when undertaken exclusively by social workers is a flaw. Indeed the Richardson Committee set up to review the need for reform of mental health legislation in England and Wales commented on just this omission (Department of Health, 1999a). Somewhat ironically, the evidence that was available arguably resulted in opening up the responsibility to other professionals, not least in that the reported disappearing workforce eligible to undertake the role would benefit from a wider professional net from which to recruit. Interestingly, latest figures suggest that this recruitment driver does not yet appear to have been effective (McNicoll, 2013).

The findings of the first notable research study that took place in England and Wales focused on occurrence, noting that variations of admission rates were determined by demographic factors (Barnes et al., 1990, p. 57). Additionally, this study, and its companion exercise in Scotland, revealed how, at the outset, approved mental health practitioners had infrequent opportunities to put their training into practice due to low levels of activity (Smith, 1991; Myers, 1999, p. 105). Further research conducted throughout the 1990s explored the workings of the Mental Health Act 1983 in local authorities in England and Wales. Approved mental health practice, here as undertaken by Approved Social Workers, was again explored in terms of admission rates and there was reported to be increased activity over time (Hatfield et al., 1992, Hatfield and Robinshaw, 1994). More recently, research carried out in Northern Ireland reported findings that include numbers and types; namely the demographic characteristics of workers and location of the work (Davidson and Campbell, 2010). The article also discussed the impact of the fact that there was a lack of actual opportunity to undertake the required role. The focus and subsequent findings echoed the earlier research carried out in Scotland, England and Wales, which was that the requirement to undertake approved mental health practice was infrequent at the start, but increased over time.

Studies also began to focus on other aspects of the responsibility. One, into the perceptions of those actually undertaking the responsibility, reported a better informed, more assertive professional (Haynes, 1990). Attention in Scotland turned to how social work practitioners negotiate their way through the process of approved mental health practice (Ulas et al., 1994). Later work concluded that approved mental health practitioners adopted different identities or, as the author describes it, 'changed hats' (Myers, 1999, p. 108). Numbers of approved practitioners and the way in which these numbers were appointed varied (Huxley and Kerfoot, 1994). Studies detailing the skill and knowledge of approved mental health practice, such as interviewing in a suitable manner and conveying to hospital, decision-making and relationships with other professionals also appeared (Manktelow, 1999; Campbell et al., 2001). Paradoxically, as the effectiveness was seen to increase with the consolidation of education and assessment, the impact on approved mental health practitioners became more negative with the increase in activity and reported decrease in numbers of practitioners (Evans et al., 2006).

An audit of approved mental health assessments, while also initially reporting numbers and types, also outlined the uneven distribution of workloads and some evidence of the knowledge and understanding of the skills needed. Interestingly, this study also reported on the psychological feelings that were being experienced by approved mental health practitioners, in this instance fear (Davidson and Campbell, 2010). Apart from the earlier work in Scotland this appears to be the first time that the psychological experience of approved mental health practitioners is considered. Is the meaning of experience important, does it exist in effective approved mental health practice and if so how? Little evidence is available to enable further discussion at this stage, which this chapter contends is an omission.

Exploring the non-clinical and extra-legal influences that affect the process and outcomes of decision making in approved mental health practice Quirk et al. (2003) again reported numbers and types, in their case the rates of commitment, which varied geographically. This variation Quirk et al. concluded, depended on factors such as the availability of other resources and support from others in the 'commitment team' to care for someone in the community. This study suggests that approved mental health practice is subject to outside influences and therefore out of the control of the approved mental health practitioner, and raises the question as to whether any theory upon which approved mental health practice is based is at the very least secondary. Do necessary practicalities simply pertain? Quirk et al. (2003) concluded that further qualitative research should be undertaken into approved mental health practice including the need to look at how approved mental health practice is experienced.

Echoing the opinion that there is a paucity of studies into how the assessment and detention process works, Bowers et al. (2003), undertook interviews with the range of professionals involved. These included doctors, community psychiatric nurses, approved social workers, ambulance personnel and the police. The focus of the research was the experience and perceptions of these professionals of assessment taking place in the community. A number of findings were reported including that most professions found difficulties in getting the right people to the right place at the right time and that worker safety, while an important consideration, was experienced as verbal aggression rather than physical. To be able to make an assessment in an uncertain environment is without doubt a crucial aspect of approved mental health practice and one which some argue is a responsibility that is particularly 'natural to social work' (Sheppard, 1993). Other studies conclude that the responsibilities of approved mental health practitioners are multifarious and often competing. These include being in role as 'applicant', 'therapist', (social) policeman-executioner, 'hate-figure' and 'stage manager' (Quirk et al., 1999). There is little evidence to suggest however that these roles or the skills and knowledge upon which they are based are specific to any profession. Maybe the social work profession has done itself a disservice in this regard in not providing this evidence. The Quirk study was an attempt to understand the role but did not attempt any analysis of profession appropriateness. This situation remained and, ironically in the light of research which suggested decreasing numbers of available Approved Social Workers in England and Wales (Huxley et al., 2005), the role was opened up to other professionals.

The development of the education and training of approved mental health practitioners itself demonstrates controversy. At first, there was little consensus as to the assessment and approval process, not just how to do it, but whether. For example, when the Approved Social Worker role was introduced, previous workers in similar roles were transferred into place with little extra or transitional arrangements. This was partly a result of trade unions, professional organizations and employers arguing over terms and conditions of employment. Formal education and assessment of competence did not appear for another decade. The twenty-first century has seen the developments of frameworks such as the *Ten Essential Shared Capabilities* (Department of Health, 2004a) requiring shared basic competences across all professions in mental health work, as well as an increased emphasis on multidisciplinary working and there are now clear approval frameworks based on competence for approved mental health practice (General Social Care Council, 2010), but some question their effectiveness (Peay, 2003). Others question the actual process: a competence framework it is said, neglects the hermeneutic, or interpretivist tradition. In other words competence-based assessment is a tick box exercise based on evidencing tasks and not a true test of a practitioner's ability to engage in reflection (Parkinson and Thompson, 1998, p. 59). Is being a reflective practitioner most usually associated with a particular profession and therefore in danger of being lost if the role is undertaken by various professionals? Parkinson and Thompson clearly are of the opinion that it is the case based upon their belief that the approved mental health practice curriculum precludes opportunity for understanding and engaging in hermeneutic reflection. Increasingly, social work literature proposes that meanings and experiential work is central to any social work role (Ferguson, 2010). For these commentators being a reflective practitioner is fundamental. Arguably the need to be approved as social work competent in approved mental health practice acknowledges this and is for that profession an excellent opportunity for its particular contribution to achieve such recognition.

Being a reflective practitioner, and its attributes, is essential to the current debate on effective approved mental health and to the challenge as to whether approved mental health practice can be 'learned'. Evaluating the impact on education of the opening up of approved mental health practice to non-social work professions, Bressington et al. (2011) report that, despite their different starting position, either as a social worker or a nurse, the outcome of the learning for those undertaking the specialist education did not correlate with any specific professional group. In other words that, on completion, both professions understood what was required of them. It remains to be seen whether such a learning outcome can be translated into actual practice or, moreover if the distinction, if any, in the way in different professions carry out this responsibility will become apparent. For some, positioning the education of approved mental health practitioners in the post qualifying framework for social work is reassuring as it means that the social perspective along with core social work values remained embedded (Parker, 2010, p. 20). This framework however is now replaced, as indeed is its regulator. Approved mental health education and training in England and Wales is now overseen by the Health and Care Professions Council (HCPC). It is not yet clear what impact, if any, changes in the curriculum which the HCPC might suggest will have upon the nature and characteristic of approved mental health training and education and, furthermore whether this will impact on the understanding of the social perspective, independence or being a reflective practitioner within that.

Conclusion

This chapter contends that the social perspective is central to approved mental health practice. Practitioners have to demonstrate their understanding in order to be deemed competent and, in turn, approved. There is some debate as to whether this perspective naturally rests with one profession, namely social work, but there is no real evidence to conclusively support or refute this. Despite whether, or if, this attribute is specific to any one or more professions, it seems to be the case that that the social perspective remains secondary to the dominant medical one. The primary challenge for all approved mental health practitioners is to engage effectively in the social. Purists might even suggest that to be effective approved mental health practice requires active engagement in espousing a social perspective which less readily accepts current statutory outcomes and instead promotes less discriminatory outcomes.

A second fundamental aspect of approved mental health practice is independence. The question as to whether independence is possible and the measurement of the extent of the impact of independence is once more contested. As with the social perspective, this uncertainty is brought sharply into focus by the challenge of the opening up of the responsibility to other professions. Again effective approved mental health practitioners must actively engage in this dialogue which is a constantly changing one and remains uncertain.

Emotional engagement, containment and dirty work are further underpinning theories of approved mental health practice. The extent and importance of their influence for effectiveness in practice, whether conscious or unconscious, is unclear in the literature. Initial attention on approved mental health practice research focuses on the outcome of approved mental health practice rather than the process. The activity required of approved mental health practitioners was, to begin with, slow. Nonetheless, education and training increased and became formalized.

While the findings of research did not overtly influence the education programmes nor indeed the role of social work in approved mental health practice, it is increasingly the case that research is now being embodied. At the beginning of this period approved mental health practice was poorly supported and it would appear also poorly practiced, either because of lack of actual opportunity to practice, or because of slow development in education and assessment. Formal training is now the norm, but its effectiveness has been questioned, especially in relation to being a reflective practitioner. Additional factors including the psychological experience of approved mental health practitioners are increasingly being reported in the literature and need further empirical exploration.

Approved mental health practice attracts controversy but, despite this, it is a responsibility that remains central to the admission process under mental health legislation in all nations of the United Kingdom. Usually carried out by a qualified social worker, the responsibility can also be undertaken by other eligible professionals once deemed competent and approved. This chapter has explored approved mental health practice through underpinning themes, theories and research. The initial premise of the chapter is that all who wish to undertake effective approved mental health practice have to be aware of and understand all of these. In examining the theory and research as is applies to approved mental health practice this early premise has raised as many questions as answers. The debate suggests that effective approved mental health practice may not be specific to a particular profession but it nonetheless depends upon the ever changing context in which the work is to be practiced. Uncertainty is a key theme for approved mental health practice and as we see in the remainder of the book a common feature of practice.

Reflective Questions

1. How important is it that effective mental health practice applies the social perspective?

2. To what extent is independence as an approved mental health practitioner compromised by professional background and employment status?

3. Consider whether approved mental health practice can only be effective if underpinned by an understanding of sociological and psychological concepts.

4. To what extent does empirical research influence contemporary approved mental health education and practice?

5. Consider whether without developing the skills of being a reflective practitioner effective approved mental health practice is simply a technical application of the law.

2

UK-Wide Perspectives: England and Wales

Tim Spencer-Lane

Editors' Voice

Chapter 2, along with its companion Chapters 3 and 4, sets the political and legal scene across all four nations of the United Kingdom. As editors we were keen to examine approved mental health practice from an intranational perspective and in so doing explore any divergence and convergence. Approved mental health practice does not happen in a vacuum but rather reflects a wider political context. Of most relevance here are the increasing moves towards devolution and the policy-led decision to modernize mental health services. Paradoxically as intranational perspectives are diverging, policy makers are recommending converging professional roles. This chapter focuses on a further tension; the legal changes within mental health law both in England and Wales depicting the bitter contemporaneous debate about the state's role in protection of the individual. We are also reminded that such tension is not inevitable. One aspect, law based upon principles, is mostly in union. Other aspects, such as those professions deemed most suitable to undertake designated roles are at variance. This chapter, therefore, continues the discussion of the underpinning themes in Chapter 1; discussing the possible impact of departing from a social work specific role in one nation while retaining it in another. Concluding with the Welsh context, the chapter brings this discussion to the fore and provides a springboard for consideration of the Scottish and Northern Irish contexts discussed in Chapter 3.

Throughout the history of mental health law, there has been a tension between, on the one hand, individual rights to liberty and physical integrity and, on the other hand, the state's duty to protect vulnerable people and the public from harm. Between 1998 and 2007, this tension erupted into a bitter struggle between the Government and its opponents which culminated in the passing of the Mental Health Act 2007 (MHA 2007) which amended the Mental Health Act 1983 (MHA 1983). While the Government argued that mental health law needed urgent reform to reflect developments in services and treatments, critics were concerned by the prominence given to considerations of dangerousness and public safety. The reforms also aroused controversy because of the fundamental changes to the workforce especially the introduction of the role of the Approved Mental Health Professional (AMHP). However, not all of the reforms to mental health law introduced during this period proved so contentious; the Mental Capacity Act 2005 (MCA 2005) for example was developed in an altogether different spirit of collaboration and goodwill. This chapter will outline the process of law reform in England and Wales which led to the enactment of the MHA 2007 and in particular the introduction of the AMHP. It will also consider the reforms post-2007 introduced in Wales, the development of the MCA 2005, and mental health policy under the Coalition Government in England.

Mental health law reform under New Labour

The policy of care in the community, implemented largely in the 1980s, saw the closure of the old Victorian asylums and a greater emphasis on integrating people with mental health problems into the community (Griffiths, 1988). This policy was the result of a number of developments including improved drugs and treatments for those with mental health problems, evidence of the ill-treatment and neglect of patients in mental health hospitals, the cost of long stay institutions and enlightened social attitudes towards the care and treatment of people with mental health problems and a rise in the patients' rights movement (Pilgrim and Rogers, 2010). However, by the 1990s concerns were being expressed about care in the community.

Two homicides, in particular, committed by persons with severe mental disorders fuelled these concerns. First, in 1992, Jonathan Zito was killed on a station platform by a complete stranger, Christopher Clunis, who was suffering from schizophrenia. The subsequent Inquiry into the case identified a catalogue of failures to provide adequate care, including the absence of an after-care plan, and failure by the authorities to manage or oversee the provision of health and social services (Ritchie et al., 1994). The influence of this case can be seen in the subsequent push by Government towards greater compulsory measures to ensure that patients living in the community comply with care and treatment plans.

Second, Michael Stone was convicted of the homicides of a mother and her daughter and seriously injuring a second daughter, in broad daylight, in a peaceful county lane in South East England in 1996. Stone was suffering from a personality disorder and it was widely believed that he was 'free to kill' because psychiatrists had deemed his mental health condition 'untreatable' and therefore had no grounds on which to compulsorily detain or 'section' him. The subsequent Inquiry found that no evidence that the local forensic unit was unwilling to admit Stone (Francis, 2006). Nevertheless, this case prompted the Government to consider whether the law should be used to detain people with severe personality disorders whether or not they could benefit from treatment and irrespective of whether they had committed a crime.

The media reporting of such cases – in particular the print media – helped to support and maintain an emphasis on the stereotypical view that people with mental health problems are violent (Cummins, 2010). Under the New Labour Government, which came to power in 1997, concerns about dangerousness and public safety, fuelled partly by these two cases, became a powerful driver for the reform of mental health legislation in England and Wales. To some extent New Labour built on the policy shift already initiated by the previous Conservative Government in the wake of the Clunis report, such as the introduction of the Supervision Register to keep track of high risk patients (Department of Health, 1994) and Supervised Discharge in the Mental Health (Patients in the Community) Act 1996. However, under New Labour this agenda was accelerated. The new aggressive tone was set by the then Secretary of State for Health, Frank Dobson, who called for 'root and branch' reform of mental health law:

> Care in the community has failed. Discharging people from institutions has brought benefits to some. But it has left many vulnerable patients trying to cope on their own. Others have been left to become a danger to themselves and a nuisance to others. Too many confused and sick people have been left wandering the streets and sleeping rough. A small but significant minority have become a danger to the public as well as themselves. (Dobson, 1998)

The Richardson Committee

The Government commissioned an Expert Committee, chaired by Professor Genevra Richardson, (the Richardson Committee) to consider the possibilities for reform. At the first plenary meeting of the Richardson Committee, the then Under Secretary of State for Health, Paul Boatang, set out what the Government expected from the Committee:

> if there is a responsibility on statutory authorities to ensure the delivery of quality services to patients through the application of agreed individual care plans, so there is also, increasingly, *a responsibility on individual patients to comply with their*

programmes of care. Non compliance can no longer be an option when appropriate care in appropriate settings is in place. I have made it clear to the field that *this is not negotiable.* (Department of Health, 1999a, p. 142 (emphasis added))

The Richardson Committee reported in November 1999 (Department of Health, 1999a) and in many respects took a very different line to that promulgated by the Government. It recommended the replacement of the MHA 1983 with a new Act which would provide a single pathway to compulsory treatment whether in hospital or in the community – consisting of a preliminary assessment by three mental health professionals, formal assessment and treatment for up to 28 days, and longer term compulsion. There would be a new broad definition of mental disorder but accompanied by rigorous entry criteria, the strictness of which would increase as the patient progressed from assessment to a compulsory order. A reformed Mental Health Tribunal would be placed at the centre of the system of safeguards, authorizing and reviewing compulsory treatment plans.

The Richardson Committee gave great emphasis to the inclusion of principles on the face of the Act which in their view would be educative and provide a guide as to how provisions should be interpreted. These principles included enhancing patient autonomy, the least restrictive alternative and reciprocity whereby duties to comply with care and treatment are balanced by parallel duties on health and social care authorities to provide appropriate care and support. As noted in the next chapter by Jean Gordon and Roger Davis, statutory principles have since become an important feature of mental health legislation in Scotland, and are being considered in Northern Ireland.

The Richardson Committee regarded the principle of non-discrimination on the grounds of mental health as central to the provision of care and treatment, and endorsed the approach that, whenever possible, the principles governing mental health care should be the same as those governing physical health care. Thus, just as a capable patient has the right to refuse treatment for physical disorders, even if the consequences are life-threatening, mental health legislation should similarly require that the patient must lack capacity to make treatment decisions before compulsory treatment can be imposed. The only exception would be in cases where there was there was a substantial risk of significant harm to the health or safety of the patient or others.

A further key issue considered by the Richardson Committee was the role of the Approved Social Worker (ASW). The ASW role had been introduced by the MHA 1983 as a potentially powerful advocate for patients' rights and means of challenging medical dominance in this field (Gostin, 1986). However, the 1990s had seen major changes in the working practice of mental health social workers. The introduction of multidisciplinary community mental health teams and the secondment of social care staff to (and sometimes their direct employment by) NHS Trusts meant that social workers were becoming increasingly integrated with health workers in their day-to-day work. New models of working increasingly promoted a relaxation of professional boundaries and shared responsibility for cases among team members. Many of these reforms were developed in England under the banner heading 'New Ways of Working' (National Institute for Mental Health in England, 2007). One of the outcomes of these changes was an increasing questioning of the actual and perceived independence of the ASW role. It was also argued that other health professionals were capable of stating independent views irrespective of status and that management of a co-ordinating role, and the need to broker arrangements for care in the community, were also no longer exclusive to social workers (Department of Health, 1999a, p. 46). However, there were also pragmatic reasons behind the review of the ASW role including low morale, stress and recruitment and retention problems. Research confirmed that the number of ASWs had halved in England and Wales between 1992 and 2002, alongside a 27 per cent increase in the number of formal admissions to hospital (see Rapaport, 2006, p. 41). Moreover, there was a very serious problem with an ageing workforce with at least a third of ASWs aged over 50 (Joint Committee on the Draft Mental Health Bill, 2005a).

The Richardson Committee concluded that in the short term the ASW role should be retained but that consideration should be given a gradual extension of this role to other professions. The Committee noted strongly held arguments that other professionals are as capable of independence as ASWs but it felt unable to express a view given the lack of data on how ASWs carry out their role. On this basis, the Committee argued that additional research should first be undertaken into the effectiveness of the ASW role before any consideration is given to extending it to other professionals.

The 1999 Green Papers

The Government response was to reject much of the Richardson Committee's report, but retain those elements which fitted in with its public safety agenda (Peay, 2003). In a Green Paper, the Government argued that questions of capacity are largely irrelevant to the question of whether or not compulsion should be imposed and instead it is the degree of risk that patients pose to themselves or others that is crucial (Department of Health, 1999b). While the Government did not reject entirely the notion of guiding principles, it argued that any such principles should be contained in a less binding Code of Practice. In general terms the Government accepted the Richardson Committee's single route to compulsion whether in hospital or in the community – and a central role for a new Mental Health

Tribunal. They also accepted the broad definition of mental disorder, but rejected the more limiting entry criteria for the use of compulsion. On the question of the extension of the ASW role to other professionals, the Government remained neutral, merely asking for further views on whether the applicant for admission must be an ASW or whether they might be a mental health professional either with specialist training or recent knowledge of the patient.

In 1999, the Government also published separate proposals for reform of the law to manage people with a severe personality disorder. The paper put forward two possible options: either strengthening the existing criminal law to make greater use of discretionary life sentences or creating a new legal framework to allow the confinement of dangerous people with a personality disordered indefinitely, whether or not they are treatable and whether or not they had committed a crime (Department of Health and Home Office, 1999).

Critics were concerned about the prominence given by the Government in both Green Papers to considerations of risk and protection of the public. Much of the opposition was mobilized through the Mental Health Alliance, an umbrella organization representing over 70 groups including service user and carer organizations, professional bodies, charities and academic groups formed in 1999. The Alliance argued that mental health legislation should provide more than just a legal framework for compulsory medical treatment, and should also ensure the provision of appropriate services to avoid the use of detention and reduce the stigma of mental disorder (Mental Health Alliance, 2005). One of the most notable features of the Alliance was, and continues to be, its ability to unite groups who had traditionally been in opposition, such as radical service user-led groups and professional bodies representing psychiatrists and other mental health professionals. Its ability to do was indicative of the widespread opposition to the Government proposals for reform of the MHA 1983.

The 2000 White Paper and 2002 Draft Bill

In 2000 the Government produced a two volume White Paper setting out its detailed plans for law reform (Department of Health and Home Office, 2000). This was followed some two years later by a draft Mental Health Bill (Department of Health, 2002). Some aspects of the new proposals were welcomed by stakeholders. These aspects included new rights to advocacy for detained patients, the use of Tribunals to authorize longer term compulsion and additional safeguards for detained children. But there was almost universal condemnation of most of the main proposals such as the breadth of the proposed criteria leading to compulsion in hospital or in the community, and the absence of a comprehensive set of principles. Indeed, the Royal College of Psychiatrists concluded that the 2002 Bill would, if enacted:

> result in poorer mental health care and reduced public safety, both being at the further expense of increased stigmatisation of mental illness, stigmatisation within medicine of psychiatry as a speciality and erosion of patients' civil rights. A Mental Health Act must be both consistent with the nature of services to which it relates and command support and respect from those directly concerned with its use. Neither condition is satisfied by the Draft Bill. (Zigmond, 2002, p. 379)

Both the 2000 White Paper and 2002 Draft Bill contained proposals for the introduction of the AMHP role to replace the ASW. According to the explanatory notes for the Draft Bill, AMHPs would be social workers and members of other professions such as mental health nurses who have undertaken special training in the competencies required (Department of Health, 2002).

The 2004 Draft Bill

As a result of the strength of opposition to the 2002 Draft Bill, the Government withdrew the Bill from its legislative programme. Instead, the Government eventually introduced a second draft Mental Health Bill in 2004 and submitted it to Parliamentary scrutiny (Department of Health, 2004b).

The 2004 Draft Bill once again retained a broad definition of mental disorder and wide entry criteria, a single gateway into assessment and treatment in hospital or the community, and a new tribunal system which would be responsible for reviewing the ongoing need for detention and all further treatment. The principles would not be placed on the face of the statute but instead would be developed in the Code of Practice. The plans to introduce the role of the AMHP were also retained.

The 2004 Draft Bill was subject to scrutiny by a Joint Committee of Parliament. The Committee's members included members of the House of Commons and the House of Lords from all of the major political parties. It received more than 450 written submissions and heard oral evidence from 124 witnesses, including professionals, carers and service users. The Committee reported in March 2005 and strongly condemned the Government plans (Joint Committee on the Draft Mental Health Bill, 2005a).

The Committee argued that the case for reform is 'cogent but is by no means overwhelming'; on balance it supported the introduction of new mental health legislation but emphasized that the need to incorporate effective risk management and public protection into mental health policy must never be allowed to predominate as the primary objective of reform. The

Committee said that 'the primary purpose of mental health legislation must be to improve mental health services and to reduce the stigma of mental disorder' (para. 10). The overall tone of the Committee's criticism was summarized by Lord Carlisle, the chair of the Committee, in the following terms:

> This is an important reminder to the Government that the Bill is fundamentally flawed. It is too heavily focused on compulsion and currently there are neither the financial resources nor the workforce to implement it. Far too many people could be forced into treatment unnecessarily. They can be detained even though the treatment they receive does not help their condition. And they can be detained compulsorily even if they are perfectly capable of making their own decisions. This is well beyond what is required and the Committee believes that ministers should consider redrafting significant sections of the Bill. At present, the draft Bill is too focused on addressing public misconception about violence and mental illness, and does not do enough to protect patients' rights. (Joint Committee on the Draft Mental Health Bill, 2005b)

In 2005, the Government published its response to the Joint Scrutiny Committee's report, which rejected many of the Committee's key recommendations (Department of Health, 2005a). In particular, there was a sharp repost to the notion that the primary purpose of mental health legislation was to improve service provision and safeguards and reduce stigma: 'the Bill is not about service provision, it is about bringing people under compulsion' (Department of Health, 2005a, para. 10).

One of the main areas of contention between the Committee and the Government was the extent to which the public safety agenda had come to dominate mental health law reform. The Government was dismissive of the views of the Committee and the vast majority of written and oral evidence that the balance was wrong:

> The Committee, while recognising that public protection is a relevant issue, does not in our view recognise the significance of this. The great majority of evidence came from stakeholders who represent health and social care professionals and service users, and relatively little from those with responsibility for protecting the public or from the general public themselves – the majority of whom do not share the Committee's belief that the Bill is inappropriately concerned with public safety. (Department of Health, 2005a, para. 13)

However, it was clear that the Joint Committee's report dealt a major blow to the Government plans to introduce a new Act, and faced with pressures on Parliamentary time the Government was forced once again to reconsider its plans.

The Mental Health Act 2007

On 23 March 2006, the then Minister of State for Health, Rosie Winterton, announced the abandonment of a new Mental Health Act. The Government, she said, had taken into account concerns over the length and complexity of the 2004 Draft Bill as well as the pressures on Parliamentary time, and instead was committed to introducing a shorter, streamlined Bill, which would be easier for clinicians to use and less costly to implement. The Bill would take the form of amendments to the existing MHA 1983 Act (Department of Health, 2006).

The resulting Bill was introduced in Parliament on 16 November 2006. The key amendments to the MHA 1983 included a single broad definition of mental disorder ('any disorder or disability of the mind') for all detentions in hospital and the removal of most of the specific exclusions from the MHA 1983. The so-called treatability test was removed from the MHA 1983 and replaced by a new appropriate medical treatment test for longer-term powers of detention. In addition, new community treatment orders were introduced for patients who have been discharged from detention, with a power to require compliance with a treatment regime and powers of recall where there are concerns about the patient. As a result of amendments to the Bill during its passage through Parliament, new rights to advocacy were introduced for mental health patients and a requirement was placed on hospital managers that they must ensure that patients aged under 18 are accommodated in an environment that is suitable for their age (subject to their needs). Principles were not included on the face of the legislation but were left to the Secretary of State and Welsh Minsters to develop in their respective Code of Practice.

Finally, the role of the AMHP replaced the ASW. The functions of the AMHP are broadly the same as the ASW, although with additional responsibilities mainly relating to community treatment orders. The introduction of these orders meant that AMHPS were now responsible for agreeing to the use of compulsion in the community and not just applications for detention in hospital. Under the reforms, an AMHP can be a registered social worker, first level nurse whose field of practice is mental health or learning disabilities, registered occupational therapist or chartered psychologist (see Mental Health (Approved Mental Health Professionals) (Approved) (England) Regulations SI 2008 No. 1206 and Mental Health (Approved Mental Health Professionals) (Approved) (Wales) Regulations SI 2008 No. 2436 (W 209)). A registered medical practitioner is prohibited from being approved to act as an AMHP. The approval of an AMHP is made by the local social services authority and the AMHP acts on behalf of the authority. Thus, an AMHP who is employed by a health body is acting on behalf of the local social services authority when performing the functions of an AMHP. Local social services authorities are responsible for ensuring that sufficient AMHPs are available in their area to carry out their roles under the MHA 1983.

The Mental Health Bill received Royal Assent on 19 July 2007; nine years after the Government announced a 'root and branch review' of mental health legislation. The Mental Health Alliance provided the following verdict on the MHA 2007:

> Overall, the 2007 Mental Health Act will go down in history as a missed opportunity. While other countries, often with less well-developed mental health services, are fundamentally modernising their mental health laws, our already outdated law has at best been mildly improved. Nonetheless, the efforts of the thousands of people who have written to their MP, signed petitions, attended rallies and lobbies and in some cases been prepared to talk about their lives in the press and on TV and radio, have been justified by events. Without them, and without the commitment of the Alliance's 77 members to a better Bill, the outcome could have been much worse. (Mental Health Alliance, 2007, p. 9)

The AMHP role

As set out above, the proposal to replace the ASW with the AMHP role was first made – albeit tentatively – by the Richardson Committee and became a constant feature of the Government's proposals to reform mental health legislation. It is notable that hostility towards the proposed new AMHP role – even from social work groups – was somewhat muted compared to the other public safety aspects of the mental health law reform proposals.

Many argued that allowing health professionals to take on a role previously reserved for social workers would increase medical influence on the decision to detain and treat individuals. For example, UNISON argued that:

> ASWs work within a framework that avoids institutional pressures and which allows the ASW to retain an independent status for decision making. Without this element, the exercise of compulsory powers would be a wholly medical decision and would lack the checks and balance of the non-medical perspective, brought by the approved social worker. The input of personnel who are distinct from the admitting care team, and who embody a social context perspective, is key. (Joint Committee on the Draft Mental Health Bill, 2005c)

However, in oral evidence to the Joint Scrutiny Committee, Unison admitted the key factor is training:

> neither Unison or [the British Association of Social Workers] is saying only social workers can do this but what we are saying I think is there will need to be training

of a sort which will give colleagues from other professions [...] confidence to be able to do their job. [...The] patient deserves to have the additional perspective of someone with a social work model or a nonmedical model. As long as that is available through the training of the AMHP we do not see it as a fundamental barrier. (Joint Committee on the Draft Mental Health Bill 2005c)

The British Association of Social Workers (BASW) also recognized that ASWs provided a social care perspective to the assessment process and thereby providing 'a counterbalance to any tendency to over-medicalize what are often multi-dimensional problems'. However, BASW also acknowledged that the independence of the ASW had already been 'seriously eroded by their secondment to joint mental health services and in some places by actual transfer to the NHS Trust as their primary employer'. Indeed, BASW had recommended that rather than introducing the AMHP, the existing ASW role should be divided, with the quasi-judicial element being separated from the co-ordination and transporting function, in order to reduce the workload on one individual and to lessen role conflicts (Joint Committee on the Draft Mental Health Bill, 2005c).

The Association of Directors of Social Services and the Local Government Association expressed concerns that it would be possible for all three examiners to be employed by the detaining NHS Trust, and therefore called for the local authority to have responsibility for the management of the AMHP role, AMHPs should be legally accountable to this body for the performance of their role and the Health and Care Professions Council should have the major role in the development of approval and training systems (Joint Committee on the Draft Mental Health Bill, 2005c).

Others however, argued that the notional 'independence' of AMHPs by virtue of their training and approval is insufficient. What is key is which organization employs them and how the influence of other professionals against which they will have to exercise their independence is kept from having influence, real or imputed, on their careers and standing (Joint Committee on the Draft Mental Health Bill, 2005c).

The response of nursing groups was also mixed. The Royal College of Nursing and the Welsh Nursing and Midwifery Committee were both concerned whether performing the AMHP role could jeopardize the therapeutic relationship between nurses and patients (Joint Committee on the Draft Mental Health Bill, 2005c). The Royal College of Nursing also acknowledged that 'there are those nurses who would not wish to take on this role ... because they have seen the rigours of the current role for social workers who undertake it and they may be reticent to engage in it' but 'there are others who would see this as an appropriate extension and development of their nursing role and would be comfortable in that way' (Joint Committee on the Draft Mental Health Bill, 2005c).

Two other points are worth noting about the introduction of the AMHP role. First, the reform was introduced despite the lack of any evidence base, as discussed in Chapter 1 and later in Chapter 12. As noted above, the Richardson Committee had recommended that additional research should be undertaken into the effectiveness of the ASW role before it is phased out. However, 5 years later, the Government admitted that no such research had been undertaken and that it would be too costly (Joint Committee on the Draft Mental Health Bill, 2005a). Second, the proposal to introduce the AMHP role had been made by the Richardson Committee in the context of a new Mental Health Act where additional safeguards – most notably an enhanced Mental Health Tribunal, which authorized long term detention and treatment, – had been introduced. The MHA 2007 – which introduced the AMHP role – contained none of these safeguards.

Policy and law reform in Wales

Health and social care (including mental health) are devolved matters in Wales, and since 2011 the National Assembly for Wales has had full legislative powers in these areas. Although devolution has been in place in Wales since 1998, it has only been since 2007 that substantive differences in mental health law and policy have emerged between England and Wales.

The responsibility for preparing and revising the MHA 1983 Code of Practice in relation to Wales was transferred to the National Assembly for Wales in 1999, but, by virtue of the Government of Wales Act 2006, this function was transferred to and is now exercisable by the Welsh Ministers. The Welsh Ministers made the Mental Health Act 1983 Code of Practice for Wales in September 2008. In contrast, there is a single Code of Practice for the MCA 2005 covering England and Wales (Department of Constitutional Affairs, 2007) and for the Deprivation of Liberty Safeguards (DOLS) (Ministry of Justice, 2008).

In their content, the MHA 1983 Codes in England and Wales are similar. But there are important differences in emphasis and presentation. For example, the Welsh guidance sets out eight guiding principles under the general headings of the empowerment principles, the equity principles and the effectiveness and efficiency principles. Under the equity principle there is a strong and detailed statement explaining the need to respect the diverse needs, values and circumstances of each patient (Welsh Assembly Government, 2008, pp. 6–8). The English guidance contains only five principles – the purpose principle, least restrictive principle, participation principle and effectiveness, efficiency and equity principle. There is no explanation given of the equity principle (Department of Health, 2008, p. 6). This difference in emphasis may have an impact in terms of how AMHPs implement the MHA 1983.

In the area of mental health the most notable difference in law is the Mental Health (Wales) Measure 2010. The Measure is based on the principle of reciprocity – which as noted above had been rejected by the New Labour Government – whereby duties to comply with care and treatment are balanced by parallel duties on health and social care authorities to provide appropriate care and support. Under the Measure, health boards and local authorities are required to agree a scheme that secures the provision of primary mental health support services for the local area. The Measure also establishes duties on these bodies to undertake a primary mental health assessment where an individual has been referred by the GP or when a request is made from a former mental health service user. There is also a requirement to appoint a care co-ordinator for every person receiving secondary mental health services and to produce a written care and treatment plan in partnership with the service user.

The Measure also makes changes to the MHA 1983 in relation to its application in Wales. There is a new duty on the Welsh Ministers to make arrangements for help to be provided by Independent Mental Health Advocates (IMHAs) to qualifying compulsory and informal patents. Section 118 of the MHA 1983 has also been amended to provide that IMHAs in Wales (but not in England) are among the group of professionals that must have regard to the MHA 1983 Code. Finally, the Measure also provides for co-operative and joint working between health boards and local authorities. This is supported by a power to share information unless this is prohibited by other legal provisions.

Reforming mental incapacity law

The reform process described earlier, which culminated in the passing of the MHA 2007, not only attempted to radically overhaul the legal framework for mental health, it also represented a concerted break from the past in the way that Governments have managed the legislative reform process. As one former Government official put it:

> I was on the bill team for the 1983 Act. That was a piece of consensus legislation, as was the 1959 Act. So the tradition is consensus. The new Act is the first departure from that. The UK has had a proud history and place in the world of mental health and is currently throwing that out. So this Act represents a blip in political history. (quoted by Cairney, 2009, p. 676)

There is a stark contrast between the approach of the New Labour Government towards mental health law reform and its development of mental capacity legislation in England and Wales. In relation to the latter, responsibility for reforming the law lay with the Department for Constitutional Affairs – rather than the Department of Health and Home Office – and a more consensual approach was adopted.

The MCA 2005 was the result of a lengthy and detailed process of consultation. In 1989 the Law Commission of England and Wales began a project to review the law affecting decisions on the personal, financial and medical affairs of those who lack capacity. This was in response to concerns raised by professional bodies, carers and mental health groups. The final report and draft Bill were published in March 1995 and received widespread support. The proposed new framework was based on the key recommendation that there should be a single comprehensive piece of legislation to make new provision for people who lack mental capacity (Law Commission, 1995). The Government accepted most of the Law Commissions recommendations and took them forward in Green Paper (Department of Constitutional Affairs, 1997), a policy statement (Department of Constitutional Affairs, 1999) and a draft Bill, which was subject to pre-legislative scrutiny by the Joint Parliamentary Committee on the Draft Mental Incapacity Bill (Joint Parliamentary on the Draft Mental Incapacity Bill, 2003). The Joint Committee made a number of recommendations for improvements, most of which were accepted by the Government (Department of Constitutional Affairs, 2004). This process of consultation and scrutiny finally resulted in the Mental Capacity Bill 2004, which became the MCA 2005. The Act came fully into effect on 1 October 2007.

The MCA 2005 defines what it means to lack capacity and set out a new integrated jurisdiction for the making of personal welfare decisions, health care decisions and financial decisions on behalf of people lacking capacity to make such decisions. It also includes provisions to promote and encourage autonomy by ensuring that people are given all appropriate help and support to enable them to make their own decisions where possible, enabling people to prepare in advance for future lack of capacity and maximizing their participation in any decision-making process. It also provides protection against abuse and neglect in the form of criminal sanctions.

However, this was not the end of the reform process. A legal case known as the 'Bournewood case' (*HL v UK* (2004) 40 EHRR 761) forced the Government to extend the provisions of the 2005 Act and introduce what would be known as the Deprivation of Liberty Safeguards (DOLS). In this case the European Court of Human Rights held that the widespread practise of admitting informally incapacitated but compliant people to hospital was in breach of Article 5 of the European Convention on Human Rights because of the lack of legal safeguards. The MCA 2005 was therefore amended to provide for a new legal framework to authorize the deprivation of liberty of a person in a care home or in a hospital who lacks capacity to decide about their care and treatment. The main safeguards include a formal authorization process, providing the person concerned with a representative, requirements for deprivations of liberty to be monitored and reviewed regularly and a right to appeal against the detention to the Court of Protection. The safeguards were implemented in April 2009.

However, the introduction of the DOLS has not been uncontroversial. As anyone who has attempted to read them will testify, the DOLS are overly complex, excessively bureaucratic and often impenetrable. The DOLS can be seen to have changed the character of the MCA 2005 from being an enabling Act for people who lack capacity to being a detaining piece of legislation. A Mental Health Alliance report found that widespread misunderstanding and confusion about the deprivation of liberty safeguards meant that applications were running at only a third of the Government's predicted rate and varied widely across the country. The report concluded that too many vulnerable people are being left unprotected and called for the DOLS to be 'drastically revised' or replaced (Mental Health Alliance, 2010a). The report follows controversial cases like that of Steven Neary, a 21-year-old autistic man who was kept in a care unit unlawfully under the DOLS for a year against his and his father's wishes (*Hillingdon Council v Neary* [2011] EWHC 1377 (COP)).

Coalition Government mental health policy

Although the Coalition Government shows no signs of reforming mental health legislation, there have been a number of important policy and legal developments that will impact on mental health in England. In February 2011, the Government published its cross-government mental health strategy (HM Government, 2011). The strategy sets out six objectives for mental health: Its six main 'shared objectives' are: more people will have good mental health; more people with mental health problems will recover; more people with mental health problems will have good physical health; more people will have a positive experience of care and support; fewer people will suffer avoidable harm; and fewer people will experience stigma and discrimination.

The Health and Social Care Act 2012 will also have a major impact on mental health care. The Secretary of State is placed under an explicit duty to secure improvement in both physical and mental health in promoting a comprehensive health service. The Act abolishes Primary Care Trusts and Strategic Health Authorities and gives consortia of GPs responsibility for commissioning the majority of health services. These reforms have caused concern among mental health groups; particularly in the light of research by Rethink which found that significant numbers of GPs admitted that they lacked knowledge about mental illness and specialist services for people with mental health problems (Rethink, 2010). In social care, the Coalition Government is also committed to reform the legal framework and funding for adult social care following the recommendations of the Law Commission and the Dilnot Commission (HM Government, 2012). This is likely to include new measures for safeguarding vulnerable service users from abuse and neglect, which will further impact on the AMHP role by providing alternative intervention powers to those contained in the MHA 1983.

Conclusion

The period between 1998 and 2007 witnessed a tumultuous period in mental health law reform, the like of which is unlikely to be seen ever again. The enactment of the MHA 2007 was the result of a long and embittered battle between the Government and the major stakeholders about the fundamental purpose of mental health law. The reforms were also contentious because of the changes in professional roles and in particular the introduction of the AMHP role. The pace of mental health law reform has slowed down in recent years, but the significant changes have taken place in Wales as a result of devolution. In contrast, the MCA 2005 was developed in consensus with most of the main stakeholders and was the culmination of a long consultation process dating back to 1989. Future potential areas of law reform might include a revision of the DOLS in both England and Wales and a further review of the MHA 1983 – and possibly a separate Act – in Wales.

Reflective Questions

1. To what extent has the undoubted tension surrounding the reform of mental health law in England and Wales created legislation based on diverging principles?

2. To what extent will the equity principle included in the reform of mental health law in Wales but not England result in differing approved mental health practice?

3. The impact of Devolution not only means mental health legislation specific to each nation but a possible divergence in approved mental health practice. To what extent do you think this will be the case?

3

UK-Wide Perspectives: Scotland and Northern Ireland

Jean Gordon and Roger Davis

Editors' Voice

Chapter 3 continues in the practical vein of Chapter 2 but in this instance considers the convergence and divergence of approved mental health practice from a Scottish and Northern Irish perspective. As we have commented earlier, intranational considerations are of increasing importance in approved mental health practice. This chapter, like its predecessor therefore, focuses on such matters, but it also has another function; it continues the thread which began in Chapter 1 and picked up in Chapter 2 of the evolution of approved mental health practice. The influence of principle based legislation is revisited, and it is also reinforced that these mirror social models of mental health. Furthermore, the 'local' debate as to whether to open up approved mental health practice to other professions, and the subsequent dismissal of this, is pertinent. It is seen that the notion of independence, the second underpinning theme of Chapter 1, is fundamental. Intranational perspectives also bring into sharp focus how policy is inspired by and reflects social and cultural contexts peculiar to local developments. In so doing a platform is provided for Chapter 4 in which the author debates the influence of policy in depth. Lastly, Chapter 1's underpinning theme of the influence of research on approved mental health practice continues here as further research into approved mental health practice is urged.

Approved mental health practice in the United Kingdom has developed in different ways and at varying rates in England, Wales, Scotland and Northern Ireland. There are many similarities between the knowledge, skills and values that approved mental health practitioners require to carry out their role effectively in different parts of the United Kingdom (UK). At the same time it is crucial that they have a thorough understanding of the policy and legislation that governs practice in their nation, and of the particular social and cultural context within which their local mental health services operate. Therefore, this chapter, like Chapter 2, has a practical function, ensuring that readers from all four nations are able to gain an overview of the framework for approved mental health practice in their locality. However, an exploration of the commonalities and differences between each nation has another important function. It provides a valuable opportunity to develop our understanding, and provoke debate, about just how and why mental health law, policy and practice have evolved differently in the four nations, and what the impact of these differences may be on people who deliver and use mental health services.

We start the chapter by building on the context set in Chapter 2 and the discussion of changing policy and legislation in England and Wales, by describing the nature and development of mental health law and practice in first Scotland, and then Northern Ireland. Threading through this discussion, we will explore commonalities and differences between legislation in different parts of the UK. The final section of the chapter will look to the future and consider how approved mental health practitioners can learn from the experiences of others in different parts of the UK, and contribute to future practice development.

Scotland

Scotland has a different legal system from the rest of the UK, and, although there are many parallels between the law in Scotland and other parts of the UK, the devolution of law-making powers to the Scottish Parliament in 1999 has brought about rapid change in Scottish policy and law. The Parliament can legislate for Scotland in many areas, including health, social work and education, although the Westminster Parliament retains a number of reserved powers to legislate on matters that affect the UK as a whole, such as foreign policy and social security. Devolution of legislative powers has partly been driven by an expectation that devolution will give opportunities to develop 'Scottish solutions to Scottish needs' (Scottish Office, 1998). It has been argued that divergence between Scotland and the other UK jurisdictions, although not as extensive as originally anticipated by many, has been greatest in the area of social policy (Mooney et al., 2006). This divergence is apparent in relation to incapacity and mental health law and has resulted in some key differences between the law and the roles of mental health practitioners, including social workers, North and South of the border.

Until 2000, the law relating to people with a mental disorder in Scotland, which was substantially based on legislation drafted in the 1960s, was 'archaic and fragmented' (Lyons, 2008, p. 89). Scottish incapacity law was yet more dated, with some provisions from the sixteenth century still in force at the end of the twentieth century. Legislation relating to mental disorder and incapacity had significantly lagged behind community care policy and practice, with 'limited safeguards' for service users (Mackay, in Davis and Gordon, 2011, p. 136). A number of major inquiries, such as the Ms P case (Mental Welfare Commission for Scotland, 1999) highlighted major gaps in society's ability to protect people with mental disorders who were subject to neglect and abuse. Two key statutes were introduced very soon after the Scottish Parliament was established in 1999, the Adults with Incapacity (Scotland) Act 2000 (the 2000 Act) and the Mental Health (Care and Treatment) (Scotland) Act 2003 (the 2003 Act). Since then legislation to safeguard the welfare of vulnerable adults, the Adult Support and Protection (Scotland) Act 2003 has been passed. Together these three statutes form the framework for adult support and protection in Scotland.

The 2000 Act was one of the first pieces of legislation passed by the Scottish Parliament. The Scottish Law Commission recommended radical reform to the patchwork of incapacity law as 'the only solution' that would ensure that the law reflected society's increasing focus on the rights of people with disabilities (Scottish Law Commission, 1995, 1.27). The legislation is based on a set of guiding principles that determine actions under the Act. The principles require that interventions should be for the benefit of the incapable adult, and the least restrictive to achieve that benefit. The reforms were based on principles of autonomy and equity, with the intent of ensuring that adults who are unable to make decisions for themselves should not be disadvantaged (Killeen and Myers, 2004).

Three years later the Mental Health (Care and Treatment) (Scotland) Act 2003 came onto the statute books. This legislation is very different from its predecessors in Scotland, and from the Mental Health Act 1983 for England and Wales and the Mental Health Act 2007 (Zigmond, 2008). The 2003 Act emerged through a broad based consultation process, spearheaded by the 'Millan Committee'. The Millan Committee had a wide variety of stakeholders and heard evidence from many interested parties, including service users and carers. It reported in 2001, setting out its recommendations for a response to 'the new directions which have emerged in mental health care: of more community based services; greater involvement of users and carers in decisions concerning treatment; and greater awareness of the need to respect human rights' (Scottish Executive, 2001, p. xv).

Like the 2000 Act, the 2003 Act is built on a set of principles, derived from those formulated by the Millan Committee. The ten principles are set out at the start of the Act and guide all decision making about interventions in people's lives. This contrasts with the Mental Health Act 2007 where the principles are set out in Codes of Practice in England and Wales rather than in the statute itself. There are overlaps between the principles of the 2000 and 2003 Act, but the 2003 Act has some important additions, including the principle of reciprocity. This principle imposes an obligation on the health and social care authorities to provide appropriate services to people who have been subject to compulsory interventions. Mackay (2012) sees this obligation as one that arises from a social, rather than medical, model of disability, supporting a 'recovery approach' (see, for example Repper and Perkins, 2006) to mental health and well being. She also suggests that the principle accords well with a commitment to social justice, and social workers' 'responsibilities to address and counter the effects of structural discrimination and disadvantage on service users' (Mackay, 2012, p. 8). At the same time, Ridley et al. (2009, p. 19), in their evaluation of the early implementation of the Act, found that professionals often found the principles a challenge to work with, especially those of 'least restrictive alternative' and 'reciprocity', when community resources were scarce or under-developed. There is not scope in this chapter to explore the major changes brought in by the 2003 Act in any detail. However, key reforms have included the introduction of Mental Health Tribunals (separate from hospital management systems, and replacing Hearings in Sheriff Courts), widening of the criteria for mental disorder to include personality disorder, the introduction of community-based Compulsory Treatment Orders (CTOs) and new rights for service user advocacy (see Patrick, 2006 for a detailed account of the Act and its impact in Scotland).

More recently, the Adult Support and Protection (Scotland) Act 2007 ('the 2007 Act') introduced new measures to identify, support and protect adults who may be at risk of harm and neglect. A major inquiry relating to the serious abuse of a woman with learning disabilities in the Scottish Borders (SWSI/ MWC, 2004), and a series of consultations set the context for this legislation (Keenan, 2010). The Act introduced new duties to protect adults at risk in the community with a wide range of community care needs, and a range of protective measures, including orders to ban perpetrators of harm from the homes of adults at risk. Like the 2000 and 2003 Acts, the 2007 Act is underpinned by principles of least restriction and of benefit for the adult concerned. It is also important to highlight the role of the Mental Welfare Commission for Scotland (MWC), which plays a key role, further strengthened by the 2003 Act, in monitoring the implementation of law relating to mental disorder, fulfilling safeguarding duties to inquire, visit, advise and publish findings of inquiries, and promoting good practice.

As in the rest of the UK, Scottish mental health law sets out criteria for the detention and compulsory treatment of individuals with a mental disorder, and the roles and responsibilities of individuals involved in making these crucial decisions. Again, there are differences between statutes north and south of the border. One important difference is that Scotland has 'much stricter criteria' (Mackay, 2012, p. 9) for compulsory intervention than England and Wales. In Scotland not only is there, in common with England and Wales, a requirement to demonstrate that a person has a mental disorder and that there is treatment available to alleviate that disorder, but in addition the patient's ability to make decisions about medical treatment must be 'significantly impaired' because of their mental disorder before measures such as a Compulsory Treatment Order (s. 57(3) (d) of the 2003 Act) can be invoked. The 2003 Act also refers to the presence of significant risk, and the need to demonstrate that compulsory intervention is 'necessary'. The last requirement is a key one for the Mental Health Tribunal to debate, since the first four tests may all be met without their being a corresponding necessity for compulsory, rather than voluntary intervention.

Key responsibilities under the 2003 Act are fulfilled by medical and legal personnel, and by social workers, termed 'Mental Health Officers' (MHOs). MHOs perform many of the same functions as Approved Social Workers in Northern Ireland, and Approved Mental Health Professionals (AHMPs) in England and Wales, although, as we will explore later in this chapter, there are some crucial differences. The title of MHO has existed since the Mental Health (Scotland) Act 1960, although the role has evolved considerably with changing legislation and patterns of service provision (McCollam et al., 2003). The Mental Health (Scotland) Act 1984 set out requirements for local authorities to appoint experienced, trained and accredited personnel to be involved in the compulsory detention of people with mental disorders. The Millan Committee saw MHOs having a key role in the detention and care of individuals with a mental disorder, and gave much thought to the question of whether professions other than social work could take on this role (Scottish Executive, 2001). Individuals and organizations the Committee consulted put strong arguments for and against a widening of the role, to include, for example occupational therapists, and clinical psychologists. Millan's eventual recommendation, based on the Committee's extensive consultations, was that MHO status should remain exclusively available to trained social workers with at least two years post-qualifying experience. Here they concurred with the MWC, which took the view that 'social workers are currently the only profession to combine independence from the health service with training and experience within a statutory framework' (Scottish Executive, 2001, p. 89). The decision, to retain the MHO role as 'a check and a balance' in compulsory interventions under the 2003 Act, contrasts with changes made under the Mental Health Act 2007 in England and Wales. Here, as Chapter 2 explained, the ASW was replaced with the AMHP, a role that can be held by a range of different non medical professionals. AMHPs are approved by, and act on behalf of Local Authorities, but may be employed by other organizations, such as the National Health Service (NHS). Mackay (2012, p. 11) has argued that in Scotland 'the degree of independence afforded by being a local authority employee' has acted as 'a buffer' against pressures that may be asserted by other workers, especially more powerful individuals such as psychiatrists, when decisions are being made about compulsory interventions. She questions whether, for example, NHS staff in England and Wales will readily be able to move between their roles in their organisational hierarchy and the independent decision making required of an AMHP. Mackay (2012, p.12) also suggests that local authorities may find it difficult to manage their statutory accountability for providing an AMHP service when some practitioners are employed by other organizations with, for example, different staffing rotas and potentially conflicting priorities.

The current responsibilities of MHOs are set out in s.32 of the 2003 Act and by the Scottish Ministers (Requirements for the Appointment of Mental Health Officers) Direction 2009. To become an MHO, a social worker requires at least two years post-qualifying experience, and the achievement of the MHO Award, a qualification set at Masters Level, and delivered by Scottish Universities. The standards and practice competences for the MHO Award are determined by the Scottish Social Services Council (SSSC, 2007). Many of the legal duties performed by MHOs relate to their work under the 2003 Act, but MHOs also have duties to make applications for guardianship orders under the 2000 Act. The Criminal Procedure (Scotland) Act 1995 also requires MHOs to compile reports to the Sheriff Court about mentally disordered offenders subject to criminal justice processes, as well as providing individuals with supervision and support.

In practice, the MHO role, especially for those social workers in community mental health settings, tends to be a much broader one than these legal duties suggest. For example, MHOs are likely to be involved in giving advice and information to service users and carers, and to colleagues, assessing the needs of adults at risk in the community, and, as representatives of the local authority, making applications for Guardianship and Intervention Orders under the 2000 Act. Local authorities also have duties under the 2003 Act to provide services, for example, to promote well being, as well as to make enquiries when adults may be at risk of harm and to co-operate with health and other authorities. There have been challenges in working with three overlapping statutes: the 2000, 2003, and 2007 Acts. For instance, there has been uncertainty about which legislation is most appropriate to use when, for example, an adult with an appointed Welfare attorney or Guardian under the 2000 Act has a mental disorder that may warrant compulsory measures under the Mental Health (Care and Treatment) (Scotland) Act 2003 (Gordon, 2004, Ridley et al., 2009). These interactions have now been generally recognized and addressed by the Scottish Government and the Mental Welfare

Commission (see also Mackay, 2009 and Keenan, 2011 for a full discussion of integrated approaches to the three statutes).

The Scottish Executive published National Standards for MHO Services in 2005 (Scottish Executive, 2005a). These set out expectations of local authorities including the provision of sufficient MHOs to provide comprehensive and responsive MHO services that respect service users' rights and promote anti-discriminatory practice. Concerns about the capacity of the MHO workforce have been regularly reported, especially in rural areas, including Scottish Islands, where services may rely on the good will of small numbers of MHOs to maintain a 24 hour service (McCollam et al., 2003), and inpatient services may be a ferry or plane journey away. 2010–11 statistics about MHO numbers and activity show reductions in numbers of MHO trainees, loss of experienced MHOs through retiral and increased MHO vacancies reported between 2007 and 2010 (Scottish Government, 2011). At the same time, the MHO role has vastly expanded since the 2003 Act (Ridley et al., 2009, p. 5) especially in relation to their major involvement, with consultant psychiatrists, in making applications for Compulsory Treatment and Interim Orders, Appeals processes and serving and attending Mental Health Tribunals (Atkinson et al., 2007, Ridley et al., 2009). Although MHOs may be employed to work in a range of roles in a local authority, there has been a trend in Scotland for increasing numbers of MHOs to work in specialist settings, such as psychiatric hospitals and community mental health teams rather than in, for example, more generic community care or children and family services (Scottish Government, 2011). This may be related to the growing complexity of the MHO role, making it hard for MHOs in non mental health settings, to feel sufficiently confident and competent to take on a major piece of work such as a CTO application. Tensions between the social work and MHO role have been reported; the sense of wearing 'two hats', with sometimes conflicting purposes (for example advocate vs. guardian of public safety) (Myers, 1999, p. 113). There have also been debates ever since the MHO role was established about the autonomy of the MHO role, and the extent to which MHOs operate as independent decision makers with accountability for their own decisions, while working as employees of hierarchical organizations (Myers, 1999, McCollam et al., 2003). While a relatively low population and a large geographical area can make Scotland a challenging place to deliver MHO services, this also enables MHOs to feel part of a relatively small community of practice in which there is a good deal of sharing of experience. For example there is an MHO Newsletter, produced through the collaboration of relevant bodies including the MWC, Association of Directors of Social Work, and Scottish Association of Social Workers (SASW) which provides a vehicle for sharing information across Scotland on legal, administrative and practice developments, and a well attended annual conference.

Northern Ireland

While Scotland has seen rapid changes in policy, legislation and practice since 2000, by contrast Northern Ireland remains the last of the four nations still to be working to the 1980s generation of mental health legislation. Indeed, Northern Ireland is also lagging behind its immediate neighbour, the Republic of Ireland, which overhauled its mental health legislation in 2001. The Mental Health Order (Northern Ireland) 1986 (the 1986 Order) was considered as ground breaking in its day as the Mental Health Act 1983 in England and Wales, and the Mental Health (Scotland) 1984. As in other parts of the UK, the Act introduced the role of Approved Social Worker (ASW), requiring qualified social workers to undertake formal competency-based training and assessment in order to carry out the role. However, by the 1990s, calls to reform mental health law to reflect a rights-based approach gathered force. In Northern Ireland the Bamford Review was convened in 2002 to independently investigate policy, service provision and law in relation to mental health and learning disability. However, a decade later and Northern Ireland still does not have new legislation to match its neighbours, currently continuing to practice law that sits uncomfortably alongside the European Convention on Human Rights (incorporated into UK wide legislation in the Human Rights Act 1998). This state of affairs is set to change; it is the intention of the Department of Health, Social Services, and Public Safety (Department of Health Social Services and Public Safety (Northern Ireland)) to place a draft Mental Capacity (Health, Welfare and Finance) Bill before the Northern Ireland Assembly during 2014/15 with a view to implementation in 2017/18.

An exploration of the background to the Bamford review, and the thinking that has gone on since it reported its findings in 2005–7, will help to capture the uniqueness of the Northern Ireland context, and the opportunity it has, for the first time in any legislature, to bring together capacity and mental health law. Like its neighbours, Northern Ireland has struggled to emerge from an institutional approach to mental health care, from its one time position of world 'leader' in psychiatric hospital beds per head of population (Robins, 1986) to more recent efforts to develop modern community-based services (McCabe and Park, 1998; Wilson and Kirwan, 2007). The significant developments throughout the UK in the 1990s in building a mixed health and welfare economy, characterized by a drive to de-institutionalize services, were, in some ways eased in relatively smoothly in Northern Ireland. This was in part due to its early establishment in 1973 of an integrated health and social care structure overseen by regionally organized Health and Social Service Boards, engendering a multidisciplinary approach consistent with a shift towards care in the community (McCoy, 1993; Wilson and Kirwan, 2007). The introduction of community-based and needs-led mental health services led to a significant reduction in the psychiatric hospital population, albeit against a backdrop of generally perceived underfunding and low priority given to funding mental health services (Prior, 1998; Wilson and Daly, 2007). In a survey of ASWs 62 per cent identified the lack of suitable community-based mental health services as a key factor in their decision making about applications for compulsory hospital treatment (Manktelow et al., 2002).

The provision of mental health services in Northern Ireland also has to be set against a background of decades of civil and political unrest. Research in the early 2000s uncovered a 25 per cent higher incidence of mental health morbidity and consequent unemployment and incapacity benefit claims than in England (Northern Ireland Association for Mental Health, 2004). A survey of qualified mental health workers found that 31 per cent reported an increase in referrals following the signing of the Belfast Agreement in 1998 suggesting that people felt more able to show the impact the conflict had had on their mental well being after the most difficult times had passed (Campbell and McCrystal, 2005). This high demand for mental health services either side of the1998 Peace Agreement stretched community-based services and resulted in increased in-patient hospital admissions and hospital out-patient referrals (Wilson and Daly, 2007). The number of involuntary hospital admissions also continued to rise, and at a rate higher than that in England. This was a reflection of a number of factors, including overstretched community resources, a culture of risk averse practice among practitioners concerned with their role of protecting the public, and was possibly also an outcome of de-institutionalization itself (Mental Health Commission for Northern Ireland, 2002; Wilson and Daly, 2007; Wilson et al., 2005). This reliance on hospital-based mental health services reflects another tension that continues to exist throughout the UK and beyond – that of the dominance of the bio-medical model, one that frames policy in order to maintain 'traditional' approaches and practices and is less comfortable with practices that promote service user rights and community care (Pilgrim and Waldron, 1998). It is this contested arena that mental health workers, who in the main are publically funded in Northern Ireland, operate.

The introduction of the 1986 Order followed broad consultations and was informed by the work of the MacDermott Committee (Northern Ireland Review Committee on Mental Health Legislation, 1981). The Order was welcomed as progressive, especially its safeguards to protect patient rights through regular medical reviews and appeal procedures, and the introduction of the requirement that mental health professionals seek the least restrictive alternative to hospital admission, with the inference that compulsion should always be the last option (Wilson and Daly, 2007; Manktelow et al., 2002). The Order introduced the ASW role with a range of statutory duties including those of: 'acting as an applicant in an admission for assessment' (Article 5), acting as a second ASW when a nearest relative objects to compulsory admission; conveying patients to hospital; interviewing patients in a suitable manner; and, exercising powers of guardianship (Manktelow et al., 2002 p. 444). These duties are broadly in line with the roles ascribed by the other UK legislatures in the 1980s and include the protective role of ensuring correct procedures are followed and acting as advocate for the patient in ensuring least restrictive options. As already noted in other parts of the UK, ASWs in Northern Ireland experience tensions when simultaneously pursuing an application and advocating for services on the patient's behalf (Prior, 1992). These tensions are not new to professional social work where practice routinely involves consideration of risk and protection cast within a clear and well understood value base. However, Wilson et al. (2005) found that ASWs experienced their social work role of advocating self-determination and autonomy and of working therapeutically undermined by entrenched imbalances of status and power and the predominantly bio-medical approach of other mental health professionals. This was reinforced by ASWs' mandatory, competency based training that tended to reflect the status quo of established professional risk averse and procedural practices (Wilson et al., 2005). In addition ASWs, like their mainland counterparts, were now making independent professional decisions and as such became legally responsible for their actions. Uncertainties about ASW accountability were exacerbated by the absence of an ASW Code of Practice until 1992 (Department of Health and Social Services (Northern Ireland), 1992).

There were then, and continue to be now, certain aspects of the 1986 Order that set it apart from its UK neighbours. These include the specific exclusion of psychopathic disorder, a unitary compulsory admission procedure normally carried out by the GP and with the consent of the ASW or the 'nearest relative', the requirement that criteria for detention must involve evidence of the specific harm the patient has or may cause to themselves or others, and that the Mental Health Review Tribunal has purely an appeal function. These features are not exclusive to Northern Ireland, but the first two alone demonstrate how currently out of date, let alone kilter, the 1986 Order is with its UK neighbours. Its apparent lack of a human rights approach, its use of stigmatizing terminology (for example 'mental handicap'), and its failure to take account of the development of new practices and models of the delivery of care all further contributed to a need for law reform. This is well illustrated in respect of the appointment of 'nearest relative' in relation to compulsory detention. A person subject to compulsory detention cannot challenge the appointment of the 'nearest relative' (although the ASW can). Bearing in mind the role the 'nearest relative' could play in making decisions that might not be in the person's best interests this provision is clearly challengeable in the European Court of Human Rights (ECHR).

The Bamford Review of Mental Health and Learning Disability,which started its work in 2002, is 'the most extensive re-examination of policy and legislation ever undertaken in Northern Ireland' (Wilson and Daly, 2007, p. 424). The Review, which heard from a very wide range of stakeholders, was informed by 'the need to respect the rights of all citizens, to provide rights for those whose freedoms may need to be interfered with on healthcare grounds, where appropriate, to protect public safety and the need to encourage best practice generally' (Department of Health Social Services and Public Safety (Northern Ireland) 2007, p. 1). In keeping with its rights-based approach the Review called for a 'single, comprehensive legislative framework for the reform of Mental Health legislation and for the introduction of capacity legislation in Northern Ireland' (Department of Health Social Services and Public Safety (Northern Ireland), 2007, p. 4). Central to the Review's findings were that the new statute, like comparable Scottish legislation, should be framed by a set of overarching principles in keeping with the ECHR:

1. Autonomy – respecting the person's capacity to decide and act on his own and his right not to be subject to restraint from others;

2. Justice – applying the law fairly and equally;

3. Benefit – promoting the health, welfare and safety of the person, while having regard to the safety of others;

4. Least harm – acting in a way that minimises the likelihood of harm to the person. (Department of Health Social Services and Public Safety (Northern Ireland), 2007, p. 4)

Initially the Department of Health Social Services and Public Safety (Northern Ireland) (DHSSPS) took the view that a single piece of legislation to cover both mental health and mental capacity was not pragmatic given the mandate to deliver during the 2007–11 Assembly session and that separate legislation would be in step with the rest of the UK. However after further consultation in 2009, which came down strongly in favour of the single Bill recommended by Bamford, the DHSSPS Minister announced that the decision had been made to prepare a single bill called the Mental Capacity (Health, Welfare and Finance) Bill ('the Bill'). Following this, and in terms laid down in section 75(1) of the Northern Ireland Act 1998, the DHSSPS conducted an 'Equality Impact Assessment' consultation and subsequent analysis in 2010 of responses aimed at ensuring that the proposed legislation would not negatively impact on equality of opportunity. As the proposed bill has yet to be tabled what follows cannot be confirmed but is an outline, not just of the direction of travel, but of as much detail that is available at the time of writing.

First, and crucially, the Bill is to be built around the Bamford approach of a single comprehensive legislative framework with impaired decision-making capacity as the gateway criterion and the principle of autonomy at its heart. The presumption was to be that a person has full decision-making capacity and should be helped to exercise that capacity. If a person is assessed to lack decision-making capacity then the Bill will allow authorities to intervene on an 'as needs be' and decision-specific basis – incrementally as required in direct relation to the incapacity as assessed. Protections will be built in to ensure that those making decisions on behalf of a person who lacks a specific capacity do so through the lens of the principles and in relation to the best interests and least restriction/harm to that person. Anyone subject to major interventions will have safeguards including a nominated person to be consulted and involved, and access to an independent advocate. The similarities with Scottish mental health and incapacity law are striking, but the way in which the new Northern Irish legislation consolidates these elements breaks new and exciting ground. The Millan Committee's original recommendation was, in fact, that Scottish mental health and capacity law should, in due course, be brought together into a single statute (Scottish Executive, 2001). At the time of writing, Northern Ireland looks set to lead the way in testing out the benefits of an integrated approach to mental health law.

Conclusion

The evolution of mental health law in the four UK nations provides a compelling illustration of the ways in which social, political, administrative and ideological contexts can influence and shape policy and practice. Mackay (2012, p. 12), comparing Scottish and English law and social work practice, argues that the UK's intra-national differences are profound, with Scotland's rights-based approach to mental health at increasing odds with the 'safety-first' emphasis that now predominates in England. Northern Ireland has now put itself behind comprehensive reform, underpinned by similar principles to those first proposed by the Millan Committee in Scotland. Although England and Wales share a legislative framework for mental health, The Mental Health (Wales) Measure 2010 seeks to provide a check to compulsory powers, conveying rights to assessment, treatment and advocacy. These contrasts between different parts of the UK also set different contexts for practice, particularly in the varying balance that mental health professionals may be required to achieve between public safety, and limiting risk and dangerousness, against the rights of service users and carers to autonomy and self-determination. This balance, and the context in which decisions are made about compulsory treatment, lie at the heart of the approved mental health practitioner role, and have profound implications for their practice.

The opening up of the AMHP role to non-social workers in England and Wales provides another contrast between legal jurisdictions, and may signal a move away from the more welfare-focused role of the MHO in Scotland or the ASW in Northern Ireland. Pilgrim (2007a) has argued that mental health law in England and Wales, set within a discourse that privileges the avoidance of risk, has been framed in ways that increase prescription, and reduce the autonomy of mental health workers such as AMHPs. These forces are at play in all parts of the UK, but the decision to continue to support the autonomy of the MHO role in Scotland signals a continuing focus on the rights of the service user to independent support and assessment. It will be interesting to see whether developments in Northern Ireland follow a parallel route; there are clear indications that, like Scotland, Northern Ireland intends to continue to restrict the ASW role to those with social work qualifications.

Although divergence in mental health law and practice raises concerns, particularly where it appears that the rights of service users and carers may be compromised, these contrasts also offer opportunities for research and debate about mental health law, and the roles of mental health professionals in different social and political contexts. More research is required about the impact of different legal systems and roles and their impact on people subject to compulsory legal measures, and their families. Greater dialogue between approve mental health practitioners in all parts of the UK about the nature of their work, and the shared, and sometimes conflicting, legal and moral values that underpin their practice can only be of benefit to the approved mental health practitioner community, their colleagues in mental health and other services and those who use mental health services in all parts of the United Kingdom.

Reflective Questions

1. How important is it that I understand other nation perspectives in order to be an effective approved mental health practitioner?

2. The different outcomes in mental health legislative reform may impact negatively on approved mental health practice. Consider whether approved mental health practitioners should only focus on those reforms that affect the nation in which they are working?

3. To what extent do I need to understand policy in relation to approved mental health practice?

4. Consider whether it is crucial to your role as an approved mental health practitioner that you keep abreast of up-to-date research and consider being involved in it?

4

'Mental Health Law' and 'Mental Health Policy' in the UK

David Pilgrim

Editors' Voice

Chapter 4 sets out to provide a space for the reader to recognize and also reflect upon the 'taken for granted', or doxa. Here law and policy is not simply a matter of rules to be followed; instead the author asks the reader to look beyond any superficial acceptance of the legal and policy framework and question its very existence. This chapter especially asks that this questioning needs also to done by specialist professionals who might otherwise not allow themselves this opportunity. How do practitioners, as the author asks, come to be doing what they are doing and thinking what they are thinking. Arguing that professional practice is a result of the societal context in which they exist and in which they are educated, the author debates the social construction of normal behaviour. In turn he questions society's way of coping with abnormal behaviour, especially where psychological 'abnormality' demands that help is provided even when not asked for. Picking up on the turmoil surrounding the reform of legislation in England and Wales, the author discusses in more detail the debate around underpinning principles of statutory mental health care and in particular the reason in England and Wales why the Government did not accept the reciprocity principle. Ideological uncertainty is a central theme for approved mental health practice to which this book returns.

This chapter's title places the terms at the centre of its exploration in speech marks not to indicate postmodern irony but because they are taken for granted notions. 'Mental health law' is not really about mental health in its broadest sense but the conditions under which some people (but not others) who are deemed to have a mental health *problem* can be coercively contained and treated by agents of the State. Similarly 'mental health policy' was until quite recently a continuation of the 'lunacy policy' associated with the Victorian period. In the past ten years that emphasis has now been extended to 'common mental health problems', as well as a very recent governmental interest in the promotion of well being in the general population being evident.

Thus what has for many years been euphemistically called 'mental health policy' has, at long last, actually started to include mental health (rather than just mental disorder) in its ambit. Another ambiguity to note at the outset is that we have to now use the term 'mental disorder', not simply 'mental illness', because it also subsumes descriptions of people with diagnoses of personality disorder, substance misuse and 'common mental health problems'. This means that 'mental health services' do not only manage madness but also common distress ('anxiety disorders' and 'depression'), incorrigible self-centred conduct and the psychosocial casualties of drug and alcohol abuse.

A central concern of the chapter is how to problematize these semantic ambiguities. In the daily life of specialist professional practice there is rarely the time and opportunity to check basic assumptions. Producing and consuming academic texts creates a protected space for that checking. Indeed, in the lifetime of a professional, it is mainly, or even only, during their basic training and subsequent post-qualification education that such a space arises. For this reason, the chapter will not spell out or enumerate the fine details of mental health policies in practice: *ipso facto* practitioners are already expert about this because it is their daily bread and butter. Moreover, changes over time about the detail of policy mean that published accounts of policy in practice are out of date and polices predominating in one national context may not in another. Instead is the chapter aims to go beneath that daily practice to trace the historical and political factors that have created a current reality for practitioners that they may have little routine opportunities to reflect upon. These more general historical and epistemological factors do have abiding or at least long term relevance for those working with people with mental health problems.

Moreover, that exploration also allows us to unpick how practitioners have come to be doing what they do and thinking what they think. Their actions, and their consciousness about them, are derived from a few observable processes involving a variety of social forces and factors. The basic mandate to practice is reflected and codified in training and education (this is sometimes called 'credentialism'). Once qualified, then a practitioner has their role and duties defined and prescribed by their employer. And employers are minded to codify those roles and duties in this way rather than that way because of the organizational goals they are pursuing. Those goals are framed by a mixture of custom and practice and current or anticipated policies set from without, by local and national government. The latter also fund services to comply with their policy expectations.

Given that this general description about the *inherently social nature* of professional practice would apply to any health and social care practitioner, we also need to consider a unique and ubiquitous factor overlaying the picture. In some forms of practice, such as child protection and specialist mental health services, statutory powers derived from the State are transferred to professionals. That transferred power, about managing those deemed to be lacking in reason, in legal terms is called *parens patriea*. The very term 'statutory' signals that power is in play. As well as the State holding powers over individual citizens, particular individual professionals can also become agents of the State. Mental health workers may not think of themselves as being an agent of the State (even when they are). This may be because part of their *habitus* (see later) leads to the assumption that their work is inherently and unambiguously about *only* working with the interests of their named clients or patients. It is not: in mental health work third-party interests constantly shape professional decision making and action. Indeed at its most coercive, mental health work considers the needs of the indentified patients only after others are protected from their prospective presence and actions. Given the extent of iatrogenesis, which can even include patient deaths in secluded psychiatric settings, it is soon evident that public safety and institutional order can dominate staff decision making.

In the case of approved mental health practice there is a clear and immediate distinction to be made between people who are in distress who are offered help which is 'anxiously sought and gratefully received', by the State or in some private arrangement, and those who have services imposed upon them. Indeed, when we say in plain English that 'services' are 'imposed' on people we see the tensions that might arise both practically and ethically. If we deprive people of their liberty without trial or intrude upon resistant bodies with our 'treatments' then this is likely to have profound consequences for all involved.

Given these opening points, I want now to follow through their implications for 'statutory mental health practice'. In particular I will utilize three orientating sociological concepts of *doxa, habitus* and *field*. These are derived from Bourdieu (1977). The term *doxa* is traceable to Aristotle and refers to the taken-for-granted assumptions that operate in a particular cultural setting or time and place. The term *habitus* refers to the habits, preferences and dispositions that are present in individuals. These are derived from our primary socialization (in the family and school) but are also open to modification over time from later experiences. In the case of mental health practice, this point about modification is evident through the secondary socialization we experience during our professional training and early professional practice.

Thus the habits and assumptions of approved mental health practitioners are under the pervasive influence of both their upbringing and their training. Approved mental health practice is shaped by the assumptions and requirements of its parent society at the time of its occurrence and learned when becoming a society member. It is embodied and enacted by workers who are part of their own society, especially that part which is 'sane by common consent'.

Bourdieu talks of *field* to indicate a particular setting and range of practices (for example the field of education or the field of local government). All fields are embedded in wider social and economic arrangements but each one is characterized by *particular* processes, or ways of working, which are different to other fields embedded concurrently in the same wider social context. This means, in our case, that the 'field of mental health work' has peculiar and distinct characteristics, which we need to think about. Put differently we all exist and operate in a shared social system but each sub-system has its particular and sometimes unique features. And this general caution certainly applies to approved mental health practice.

These orientating sociological concepts might seem esoteric but, as we will see below, they allow us to address in a very direct way some of the basic questions about approved mental health practice that can be glossed over under the daily pressures and taken-for-granted arrangements of professional practice. I will illustrate this advantage by using the terms from Bourdieu within the headings for sections.

Doxa and mental health work

You can do this section on your own in a simple reflective exercise. Ask yourself 'what do I assume about the nature of mental health problems and how does the society I am in typically respond to them?' The sort of assumptions that could flow from this exercise might look something like this from mental health professionals:

- People with mental health problems need help.

- Because of their problems they do not always seek help.

- It is in their interests for somebody to provide the help that they need because of their lack of insight. This might involve decisions the person identified with the mental health problem may not like, but it is for their own good to accept what is imposed upon them.

- In order that this fraught process of help is offered appropriately, we need a defined legal frame of reference to be clear what is being done to whom, by whom and for what reason.

- Therefore the existence of mental health legislation reflects social progress and it protects the interests of all parties involved.

This list could be elaborated in the lay arena by others that might include:

- People with mental health problems are a greater risk to themselves and others than sane people – they cannot be trusted about anything because they have lost their reason.

- But when people with mental health problems comply with treatments given to them they might get better and will not be a risk to self and others.

- What is happening in the minds of mentally ill people is distinct and different from other people.

- We should not trust people with mental health problems to look after their children or do difficult jobs.

These points above are not adhered to by all professionals and lay people all of the time but they are common enough. They are sufficiently common for us to interrogate them with justification. For example, in response, I could make the following challenges on both logical and empirical grounds:

- The need for help is not self-evident in life. It is socially negotiated. It can be defined by others or by the person with the problems.

- Many people with problems do not seek help: this fact is not peculiar to those with mental health problems. Also, it is not self-evident that paternalism should be invoked legitimately when people are deemed to have lost their reason in the view of others. That invocation and the mandate for coercion it creates in particular cases are culturally-derived, self-reinforcing, self-serving and they reflect particular contingencies during social crises.

- Many people in life lack insight and pose a risk to self or others, not just those deemed to be mentally disordered. When corrective action is imposed on *some* of these people then those benefitting may well be others, not the person identified with the problem.

- Legal frameworks about controlling people who are psychologically different in society have been around now for nearly 200 years in developed societies and there is still no consensus about what they should be and how effective they are at: ensuring good care; improving the well being of identified patients; and protecting their human rights. Indeed, the very existence of such frameworks is inherently discriminatory because powers of social control are imposed differentially on some risky people in society but not others.

- Therefore the existence of mental health legislation does not self-evidently reflect social progress and it does not inevitably protect the interests of all parties involved. This is not social progress but legally sanctioned discrimination and social exclusion.

- Some people with mental health problems are a greater risk to themselves and others than sane people but some of the latter are a far greater risk to self and others than psychiatric patients.

- When people with mental health problems comply with treatments given to them then they do not inevitably get better and their risk to self and others may not be reduced.

- What is happening in the minds of mentally ill people is not distinct and different from other people. The psychological processes manifested by psychiatric patients are much the same as those of non-patients.

- We should not trust some people with mental health problems to look after their children or do difficult jobs but that is also the case for some people with no identified mental health problem.

Despite all of the ambiguities set in train by my responses to the prior *doxa* list it is significant that so much of British mental health policy adheres to the assumptions in that prior list in an unquestioning manner. In England, for example, New Labour epitomized the *doxa* list in its period of office between 1997 and 2010.

New Labour and its '*mental health policy*'

As discussed in Chapter 2, in 1998 the then Secretary of State for Health, Frank Dobson, lamented that 'care in the community has failed' and that more beds were needed of 'the right kind in the right place'. He was particularly concerned about patients who were 'a nuisance' or a 'danger to themselves or others' (Dobson, 1998). This position was formally codified in *Modernising Mental Health Services: Safe, Sound and Supportive* (Department of Health, 1998b). Note that the sub-title of the document and its contents tellingly puts safety first and supportive last.

Dobson's statement was not idiosyncratic and it could appeal to the fears in the public imagination about the risks associated with mental disorder. It was not about his *individual* prejudices or assumptions but reflected *doxa*. As a politician he was playing to a well-populated public gallery and as a citizen he was simply replaying his own acculturated assumptions, shared by others in his society. However, a counter-discourse was also provoked and the government faced organized opposition from the Mental Health Alliance, an umbrella organization subsuming over 70 groups. It contained representatives from all communities of interest, including traditionally conservative groups (doctors and lawyers) as well as radical service users.

Although advice was sought by government about reforming the 1983 Mental Health Act in the new post-institutional context from a group chaired by an academic lawyer (Professor Genevra Richardson) it was not happy with some of the returning messages. The group were asked to suggest reforms but not permitted to countenance abolition of the 1983 Mental Health Act. They offered advice accordingly but some of this was not welcomed by New Labour. The problem centred on Richardson pointing out that if new powers of compulsion in community settings were to be sanctioned then, in return, patients had a right of ensured optimal care in every locality. This ethical trade off is known as the 'principle of reciprocity' and it was not deemed to be politically feasible by government, because of the unspecified resource obligations implied. With the exception of anti-terrorist legislation, mental health legislation is unique because detention without trial is permitted and sanctioned as lawful. Moreover, 'mental health law' is enacted daily in all localities, whereas anti-terrorist powers are deployed rarely and very selectively. Also, with the exception of mentally disordered offenders most formally detained patients are not even suspected of criminal acts (compare the target of anti-terrorist legislation). Lawful judgments are made in the practical application of mental health legislation about the *prospective*, rather than past, actions of deviant individuals. These ethical and legal complexities were reflected in the Richardson Report and the Westminster government, thereafter, was accused of a preoccupation with public safety at the expense of service quality and human rights. As a consequence, the Westminster government ignored that piece of advice and simply cherry picked recommendations that supported its preferences about risk minimization.

The Richardson review emphasized this principle of reciprocity and even noted in passing that the *very existence* of mental health law signalled a discriminatory position (by singling out one social group as uniquely dangerous to be subjected to control without due process of trial, and not others). Thus, although the abolition position was pre-empted in its given brief, this did not prevent Richardson rehearsing the potential *grounds* for abolition in principle. Indeed some lobbyists at the time (such as the British Psychological Society) were arguing that mental health law was not necessary and that we should instead have law on dangerousness, which bracketed mental state and could be supported by pre-existing disability legislation to define patient rights.

In the midst of this period of policy contention, strategically the government rigidly separated out legal requirements from service obligations. For example, the Department of Health issued this frustrated statement in response to a critical report offered by the cross-party Joint Committee on the Draft Mental Health Bill:

> the [Joint Committee] report says that the legislation should be about improving services. The Bill is not about service provision. It is about the legal process for bringing people under compulsion. (Department of Health, 2005a, p. 4, para. 10)

However, Cabinet decisions about 'safety first' legal reforms did not go unchallenged by colleagues in the Parliamentary Labour Party. For example, the Commons Health Select Committee, chaired by the Labour MP David Hinchliffe, was highly critical of the emerging policies that reinforced prejudices about mental health problems. The Committee's report (Department of Health, 2000a) attacked the government for dismissing the benefits of community care, calling that official message 'misleading and unhelpful' (Department of Health, 2000a, para. 39). The government were also admonished for being obsessed with risk, which 'conveys a highly misleading message to the public' (Department of Health, 2000a, para. 66).

The contention surrounding the English legislation of 2007 reveals both the existence of *doxa* and its tendency to provoke dissenting voices. This tension reminds approved mental health practitioners about the lack of ideological certainty operating in their field of operation. We now then can turn to the characteristics of that field.

The field(s) of mental health work in the UK

Some of the tensions just noted about English mental health policy were thrown into even greater relief when we consider the difference between Scotland and England during the 'noughties'. These distinctions highlight the need to understand the *particular* aspects of *field*. While both the English and Scottish policies appeared to share a single set of *field* characteristics (especially the legacy of the Victorian lunacy laws and asylums) the fine grain differences between the two national cultures led to different outcomes.

Different policy paths in England and Scotland in the 'noughties'

The Mental Health Alliance would probably not have come into being or would have collapsed quickly were it not for risk minimization being privileged over human rights by New Labour in England. What supports this hypothesis is the relative ease of passage of new legislation in Scotland, where far less opposition was encountered compared with that south of the border. In Scotland the policy included safeguards about the need to demonstrate therapeutic benefit, as a pre-condition of compulsory detention and treatment. Scotland was able to proceed to full legislation quickly (Scottish Executive, 2003a), with the Mental Health (Scotland) Act 2003 coming into operation in 2004. In England a process started in 1998 had to wait until 2007 before new legislation was established.

Moreover, in Scotland professional and user groups had the additional political reassurance there that the promotion of mental health was being taken as seriously as the control of mental disorder. There the government laid out a plan of action, in that regard, for the country (Scottish Executive, 2003a). This proactive Scottish government commitment to mental health promotion was notably absent south of the border. The Westminster government published both the Richardson Report (Department of Health, 1999a) and the 'cherry picked' Green Paper (Department of Health, 2002). This early attempt to proceed with legislation emphasizing risk minimization and refusing the principle of reciprocity provoked the anger of the Mental Health Alliance and so slowed down successful legislative changes. The English government placed an emphasis on developing some form of compulsory community treatment order (CTO), which highlights this skewed balance between risk minimization and human rights. A further indication of the English preoccupation with risk was the dedicated policy on people with 'Dangerous and Severe Personality Disorder' (Department of Health, 2000a). We can see that the *field* of mental health work in Scotland had a different feel to that in England. This reminds us that ways of working in mental health, even in statutory services, are not uniform and given but are shaped by particular cultural norms and priorities. Moreover, mental health work remains variegated and contested for other reasons to do with the epistemological differences evident in different professional groups or disciplines.

The role of *habitus* in applied mental health policy in the UK

The secondary socialization (the shaping of our values and actions *after* childhood) has a double significance for mental health work. The first is that mental health work itself can be framed as a process of secondary socialization. Mental health workers, whether involved in voluntary or coercive interventions are responding to rule infractions and attempting to encourage conformity in the interests of the socioeconomic stability and functioning of their parent society (Bean, 1986; Pilgrim, 2012a). The second significance is that mental health workers themselves are products of their own secondary socialization (via their higher education and under the ongoing scrutiny of their professional bodies and expectations of their employers). It is in this second sense that Bourdieu's notion of *habitus* is relevant because our assumptions, habits and values are open to modification for our whole lives.

The daily work of mental health practitioners is a function of both *doxa* and *field*, as the above sections indicate. But the self-evident sense of what is 'good' approved mental health work emerges as well from the habits, values and preferences of each practitioner, with their *habitus* being under the particular influence of their professional training. The division of labour in mental health services positions the outcome of that training in practice.

And as Goldie (1977) noted this division of labour is a negotiated, not an imposed, order in two senses. First, because mental health work contains, within in it, contrasting perspectives, sometimes people have more in common with those in *other* disciplines rather than their own (with a shared perspective encouraging a shared approach to mental health work). Second, governments may intervene at times to re-orientate interdisciplinary relationships rather than simply letting a custom and practice of work relationships and roles grow organically over time. And that custom and practice contains within it a range of professional understandings and approach to work. Mental health work in the UK contains within it four broad approaches, which at times mix with each other at their boundaries. These four approaches broadly describe the ideological and epistemological assumptions operating inside the mental health workforce (each reader may wish to reflect on their own position in their daily practice, as they read the descriptions):

- The starting orthodoxy is that derived from eugenic biodeterminism typified in the later Victorian period and adopted from German psychiatry. Kraepelin in particular argued that mental illnesses are genetically determined deteriorating brain conditions which are *naturally occurring categories* (Kraepelin, 1858; Guze, 1989; Hoff, 1995; Kingdon and Young, 2007). This emphasis on categories has been retained in nosological systems, such as the Diagnostic and Statistical Manual of the American Psychiatric Association, but which no longer assumes aetiological certainty (hence it is now dubbed as 'neo-Kraepelinian'). This approach is often called the 'biomedical model' or sometimes simply the 'medical model'.

- A minority position in early psychiatry was at odds with the above orthodoxy and was associated with the work of Adolf Meyer, a Swiss psychiatrist who develop his career in the USA and was highly influential in laying the ground for what was to become the 'biopsychosocial model'

(Engel, 1980; Pilgrim, 2002). The latter has been associated with the inter-disciplinary project of 'social psychiatry' which has involved many sympathetic psychologists and sociologists and was boosted in confidence by the strictures of General Systems Theory. Meyerian psychiatry was adopted extensively in academic Anglo-American psychiatry in the first part of the twentieth century (Henderson and Gillespie, 1927; Meyer, 1952) and retained a strong legitimacy by the turn of the twenty first century (Double, 1990; Clare, 1999).

- Another strong tradition of relevance to mental health work is psychoanalysis. This is a form of biographical psychology, which has been contrasted strongly on epistemological grounds with the medical naturalism of the orthodoxy noted in the first point above. In a radicalized libertarian form psychoanalysis challenged the coercive norms of institutional psychiatry (Laing, 1967). Other psychoanalysts have also argued that mental illness is a category error, used as a political rationalization to justify the social control of some forms of deviance. For example, the psychoanalyst Thomas Szasz argued that mental illness is a myth (Szasz, 1961) and that all coercive 'mental health law' should be abolished.

- The fourth and more recent development *within* psychiatry has been the emergence of 'critical psychiatry'. This network of British psychiatrists debate the reform or abolition of their own profession and adopt a critical stance derived from Foucauldian analysis or from a demand to adopt, in a more thoroughgoing manner, the Meyerian position above of the biopsychosocial model (Double, 2006; Bracken and Thomas, 2006). The shared emphasis in this network is the willingness of its participants to concede the limits of the profession and to open up debates for us all about how to respond in society to psychological difference.

As well as the above sets of starting assumptions characterizing the mental health workforce, its character has been shaped by its State paymasters. By the turn of this century politicians setting out to improve the quality and quantity of the mental health workforce were faced with two major problems. First, it was a relatively unpopular field of employment. Second, its traditional division of labour and power hierarchy, focused on Consultant Psychiatrists, worked reasonably well (the State cares little about professional turf wars provided that 'the job gets done'). However, in some circumstances the job was *not* getting done, especially around risk management. Incorrigible risky people who were not psychotic were not favoured by psychiatrists because a biomedical approach has little to offer in the case of those diagnosed with a 'personality disorder' or where that aspect of a psychotic patient's functioning was the main practical challenge. Indeed general psychiatrists are quick at labelling personality disorder but find ways of debarring them from their service with equal alacrity. A variety of government policies around case management had, over a 20 year period, increasingly focused not on 'diagnosis and treatment' but on risk and need, with the latter being divided between 'expressed need' and 'defined need'.

Discussion

In the light of the above descriptions of the complexities of applied mental health policy in the UK, we can identify some interesting points of contention, especially about what exists (ontology), what knowledge is legitimate (epistemology) and what is to be done, if anything, (methodologies of research and intervention) when people report or are deemed to be manifesting the transgression of 'emotion rules' in society (Thoits, 1985). As readers working in the field of approved mental health practice know all too well, contestation dominates the picture. We cannot even agree for certain whether 'mental illness' is a fact or a myth. However, one thing that is evident is that society *expects something to be done* when someone is vulnerable and distressed or they are distressing others (the latter is as important to think about constantly for our topic).

This is where 'the mental health workforce' comes into its own because those who are sane by common consent are more than happy to let *someone* sort out problems in their midst, which threaten the smooth running of their lives or provokes their fear or concern. Because people with a diagnosis of mental disorder are inherently unreasonable (Pilgrim and Tomasini, 2012) those around them will readily encourage *parens patriea*, as well as tolerate actions by agents of the State that, in other circumstances, would be seen as grievous offences against basic human rights. It is quite possible to have clearly discrepant views about what causes mental health problems, what to call them and even how to respond to them technically provided that *something is done by somebody* to deal with the social crisis.All psychiatric crises are social crises. And without the mental health workforce, lay people still do something about madness in their midst and the fear and social disruption it provokes in the sane, as is exemplified in peasant societies (Westermeyer and Kroll, 1978). The need to socially exclude and socially control psychological abnormality in society was not created by psychiatry and other professions but the latter take on those roles on behalf of their parent society in modern times.

That pragmatic driver about crisis resolution keeps the mental health workforce in employment even if, by its own criteria, it cannot achieve its own grand ambitions to 'temporarily fix' or, even more ambitiously, 'cure' mental health problems. What is striking about mental health work is the glib tolerance by all (apart from some disaffected professionals, users and their significant others) of its failures. The latter are particularly about problem definition and human rights; the tension between paternalism and simply letting people be who speak and act in ways which others do not understand. Approved mental health practice is inherently so problematic that to not recognize these tensions and contradictions is itself a form of poor insight or 'wilful blindness'.

Mental health services deprive liberty without trial with the backing of an elaborate State apparatus, including a legal framework. The simple administrative dichotomy it appears to create between voluntary ('informal') and coerced ('formal') patients is a logical nonsense because the system contains a ubiquitous threat of coercion. Patients then might be recorded as 'informal', when they have actually been subjected to the threats about 'coming quietly or else'. Researchers call this mystification of everyday practice *coactus voluit* ('at his will although coerced') (Bean, 1986) and we know that it contains 'levers and inducements' (Szmukler and Appelbaum, 2001). This generates the mystification of a population of 'pseudo-voluntary patients' (Rogers, 1993).

Given this politically and ethically fraught field of activity, mental health workers each find their own ways of justifying the roles and actions (readers could reflect on this point now for themselves, if they are practitioners). One option is to simply inhabit the biomedical model as providing us all with a given 'truth' about mental disorder being a natural occurrence (and not a socially negotiated set of challenges) and to accept the wisdom of *parens patriea*. At this point it is worth recollecting earlier notes about *doxa*. Approved mental health practitioners are also citizens and they were often raised and trained in the very society that funds their work and provides them with particular legal powers and professional duties. Approved mental health practitioners, like politicians such as Frank Dobson, are subjected, just as much as anyone else in society, to the power of *doxa*. For this reason, their role as rule enforcers for their parent society may be deemed self-evidently legitimate by them in their daily work and they may not even see that they are indeed rule enforcers.

However, the dissent evident in the build up to the English 2007 Mental Health Act, which lasted a good nine years, flushed out a set of political matters that we can no longer simply ignore in a process of wilful blindness to avoid our anxiety or guilt about the complexity of coercive mental health work (Heffernan, 2011). That period of fundamental questioning illuminated some recurring questions for us all. What exactly are 'mental health problems'? If 'mental disorder' exists, what is 'mental order'? If mental disorder indeed involves unreasonable actions and people, are all unreasonable acts and people in society dealt with in the same way and if not why not?

Also, if our treatments are not always successful then why do we demand their imposition on all patients? (For example, two-thirds of patients receiving anti-psychotic medication break down again or retain chronic residual symptoms and yet *all* patients receiving them are subjected to a range of serious iatrogenic risks.) If some people with identified mental health problems are indeed a risk to themselves, why do we not also lock up others without trial, such as smokers or rock climbers? If some people with identified mental health problems are a risk to others, why do we not lock up others without trial such as speeding motorists or politicians taking us into illegal wars?

Broadening these questions out to a scenario now well known to us all, why does 'mental health legislation' exist but there is no legal curfew from Friday night to Monday morning to ban people under 30 from our streets? The latter would have massive advantages to society as a risk management strategy in relation to sexual and non-sexual offending, sexually transmitted diseases, unwanted pregnancies, road traffic accidents, domestic violence and savings to the NHS Accident and Emergency budgets. Why does it seem absurd to pose this quite reasonable question and yet not only is it not considered absurd to query the very existence of 'mental health law' but the latter is deemed to be an example of social progress?

For practitioners involved in coercive mental health work, when dealing with mentally disordered offenders or with those detained formally under 'civil sections' of 'mental health legislation', it is useful to occasionally re-visit such questions. Struggling with them might be a helpful reminder to practitioners of their taken-for-granted reality in their place of employment and of their sanctioned role in society.

Reflective Questions

1. Consider whether approved mental health practitioners are carrying out duties under legislation that might not remain in its current format nor be based on a taken-for-granted definition of mental 'ill health'.

2. Approved mental health practice is a complex role which needs time for reflection. How can this be achieved effectively?

3. Consider whether approved mental health practice that is conducted without questioning the status quo is ineffective.

5

The Problem of Psychiatric Diagnosis

Helen Spandler

Editors' Voice

This chapter reflects on the approved mental health practitioner's approach to diagnosis and its significance. It recognizes that this is more than an academic debate in that the degree to which a practitioner accepts a diagnosis will have a clear impact on the outcome of assessment and their understanding of appropriate treatment. As the author indicates, approved mental health practitioners are not asked to take a 'pro' or 'anti' stance in relation to diagnosis, but to search out and embrace the complexity of any service user's lived experience. Sadness, madness and distress are very much a part of this, but these can be masked or overlooked by the diverting aspects of diagnosis. Being diverted in this way limits reflection and continues to give priority to all that follows from this – including loss of meaning and understanding within assessment. The author locates the process of diagnosis within a social context and recognizes the inherent undercurrents of power. The author goes on to balance these ideas with arguments that exist in defence of diagnosis, and also then to review some viable alternatives. Clearly, approved mental health practitioners will not in the short term be enabled to overhaul the systems and processes as they currently exist. However perhaps simply accepting that there is an alternative will enable them to use a language that influences their understanding of human suffering and any consequent ideas around treatment. As the author concludes, the way that we conceptualize mental ill health and its attendant crises structure how it can be understood, experienced, assessed and addressed. An approved mental health practitioner who is unable to embrace an appropriately critical perspective risks colluding with a rigid, limited perspective that affects their ability to act creatively when considering alternatives to hospital and treatment options.

Debates about the problems with psychiatric diagnosis have been well-rehearsed in the academic literature. It is important that approved mental health practitioners actively engage with these debates and do not sit back and see them as irrelevant or merely theoretical. These debates are important because the different ways we describe and talk about mental health problems lead to very different understandings, treatment strategies and ways of relating to service-users (Johnstone, 2000; Warner, 2009).

Approved mental health practitioners need to have the capacity and competence to understand whether psychiatric diagnosis is helpful or not in any given situation. Take, for example, the following legal definitions of mental disorder within the respective UK mental health legislation.

- Northern Ireland: Mental Health (Northern Ireland) Order 1986:

  3(1) "mental disorder" means mental illness, mental handicap and any other disorder or disability of mind;

  "mental illness" means a state of mind which affects a person's thinking, perceiving, emotion or judgment to the extent that he requires care or medical treatment in his own interests or the interests of other persons;

  3(2) No person shall be treated under this Order as suffering from mental disorder, or from any form of mental disorder, by reason only of personality disorder, promiscuity or other immoral conduct, sexual deviancy or dependence on alcohol or drugs.

- Scotland: Mental Health (Care and Treatment) (Scotland) Act 2003: Definition of "Mental Disorder"

  16 Section 328 of the Act provides that "mental disorder" means any mental illness; personality disorder; or learning disability, however caused or manifested.

  17 The definition of mental disorder has been drawn widely to ensure that the services provided for in the Act are available to anyone who needs them. A person with mental disorder will only be subject to compulsory measures under the Act if they meet the specific criteria for those measures. However, sections 25 to 27 of the Act also provide for a range of local authority duties in relation to the provision of services for any person who has, or has had, a mental disorder.

- England and Wales: Mental Health Act 1983 (as amended):

  1(2) In this Act – "mental disorder" means any disorder or disability of the mind

For approved mental health practitioners, an understanding of legal definitions connects with their competence in relation to knowledge of mental disorder as a central requirement of their training and education (Health and Care Professions Council, 2013). The starting point for most assessments for compulsory admission is that the service user meets the requirements of these definitions and there is an implicit need for approved mental health practitioners to engage with the applied understanding of the medical model in this context. This may be a pre-requisite to be able to challenge and concur with clinical definitions of mental disorder from a social perspective. However, there is equally a danger of collusion with a process of clinical diagnosis where the approved mental health practitioner is unable to articulate a critical standpoint.

It can be argued that psychiatric diagnosis rarely aids complex decision making in the application of mental health legislation. Good decisions about compulsory mental health care should be based on an understanding of the prevailing context, a person's needs and the relationship the professional has with the person concerned. This is often difficult for approved mental health practitioners who usually have insufficient time to develop relationships with a person who is being assessed for compulsory admission. This may be one of the reasons why they frequently refer (or defer) to diagnostic categories.

Although many approved mental health practitioners often talk of adopting the social model (as opposed to the medical model) or social perspectives (Tew, 2011), in practice they often still fall back on diagnosis as a short-cut to articulate their understanding of mental health service users and crises (see Anderson et al., 2012). However, it is important that social perspectives go beyond a surface and rhetorical level that narrowly focuses on external environmental considerations like housing, social inclusion, employment and discrimination. These considerations are absolutely crucial to a person's lived experience and their crisis. However, this kind of social perspective does not necessarily question the bio-psychiatric orthodoxy of assuming the presence of certain *pre-existing* mental disorders, which are seen as relatively untouched by social factors (except perhaps being reduced to environmental triggers). In effect this just lets traditional diagnostic categories back in 'through the back door' (Spandler, 2012).

The purpose of this chapter is to equip approved mental health practitioners with the knowledge to question, challenge and understand the broader meaning of mental disorder and diagnosis. Hopefully it will encourage practitioners to be more cautious and thoughtful about the language we use to describe mental health crises. As we shall see, this is not necessarily about taking an abstract pro- or anti-diagnosis position. Rather it is about seeing the complexity in every situation and about being able to make the best decisions with the information at our disposal. As others will discuss later in this book, this is not a linear process.

Psychiatric diagnosis has become the dominant way of contextualizing mental health crises. In this way it can be seen as culturally hegemonic. It is the psychiatric equivalent to 'there is no alternative' (for example, to capitalism) which has been referred to as TINA. A person appearing to be suffering with sadness, madness or distress is often understood within a bio-psychiatric frame in the absence of any alternative viewpoint. In the spirit of the recent anti-capitalist occupy movement, I want to show that there *are* (or, at least, can be) alternatives to psychiatric diagnosis. However, they have to be used and developed in practice. But first we need to look at psychiatric diagnosis in a bit more detail.

Psychiatric diagnosis

Current definitions of mental disorder all offer wide discretion in terms of who falls within the scope of the respective statute and who does not. Arguably too many behaviours are being classified as disorders and this is what is often referred to as 'psychiatrization' (Castel et al., 1979) or the 'medicalisation of misery' (Pilgrim and Bentall, 1999). Some reason that this is about widening the net of psychiatry and the potential for medicalization and marketing new drugs and treatments: "psychiatric waters muddied by the allegedly miraculous 'psychiatric drugs' for treating non-existent diseases" (Szasz, 1991, p. viii).

It is important to recognize that various diagnostic criteria were originally devised for research purposes and were never intended to be sufficient for legal purposes (Jones, 2011). The Diagnostic and Statistical Manual (DSM) (American Psychiatric Association, 2000) and the International Classification of Diseases (ICD) (World Health Organization, 2010) both classify human experience and behaviour into hundreds of categories of disorder. The DSM has undergone another revision (American Psychiatric Association, 2013) and has become the focus of intense debate and contestation (Boseley, 2012). This has, once again, brought into question the whole diagnostic enterprise.

The first and most obvious problem relates to decisions about what should be included. Historically there have been a number of contentious examples such as drapetomania (trying to or actually succeeding in running away from slavery) and homosexuality (Bayer, 1987). More recently, the medicalization of men's violence has led to a proposed new category of 'paraphilic coercive disorder' (Tosh, 2011a; American Psychiatric Association, 2012). Some diagnoses such as Gender Identity Disorder (GID) specifically relate to girls and boys not adhering to gender expectations and have inspired extreme approaches such as the work of Ken Zucker in curing children of GID (Zucker, 2006; Tosh, 2011b).

Some have argued that the whole business of diagnosis should be scrapped entirely. This debate is not new (Laing, 1960; Szasz, 1960; Cooper, 1978).

It has plagued the history of psychiatry with many critics arguing that the DSM operates more like a mythology, than a scientific text. As a culmination of this, and in anticipation of the revised DSM, members of the Critical Psychiatry Network in the UK recently launched the *Campaign against Psychiatric Diagnosis* (Timimi, 2011). The following section looks at the critique of psychiatric diagnosis in more detail. As we shall see, these critiques have come from a number of different angles: from within psychiatry itself; clinical psychology; social science; social constructionists; and service users. We will look at these critiques in turn.

Critiques from psychiatrists

There have always been some dissident psychiatrists who have been critical of the centrality of diagnosis within their profession. The campaign to abolish psychiatric diagnosis is basically trying to 'hoist psychiatry by its own petard' by maintaining that diagnosis is not a properly scientific enterprise as it merely puts a name to a set of vaguely connected traits. The following main arguments are used (summarized from Timimi, 2011).

Diagnosis rests on the assumption that there are a definable number of discrete disorders made up of interconnected symptoms that differ from each other according to aetiology, prognosis and intervention. However, critics argue that there is insufficient scientific evidence available to support the majority of diagnostic categories used. Moreover, by itself, a psychiatric diagnosis cannot tell you about cause, meaning, or best treatment. While validity and reliability are the key determinants of scientific rigour, critics argue that psychiatric diagnoses are neither valid nor reliable.

Diagnoses would be valid if they actually correspond with something that exists in the real natural world. However, critics argue there is little, if any, research that reveals any specific biological abnormality or even any physiological or psychological marker that identifies a psychiatric diagnosis. Rather than any recognized scientific process of identification of illness or disease, new categories of mental disorders are proposed and voted upon by boards of psychiatrists who make decisions about new diagnostic categories. This is how the category of homosexuality was eventually de-classified as a mental disorder in 1973 (Bayer, 1987). This lends support to the idea that, although cloaked in the language of science, psychiatric diagnoses are highly subjective and value-laden.

Without any independent corroboration of a disease category (such as a blood test) critics argue that psychiatric diagnosis is based on circular reasoning. This can lead to unhelpful and lazy explanations such as 'Why do I hear voices?... 'Because you have schizophrenia'... 'How do you know I have schizophrenia?'... 'Because you have auditory hallucinations' (that is, you hear voices). Or 'Why do I self-harm?'... 'Because you have borderline personality disorder'?... 'How do you know I have BPD?'... 'Because you persistently mutilate yourself' (that is, you self-harm) (Pilgrim, 2005).

Diagnoses would be reliable if clinicians generally agreed on the same diagnoses when independently assessing a series of presenting cases. However, many argue that psychiatric diagnoses actually have poor reliability. Patients frequently report being given different diagnoses by different doctors; being given multiple diagnoses; and that their diagnoses frequently change over time. It is significant that diagnoses evolve to *sound* ever more precise and scientific yet with little accompanying evidence to back up their claims to legitimacy. A good example of this is the way that manic depression has recently evolved into bi-polar disorder. While manic depression might be considered a useful *description* of the experience (of extreme mood swings), bi-polar disorder appears to turn into a more *medical-sounding disease*, despite little accompanying evidence of any bio-chemical causes (Spandler, 2010).

In addition, it is argued that psychiatric diagnosis is inadequate in helping us know what to do in terms of treatment and support. For example, there is not necessarily any correlation between a person's diagnosis and their level of impairment and functioning (Timimi, 2011). Some people with a diagnosis of severe mental illness such as bi-polar disorder have high levels of functioning, are able to work and have a relatively good quality of life. In contrast, some people with low level but chronic anxiety and depression are unable to work and have an extremely low level of functioning and poor quality of life. Yet these conditions are considered mild or moderate or even common mental health problems. While they may be common, the experience can be debilitating. Therefore, diagnosis in itself is not very helpful in determining the appropriate level of services and support. In addition, people with the same diagnosis often find very different treatments and support helpful or unhelpful, and this is rarely determined by diagnoses but usually relates to the person's personality, life experience and personal preferences.

Critiques from clinical psychology

While many psychologists accept psychiatric diagnostic frameworks and attempt to work within them, a significant number argue that diagnosis actually impedes their work. Rather than seeing mental disorders as diseases, many propose that they can be understood psychologically (see, for example, Boyle, 1990; Bentall, 1993; Johnstone, 2000; Warner and Wilkins, 2003; Read et al., 2004; Warner, 2009). For example, they argue that (what is seen as) mental illness is often an understandable reaction to difficult life events (such as abuse, bullying and neglect) and the way the person makes sense of these events within the context of our lives. Indeed there is increasing evidence that a variety of mental health problems such as anxiety, depression, self-harm, hearing voices and paranoia are more common among trauma survivors and people who have experienced different kinds of oppression and discrimination (including racism, bullying, homophobia and so on) (Bentall, 2011).

Arguably, psychiatric diagnosis does not help us understand these complex, deeply individual psychosocial processes. In effect, diagnosis transforms what should be viewed as socially meaningful feelings, beliefs and actions, into disembodied, negative and stable indicators of an alleged and pre-existing disease (Warner, 2009; 2010). Psychiatric diagnosis can function to cover up (or hide) not only social factors (such as past and current experiences of abuse and oppression) and personal factors (such as individual belief systems such as spirituality) but it can also obscure other possible underlying conditions.

For example, it is increasingly being recognized that some people who are given a psychiatric diagnosis, especially of schizophrenia, could actually be struggling with various neurological conditions such as autism. People involved in the neuro-diversity movement often describe the experience of being neuro-diverse in a neuro-typical world. Trying to negotiate a frightening and incomprehensible social world may lead to behaviours which are then interpreted as symptoms of an emerging mental disorder such as schizophrenia. Instead these behaviours might be better seen as a reasonable and understandable reaction to living in a society where the prevailing (normal) emotional and social cues do not make sense. This approach is more akin to advocates of the social model of disability. Indeed there is some evidence that diagnosing, treating and medicating people who experience autistic ways of relating (such as Aspergers Syndrome) can actually lead to further social isolation and distress, rather than understanding and support (Tierney, 2011).

It is clear then that diagnosis shapes our assumptions about the presenting problem and how we deal with it. Indeed many have argued that meaning and understanding are the first and greatest casualties of psychiatric diagnosis. As one commentator argued diagnosis is a form of medicalization which 'plucks human suffering out of its context' (Worrell, 2001, p. 342). The person, in all their human complexity – their internal and external world – gets lost. Diagnosis also appears to offer a false certainty – we know why a person is behaving in a particular way – *because* they have a particular disorder. This can prevent us being reflective and open-minded about a person in distress, within context (Coppock and Dunn, 2010).

One result of this is the assumption that people cannot really understand a person's distress. This assumption of unintelligibility can lead to another (unintended) result. Some research suggests people are more likely to be afraid of the mentally ill person and see them as unpredictable and potentially dangerous, precisely because they are seen to be at the mercy of a disease process over which they have little control. Indeed there is actually evidence that campaigns to reduce stigma by using psychiatric diagnosis might inadvertently lead to increased fear and discrimination of psychiatric patients (Read et al., 2006a). In addition, utilizing the idea that 'mental illness is like any other illness' (and is therefore deserving of our sympathy, care and support) has also been criticized for imposing the truth of psychiatric diagnosis.

Critiques from social science

Social scientists have often highlighted how the practice of psychiatric diagnosis fails to fully understand the importance of the wider social context. They have pointed out that diagnosis is inextricably related to particular social categories and cultural values especially class, gender and race (see Pilgrim, 2007b; Jutel, 2009). For example, women are more likely to receive a diagnosis of Borderline Personality Disorder and men a diagnosis of Anti-Social Personality Disorder. It is also well-established that white and middle class service users are more likely to receive a diagnosis of manic depression or bi-polar disorder and black and working class service users are more likely to receive a diagnosis of schizophrenia. This can influence how a person sees themselves and is seen by others and helps determine what support and treatment people do (or do not) receive. It can be argued that the diagnostic process can never be divorced from a social context which is governed by prevailing unequal power dynamics of knowledge, professional status, class, ethnicity, gender, sexual orientation. For example, there are many anecdotal examples of articulate middle class service users and families getting their diagnosis changed to a less stigmatizing one – which raises the question of how objective and value free these diagnostic criteria actually are.

However, it is important to recognize that the way cultural values impact on diagnosis and treatment is rarely simple or straightforward. For example, while it is well known that black men rarely get offered psychotherapeutic support and are more likely to receive custodial and coercive treatments, paradoxically they are also less likely to receive a diagnosis of personality disorder (Stowell-Smith and McKeown, 1999). Some have speculated that despite (or perhaps because of) the cultural stereotype of the 'big, black and dangerous man', professionals are more likely to attribute dangerous to a supposedly organic cause (like schizophrenia) rather than anything which might suggest more of a psychological mechanism (such as personality disorder) (McKeown and Stowell-Smith, 2001).

Indeed decisions relating to approved mental health practice usually relate to questions of harm to self and others. These questions may actually be helped by a greater awareness of social context rather than referring to diagnoses which actually are a poor predictor of behaviour. For example, although there is a high proportion of suicides among mental health service users, suicide risk is rarely related to particular diagnoses, other than the obvious descriptions of depression and low mood. It is far more helpful to refer to professional judgement; awareness of a person's psychosocial history (especially of self-harm, suicide attempts, harm to others and so on) as well as other non-diagnostic factors such as drug and alcohol use and social situation such as homelessness, social isolation and relationships.

There is some useful sociological research which can help shed some light on these contextual issues (for example Fincham et al., 2011). There is a relationship between break up of relationships and suicide in men; and losing custody of children and in suicide (Scourfield et al., 2010). Despite a cultural focus on young men being a particular risk of suicide, men in their mid-life and older men are more at risk of suicide than younger men, in terms of percentage rates. The fewer numbers of elderly men in the population disguise their vulnerability. These often relate to social (as well as psychological) processes relating to how gendered relationships and expectations are internalized and played out in an individual's manifestation of distress.

Critiques from social constructionists

Various theorists and clinicians influenced by social constructionist and post-structuralist ideas have criticized the practice of diagnosis (for example Parker et al., 1995). In a more recent example, critics have drawn on Judith Butler's ideas of 'performativity' (Butler, 1993) to argue that diagnostic categories do not represent (or reveal) an underlying reality but actually *create* what we think of as reality through language (LeFrancois and Diamond, forthcoming).

Even though mental health and mental illness are not natural facts, these categories are made real through citation from a professional authority, repetition and enactment. In this way, psychiatric diagnosis can be seen as a performance whereby we create various categories as if they refer to something real outside of the language we use to describe it. A related argument is that diagnoses are used to separate and distance ourselves from our fears about (our own) madness. Thus we project our own fears about the 'other' or the 'monstrous' into certain people who experience the world differently from ourselves, rather than try to take on board the painful reality of people's distressing experiences and behaviours. This is particularly the case when it comes to certain categories of psychiatric disorder wherein, through diagnosis, these 'dangerous' people are physically separated from ourselves. This gives the rest of us a sense of comfort and security (Mckeown and Stowell-Smith, 2006).

These diagnostic manoeuvres can be seen as societies' own coping strategies. However, they appear to become solidified as truths. Moreover, in our culture, diagnosis has become popularized and increasingly used to regulate, monitor and control ourselves as well as others (Rose, 1989). We witness this in tabloid speculation about the possible psychiatric diagnosis of famous people and celebrities. Here 'experts' are often called upon to 'verify' these diagnostic accounts. For a good example of this, see the analysis of the media coverage of the pop star Britney Spears (Voronka, 2010). We can also see this when people refer to themselves (and others) through diagnostic categories. For example, 'I *have* schizophrenia' or 'he *has* bi-polar' or (even worse) 'he *is* a schizophrenic' or 'she *is* borderline'.

This would perhaps be irrelevant and fanciful social theory if it was not for fact that these categories can have a profound and real impact on all our lives, especially those who are diagnosed. This is why perhaps the most important critiques of diagnosis have come from users and survivors themselves.

Critiques from service users

Many service users are critical of diagnosis because it limits our ability to represent and understand lived experience outside of a particular bio-medical frame. This makes it impossible to imagine *alternative* ways of understanding experience. In particular, a significant number (but, it is important to stress, by no means all) of service users and survivors find diagnosis a dehumanizing process of invalidation (Stastny and Lehmann, 2007). Indeed, the problem with diagnosis is that it tends not to focus on the problems that people *themselves* identify as being most important in their lives (such as stress, trauma, abuse, neglect, oppression and poverty). Indeed this process of dehumanization is seen to reinforce certain experiences which may have led to mental distress in the first place.

> People are not objects to be categorized. When people are objectified they almost always end up dehumanized. The use of labels conveniently allows us to classify whole groups of people, usually in ways that disregard them as individuals and diminish their humanity...This process of objectification and dehumanization mimics that which occurs with bigotry and experiences of abuse, especially sexual abuse. (Mazelis, 2006, p. 5)

A number of service users have said that they feel as oppressed by the labels given them as the illness itself. This is because they start to see themselves (and others to see them) through these diagnostic categories which often feel limiting, unhelpful and pathologizing. This can become a form of internalized oppression or psychoemotional disablement (Reeve, 2012). As a result, emerging experiences that do not fit within the existing psychiatric framework are rendered invisible. In other words a person's complex personal narrative gets re-told by 'experts' and re-framed in bio-psychiatric terms. This prevents people from having the opportunity to understand their experiences outside of this framework – for example, by finding meaning or value in their experiences or crises. This mismatch of understanding can also create communication barriers and trust problems between service users and practitioners. In addition, service users often report that their rejection of diagnostic categories is used as evidence to confirm the diagnosis anyway. Alternatively, however, if they reject diagnosis it is difficult for them to access support, a point we return to later.

One of the reasons why the challenges to psychiatric diagnosis have gone largely unheeded is that it is the *raison d'etre* of psychiatry and operates as the key to its continued legitimization. Critics, especially service users and activists, have often specifically highlighted schizophrenia and Borderline Personality Disorder as two diagnoses which are especially vulnerable to these criticisms. As a result they have been the subject of *specific* anti-diagnostic campaigns.

The cases of 'schizophrenia' and 'borderline personality disorder'

The category of schizophrenia has come under the most intense and sustained critical scrutiny (for example Laing, 1960; Laing and Esterson, 1964; Boyle, 1990; Jenner et al., 1993; Johnstone, 2000; Romme and Morris, 2007). While such rational argument has done little to dismantle the diagnosis, perhaps the international hearing voices movement discredited the category of schizophrenia on a more profound level, through the lived experience of voice hearers themselves. First, they established that many people hear voices and do so unproblematically. This made it hard to see hearing voices *itself* as a main symptom of the disease of schizophrenia. Whether hearing voices is a problem relates to how the person experiences the voices, and the effect it has, rather than the voices themselves. This is difficult to account for in a traditional schizophrenia diagnosis because it would see hearing voices (or auditory hallucinations) as inherently pathological. The Hearing Voices movement also established that symptoms of schizophrenia might actually be a meaningful, understandable and reasonable response to difficult experiences such as hearing (primarily negative and persecutory) voices.

Moreover, these negative voices themselves often result from traumatic life events (Romme and Escher, 2005; Read et al., 2006b; Romme et al., 2008). In other words, the *content* of voices, far from being irrelevant (as the notion of schizophrenia-as-disease would suggest) might be really important.

The Hearing Voices movement has been very influential, and the implications of the hearing voices approach to social work have recently been considered (Sapey, 2013; Sapey and Bullimore, forthcoming). However, the wider implications of this critique – in relation to the category of schizophrenia itself – have yet to be fully realized (Thomas, 1997; Romme and Morris, 2007). As a result, an independent Inquiry into the 'Schizophrenia' Label was launched in 2012 by a group of organisations and individuals concerned about the meaning and usefulness of schizophrenia (www.schizophreniainquiry.org).

Similarly, and more recently, service users and activists have challenged the Borderline Personality Disorder (BPD) diagnosis and have launched a Campaign against the Borderline Label (Timimi, 2013). Despite its well-known correlation with childhood trauma, a BPD diagnosis often elicits intensely judgmental and punitive treatment and has been described as 'little more than a sophisticated insult' (Herman, 1992, p. 123). Many feminist therapists and survivors have argued that the symptoms that define a BPD diagnosis can often be better understood as memories, thoughts and feelings associated with living with histories of complex abuse and trauma. Like symptoms of schizophrenia, indicators of BPD may be understandable ways of coping with these experiences (Herman, 1992; Worrell, 2001; Warner and Wilkins, 2003; Proctor and Shaw, 2004; Shaw and Proctor, 2004: Proctor, 2007; Warner, 2009; 2010).

Indeed, some have argued that that the diagnosis of BPD itself might become part of a person's ongoing experience of trauma, where their experiences are disbelieved, and their behaviour controlled and punished. Similarly, Sapey (2013) questions whether detaining people who hear voices as a result of abuse might actually compound their experience of trauma. This can be considered an example of 'iatrogenesis' (medically induced harm) or what (in relation to treatment of self-harm) has been called 'malignant alienation' (Watts and Morgan, 1994).

It is, however, important to bear in mind that while people should not be seen as determined by their presumed biology, bio-chemistry or personality, neither should they be seen merely as victims of their assumed social histories (of trauma and abuse). Assuming a person's mental health problems arise from past experiences of abuse in any simplistic fashion may obscure the person's *current* situation which can reinforce (or exacerbate) their underlying difficulties (Warner, 2009). This is particularly important to approved mental health practitioners who need to put the person's current living situation at the forefront of their minds.

Taking more of a social justice (rather than a narrowly scientific) angle, perhaps it is worth putting less focus on whether diagnosis represents anything real or not, and concentrated more on what it does (or doesn't) achieve. Therefore, it is worth considering the counter-arguments about the possible usefulness of diagnosis.

In defence of diagnosis?

The case for using diagnostic categories tends to fall into three main arguments. These are outlined below:

Diagnosis has utility

Kendall and Jabelensky (2003) argue that both defenders *and* critics of psychiatric diagnosis confuse validity and utility and conflate them as if they mean the same thing. They maintain that while psychiatric diagnoses might not be valid (or true) they may have utility (or usefulness). While they agree that most contemporary psychiatric disorders cannot yet be described as valid disease categories, they maintain that this does not mean that they are not valuable concepts. They argue that diagnosis can provide useful information about a person, whether or not the category in question is valid. They make the important point that while something either *is or is not* valid, utility very much depends on context. Because of this, they argue that we should use diagnosis carefully according to context and understand that we are not talking about something that actually exists but rather something that may (or may not) be useful in a particular context 'including who is using the diagnosis, in what circumstances and for what purposes' (Kendall and Jabelensky, 2003, pp. 9–11).

Diagnosis provides relief

The second issue to bear in mind is that regardless of the problems with psychiatric diagnosis, it does appear to offer service users (and their friends/families/carers) some comfort and relief. This is because it seems to appreciate that 'something is wrong', and acknowledges the suffering experienced by the person considered and/or the people around them. Perhaps most importantly, diagnosis seems to indicate that the problem isn't anyone's fault in any obvious way. It, therefore, can alleviate the concerns of families and carers that perhaps they are to blame.

Diagnosis isn't just a problem in psychiatry

The third point that can be made is that critics of psychiatric diagnosis tend to overstate the scientific nature of physical medicine. They 'draw a sharp distinction between the natural-scientific, value-free language of physical medicine and the socially and politically loaded language of psychiatry' (Sedgwick, 1987, p. 17). Indeed many medical diagnoses of physical diseases are not an exact science either. This means that many of the problems that beset psychiatric diagnoses also best other medical diagnoses, for example a lack of objectivity and validity. Thus to posit psychiatry as unscientific and medicine as scientific is perhaps to misunderstand the way science works, because *all medicine* involves subjective value judgements (Sedgwick, 1987). In other words, all judgements of illness involve contrasting a person's condition with prevailing social norms of health. There are also many physical illnesses which do not have any accompanying tests or understanding of underlying causes and treatments. This is especially the case when it comes to medically unexplained symptoms and illness with no obvious cause or biological tests. Thus some philosophers argue that singling out *psychiatric* diagnosis, while accepting other form of diagnosis, is to commit crude 'mind–body dualism'.

However, despite these concerns they are specific *consequences* of psychiatric diagnosis that are different from physical illness. This is because it results in a particular form of discrediting – not only is part of the body diseased or ill but being mentally ill implies something far more profound. Being designated mentally ill can, *in itself*, justify practices of detention, forced treatment and discreditation as well as provided justification for human rights exceptions (Cresswell, 2008; Spandler and Calton, 2009).

With these arguments in mind, the main concern with abandoning psychiatric diagnosis is the lack of alternatives. This could leave professionals, families and service users themselves without an adequate language to assist them to understand and make sense of their difficult experiences. It is clear that psychiatric categories do refer to something, be it mental disorder, madness, suffering, distress, existential crisis, problems in living or whatever. Whether we use psychiatric diagnosis or not, in the way we describe mental health crises it must be useful for the person and their situation. The next section considers this in more detail.

Constructing more helpful alternatives

Bearing in mind these debates about psychiatric diagnosis, some have argued that it is the responsibility of other mental health professionals (that is, not psychiatrists) to not only expose the shortcoming of diagnostic approaches, but also to demonstrate why any alternative ways of understanding problems are *more useful and compelling* (Pilgrim, 2000). Taking this on board, we need to consider the following issues when considering whether we utilize diagnosis or use alternatives.

If we question diagnosis, it is important that this does not result in nihilism; a denial of suffering; or an inability to make demands on our health and welfare services (Sedgwick, 1987; Cresswell and Spandler, 2009). It seems necessary to find ways of enabling a person to receive the support and sanctuary they may need which does not rest upon problematic constructs of disorder. However, if we stop 'doing' diagnosis then we need to try doing something more helpful instead. This is more important than dogmatically adopting positions either for or against psychiatric diagnosis, regardless of context or need.

Some critical psychiatrists have developed the idea of a 'drug centred' as opposed to 'disease centred' model of understanding the way that psychiatric drugs work (Moncrieff, 2009). This ultimately means de-centring psychiatric drugs from intervention. This doesn't necessarily mean not using them, but it means that it should not necessarily be seen as the first mode of intervention (see also Calton and Spandler, 2009). It means asking 'what does a person need in a particular context' rather than, 'what drugs treat this particular mental disorder?' Similarly, it is worth de-centring psychiatric diagnosis from mental health practice.

It is clear that we can't just impose an easy alternative to psychiatric diagnosis. Indeed any alternatives should not impose new certainties and orthodoxies for example hearing voices or self-harm is *always* a reaction to trauma or abuse. Therefore, it is important not to merely replace psychiatric diagnosis with alternative definitions which might result in new fixed and immutable truths that can feel just as oppressive. While we do know a lot about human distress, there is still a lot we don't know. Therefore, any knowledge needs to be conditional. While there are no biological 'tests' for most psychiatric diagnoses – and there may never be – we need to stay open-minded to advances in scientific and other ways of understanding distress.

Whether we use psychiatric diagnosis or not it is important to be aware of the following considerations. Alternatives should provide:

- relief (that is an acknowledgement of, and reduction in, suffering);
- understanding (which will help increase compassion towards the person's situation);
- access to support and assistance (including services and welfare benefits); and

- recognition of the complexity of human experience (which doesn't artificially separate the mind and the body).

With these issues in mind, the following section suggests some alternative strategies. These are by no means mutually exclusive. They can potentially be used together or drawn upon in different contexts and situations.

Level of functioning or impairment

As there is often a poor correspondence between levels of impairment and the required number of symptoms for a given diagnosis (Timimi, 2011), it seems preferable to focus on the person's level of impairment and psychosocial functioning. This approach is frequently used in hearing voices and self-harm support groups which focus not on whether someone hears voices or self-harms, but how disabling they find the experience in a society that does not recognize or accept hearing voices or self-harm (Romme and Esher, 1989; Spandler, 1996; Spandler and Warner, 2007). Making decisions about levels of impairment and functioning (rather than diagnosis) may be more useful in determining access to services and using mental health legislation.

Using service users own frameworks

There is nothing *inherently* wrong with using any framework or diagnostic categories, as long as the person finds it helpful to understand themselves and their situation. Organizations like the Hearing Voices Network argued that we need to be open to all explanatory frameworks as they might be helpful to some people in coping with mental health difficulties. Therefore, approved mental health practitioners need to work within a person's own frameworks of understanding their distress. This may include diagnostic categories but it may also include others ways of understanding such as responses to trauma, spirituality, philosophical and other frameworks (Knight, 2009).

Some service users may prefer to construct an alternative *self-diagnosis* which they feel makes sense of their experiences. For example, Park (2012) constructed his own self-diagnosis of 'creative suicidal anxiety'. Others see *self-description* as preferable (Spandler, 2010). These descriptions may mimic some earlier diagnostic categories (for example manic depression rather than bi-polar) or just refer to the distressing experience itself (for example, voice hearer rather than schizophrenia). Sometimes these strategies are necessary to communicate one's own understanding of distress to others.

Strategic use of diagnosis

Sometimes it may be necessary to use diagnosis *strategically* in order to get adequate support and welfare assistance, regardless of whether we believe in the truth of the categories or not. For example, psychiatric diagnosis is often required in order to refer service users to specialist services (for example the diagnosis of dissociative identity disorder might help a person access alternative therapeutic support regarding their experience of dissociation). As described above, this often involves using more descriptive diagnostic categories such as post-traumatic stress disorder (PTSD) or attachment disorder which may also open doors to services.

Many feminist therapists have argued that people who display the characteristics of survivors of sexual violence, within the mental health system should be given a diagnosis of complex post-traumatic stress disorder (Herman, 1992). While there may be problems with merely replacing one category of disorder with another, at least this offers a more accurate description of the person's situation, as it highlights the links between external factors and a person's responses, rather than being something internally or intrinsically wrong with the person (as the categories of personality disorder tend to suggest). Therefore, it is important to make sure that individuals are sensitively and adequately assessed in relation to current experiences *and* histories of abuse and trauma.

It is also important to ensure that people in the mental health system are assessed in relation to other conditions such as autism or neuro-diverse conditions. This may result in *re-diagnosis* and possible re-classification (for example, from schizophrenia to Aspergers). This is often a strategy used by families of people in the mental health system in order to open up opportunities for the person to get more socially orientated and less medicalized therapeutic support. This can then assist the person to understand, and make decisions about, how they relate to the normal neurotypical social world (Tierney, 2011).

Formulation

Formulation has gained more prominence as an alternative to diagnosis in clinical psychology (Butler, 1998; Johnstone and Dallos, 2006). The idea of formulation is to attempt to: summarize the person's core problems; show how difficulties relate to each other drawing on psychosocial theory; explain why the person has developed these problems, at this time, and in these situations. It is a way of summarizing meanings; negotiating shared understandings; and communicating them to others in a process of 'on-going collaborative sense-making' (Harper and Moss, 2003, p. 8). Formulations are basically shared hypotheses or hunches.

When informed by a social constructionist perspective, formulation becomes a structured story that helps to orientate the professional and integrate others' perspective from within a particular social context. It acknowledges that it is a view from somewhere (and from someone) with a particular purpose, and does not signify an objective truth. A formation is constructed rather than discovered and therefore it puts the professional at the centre of the story making and helps then consider how useful it is, rather than whether it is true or not (Harper and Spellman, 2006; Miller and McClelland, 2006; Warner, 2009). Therefore, this explicitly addresses the utility argument discussed earlier.

The benefit of formulation is that it is more contextually driven and more open to social and cultural factors:

> As social constructionists, we are more interested in making sense of Jack's so-called 'delusions' in terms of his local and cultural context, than in categorising his experience to it with particular diagnoses. (Miller and McClelland, 2006, p. 140)

Formulations should make professionals' thinking and underlying assumptions more explicit and therefore open to challenge and revision. This seems preferable than relying on more fixed categories of psychiatric disorders. While formulation has arisen in clinical psychology and there is an acknowledgment that formulation requires a high level of psychological insight and skill, it also need not be confined to psychologists. Again, this is important to approved mental health practice in ensuring that practitioners have alternative strategies to see each person's current situation and circumstances as unique (rather than diagnostically determined).

Issues of practitioner reflexivity

It is important to be aware that both diagnosis and alternatives like formulation still involves a relational process within all its attendant power dynamics between service users and professionals (Johnstone and Dallos, 2006; Miller and McClelland, 2006). In addition, this is more than just not using diagnostic *words* but continuing to behave as if the person meets traditional diagnostic criteria. Any change has to go deeper than this – even if this sometimes involves strategically using diagnostic categories in certain circumstances to get appropriate support.

As with all professional decisions, it is crucial to bear in mind not only the context within which professionals are working (the external environment) but also one's own self-awareness, process and position (one's own internal world). This is why reflexivity is important to practice. For example, practitioners might want to consider the following questions:

- Are you for or against psychiatric diagnosis and do you impose this view on others, despite their own preferences?

- Do you use diagnosis selectively, in order to dismiss a service user's views and opinions depending on how you feel about a particular service user?

- Do you have certain prejudices, fears and judgements about people because of their particular diagnosis (this may be based on previous negative experiences)?

It is important that professionals are self-aware and honest enough about how these might impact on decision-making. Thus it is important not to let the endorsement or criticism of diagnosis get in the way of decision making. For example, while we may wish to minimize using certain stigmatizing or unhelpful diagnoses, this must not be at the expense of making sure the person gets the support they need. The problem arises when access to support is too heavily tied to particular diagnostic criteria. Unfortunately, this is likely to be increasingly the case, given cuts to service provision and changes to eligibility criteria that make it harder to access services. Therefore, if we want something different to diagnosis, it must result in better consequences for people in terms of gaining the more appropriate support and assistance.

Conclusion

The ways we describe mental health crises are important because they structure how it can be experienced, talked about and addressed. This chapter has outlined the main problems with psychiatric diagnosis, especially focusing on the categories of schizophrenia and borderline personality disorder. It has highlighted some of the ways psychiatric diagnosis may be helpful and then identified how alternatives to psychiatric diagnosis need to be more useful and compelling than this. Whether we use psychiatric diagnosis or not, the frameworks we use need to: reduce suffering; provide relief; not attribute blame; increase the likelihood of the person getting the support they need; and aid understanding of, and therefore compassion for, the person in their situation.

Many services and support mechanisms are still tied to diagnosis, and therefore practitioners might sometimes need to utilize them to advocate for people's needs in times of crisis and ongoing difficulty. However, beyond this, I have argued that diagnostic frameworks are not terribly helpful and there may be alternative, and more helpful, ways of referring to people's difficulties that will open up alternative ways of working with, and supporting, people in severe crisis.

Reflective Questions

1. What is the impact of diagnosis on an individual?

2. How easy or difficult is it to discuss alternatives to diagnosis in approved mental health practice?

3. How can an approved mental health practitioner's language and choice of words be influential?

4. In what way do people (including professionals) change their minds about a person when they hear the diagnosis?

6

Ethics and Values

Daisy Bogg

Editors' Voice

This chapter is concerned with the values and ethics underpinning approved mental health practice, these terms are often used interchangeably and it should be noted that while linked they are in fact separate considerations. The understanding of both is crucial for any textbook exploring the complexities of approved mental health practice. Here, the author considers how ethics and values are subject to changes over time and are dependent on context. Mental health legislation is underpinned by principles. In turn, approved mental health practice is based on a values-based approach. But, does it follow that approved mental health practice is therefore always ethical? This chapter seeks to discuss the dilemmas that this question poses. It discusses the balance required between personal values and the requirements of approved mental health practice alongside the impact of professional and organizational perspectives. In addition other considerations such as economic pressures and practical considerations complicate decision making. A balance is not always possible and conflict can emerge. Underpinned by philosophical considerations pertaining to risk taking, the chapter concludes with a discussion about the needs of the individual and those of society. Consideration of the literature concerning the use of Community Treatment Orders is provided as a contemporary challenge to ethical decision making. As is the case throughout the book this chapter raises the issues for consideration and concludes that there are no certain answers.

Ethics, and the ethical use of power, are key concerns for approved mental health practitioners, who are required to balance ethical dilemmas in practice on a regular basis (Bogg, 2010b). However, this is not a straightforward task and, what is considered to be ethical, changes over time and is also dependent upon social context. As first discussed in Chapter 4, the concept of mental health is one example of how service delivery and preferred intervention changes over time. Over the last two centuries psychiatric treatment has moved from understandings informed by religion and super-stition (Loschen, 1973; Porter, 2003), to asylum-based containment focused on separating those considered to be dangerous or otherwise different (Porter, 2003; MIND, 2010), and towards community-based care and sup-port focusing on independence and social engagement (Gillard et al., 2012). Each approach has been considered to be ethical at different periods in time (Bloch and Green, 2006; Lolas, 2006) and now serves to demonstrate both the change in what is considered to be ethical practice and the huge shift in thinking that has taken place internationally towards individuals experiencing mental distress.

There are two contrasting models of intervention evident within men-tal health services, the medical or health-based approach, and the social or psychosocial approach. Each offers an understanding of both the causes and treatment of mental health difficulties and how they are applied will depend on the professional background of the practitioner and the way services are delivered in the local area. As was first discussed in Chapter 1, understand-ing such models is crucial to approved mental health practice. The medical model focuses on mental illness, seeking to diagnose and medically treat individual symptoms. The anti-psychiatry movement of the 1960s and 1970s (Laing, 1960; Szaz, 1961), and the subsequent critical psychiatry network which it bore (Double, 2006), has been one of the harshest critics of the med-ical model, with terms such as 'toxic psychiatry' and 'pseudo-science' found in the literature. Despite these criticisms, this approach to mental illness has remained prevalent since the 1870s, when Emile Kraeplin first published his 'Compendium of Psychiatry' which was the beginning of the diagnostic sys-tem still in place across the world in the twenty-first century (Berrios and Hauser, 1998).

The social approach began to find its voice in the 1970s arising from the disability and civil rights movements (Duggan and Foster, 2002; Bogg, 2008; 2010a; Gilbert, 2010). It focuses on the social context of the individual and seeks to strengthen social networks and inclusion in local community life as a means of improving the individual's situation and help them move towards social recovery (Bentall, 2004; Tew, 2005; Social Care Institute for Excellence and Royal College of Psychiatrists, 2007). Issues such as occu-pation, self-reliance and a sense of hope are all key elements of the social approach, and it has been argued that these factors are essential to recovery (Frese and Davis, 1997; Social Care Institute for Excellence and Royal College of Psychiatrists, 2007; Bogg, 2010a; Barnes, 2011). Within this context it sug-gested that compulsory treatment can never be considered ethical and while there are clearly situations that warrant intervention, the practitioner role is to balance these rather than seek to remove the individual and contain them against their wishes (Kinney, 2009).

While there are commonalities between the medical and social approaches, including a duty to act in an individual's best interest (Department of Health, 2008), what this actually consists of, and what is considered to be the ethical course of action can be affected by a whole range of variables, including the theoretical perspective of the practitioner. The Approved Mental Health Professional role in England and Wales, and the Approved Social Worker role that preceded it, is designed to provide a counterbalance to the medical perspective, with an explicit remit to consider the whole circumstances of an individual's situation and provide a social perspective (Department of Health, 2008; Welsh Assembly Government, 2008) to inform any decisions or actions that are taken.

As noted in the introduction to this book the terminology in use in formal mental health is at times complex and can be ambiguous. For example, risk is a concept that is used extensively in mental health contexts and can mean different things to different people depending on the individual's perspective. For the purposes of this chapter the term is used to mean the chances of some form of harm, or other negative consequence, occurring to either the individual or to other people.

The definition of values

Whereas ethics are a set of characteristics based on what is considered right and wrong, values can be defined as broad preferences that determine what is considered important by the individual, profession, organization or cultures concerned (Bisman, 2003; Banks, 2005; Bakshtanovskii and Sogomonov, 2007; Petr, 2009; Bogg, 2010b).

For example as an individual you may personally value independence and self-determination, but as an approved mental health practitioner you are required to balance this individually held value with the need for intervention. The Mental Health Act Code of Practice in England and Wales (Department of Health, 2008) provides a set of guiding principles that should be used to underpin this decision, and which set out factors to be considered in the ethical use of formal powers. In England these include considering issues such as the purpose for which any powers are applied, the involvement of the person and their family where relevant, and a focus on applying the minimum amount of restriction upon an individual as is possible. The decision to detain someone will be influenced by both your own values and the requirements of approved mental health practice, including application of the guiding principles, and in some instances it is likely that your personal values and professional ethics may be in conflict. Where this is the case it becomes a matter of professional judgement and application of the legal framework to determine what actions are ethical in the given circumstances.

While, as we have seen in Chapters 2 and 3, legal requirements will vary across countries, the premise of balancing need, risk and protection remains common and approved mental health practitioners are required to undertake a complex balancing act between their own values and the ethical framework within which they are working.

The definition of ethics

Ethics is essentially a branch of philosophy concerned with the concepts of right, wrong and human morality (Ford, 2013). Ethical practice in most fields adheres to four key principles within which practitioners act, these include:

1. Actions are appropriate to the problem identified;

2. Actions are beneficial to the individual;

3. Actions take account of individual autonomy; and

4. Actions are socially just. (Bloch and Green, 2006; Robertson and Walter, 2007; Bogg, 2010b)

Compulsory mental health assessments are complex interventions that involve a whole range of individuals and services. They are not an exact science and the practitioner's own knowledge, values and experience all impact on the outcome. In some situations it may not be clear what the consequences of interventions will be, and approved mental health practitioners will need to make sure that their decisions are underpinned by the appropriate ethical approach. Professional and structural ethics are likely to have an impact, and there is a need to consider ethics from a broad perspective to ensure that systems and processes, as well as practice, are providing an ethical intervention option for the individual.

Professional ethics applies the concepts of ethics, and its associated social norms and attitudes to the accepted actions of a professional group, which then acts as a means of governing the provision of professional services (Abbott, 1983; Bakshtanovskii and Sogomonov, 2007; Bogg, 2008). In a health and social care context the service user or carer, is arguably, by virtue of their status as a 'user of the service' at a disadvantage in terms of knowledge, skills and power;

> People who are able to do something that other people do not know how to do, immediately, at the outset, bear certain duties and responsibilities to those who use their services. (Bakshtanovskii and Sogomonov, 2007, p. 78)

The professional acts as the gatekeeper of the service, and the service user or carer has to rely on the knowledge and skills of that professional to access what they need, when they need it. Within this relationship the power differential is significant, and how the professional responds and behaves is underpinned by professional ethics which underpin any decision or action they take.

Professional and organizational cultures

Approved mental health practice now operates across a number of professional and organizational cultures, and those undertaking the role are required to complete prescribed training and approval processes. This means that, as with other professional groups and roles, the practitioner's own values and ethics will be subject to a degree of professional assimilation which will inform their decision making process. One such example is the use of Section 136 of the Mental Health Act in England and Wales, which has been studied in terms of trends in its use (Dunn and Fahey, 1990; Turner et al., 1992; Simmons and Hoar, 2001; Royal College of Psychiatrists, 2011). These studies have identified common trends which can, in part, be associated with common responses to specific situations (Royal College of Psychiatrists, 2011). Some of the themes identified include:

- The behaviours least likely to lead to admission are threats or acts of deliberate self-harm.

- Those who present as agitated, mute or have some form of weapon are more likely to be admitted under the act following being detained under Section 136.

- The most common reason for initial detention under Section 136 are threats or actual violence, either to property or to others. (Royal College of Psychiatrists, 2011)

These trends suggest that there are professional cultures in place which attach meaning to particular aspects of behaviour and which influence professional decision making. In this instance it has become a professional norm that particular presentations of mental distress indicate the need for intervention for the purposes of both treatment and containment, and in these cases the risk will outweigh the rights of the individual. While particular factors that have been shown to indicate an increased risk of self-harm and/or aggression towards others, and as such should always form part of the analysis and decisions made, the task of the ethical practitioner is to identify the impact that professional norms and cultures are likely to have and balance these against both the objective and subjective evidence available (Banks, 2005; Bogg, 2010b).

The structures and organizations that approved mental health practitioners work within can have a significant impact on practice, and these also need to be considered from an ethical perspective. Organizational ethics are the attribution of characteristics to the way organizations operate and respond to situations. These inform the various structures, but take a wider view of whether organizations conduct themselves in an ethical way. As with other branches of ethics the dominant morality of the community or society the organization operates in will set the parameters of its approach. Structures operate within and across organizations, and these too can be considered in terms of whether they are ethical. These structures are developed within a socio-technical context (Harteloh, 2003; Airoldi et al., 2011), influenced both by current knowledge and evidence and also the expectations of the community and wider society (Tew, 2005; Bogg, 2010b) As such structural ethics are essentially the consideration of whether processes and mechanisms in place to facilitate or deliver services are underpinned by an ethical framework. (Emanuel, 2000; Borovečki et al., 2005).

Medical treatment for mental distress is the one area of healthcare where a patient's consent is not a necessary pre-requisite for medical intervention. Under the powers provided by the Mental Health Act individuals can be detained in hospital, forcibly treated and made subject to certain conditions in the community, a situation which is not mirrored in any other area of health care. The structures and systems underpinning mental health service delivery have an emphasis both on protecting and intervening in cases where the person is not willing, or able, to do so themselves, and as such the structural and organizational ethics are weighted towards the most appropriate management of risk to either the person or to others, rather than the autonomy and independence of the individual.

In the context of approved mental health practice there are a number of individuals, professions, organizations and structures involved and each will have its own cultures, behaviours and ethics. Pressures and priorities on both individuals and organizations can have an impact on both decision-making and actions, and practitioners are required to make complex decisions within the context of a whole range of organizational, structural and professional demands.

For example, hospital services may be operating a triage system and be balancing a number of admissions at a time, police services may be short of officers and prioritizing violent crimes as a result or, ambulance services may be experiencing a high call demand and prioritizing life or death cases. In each instance the actions of the organization will be dictated by their organizational ethics and principles, and their responses may have a direct impact on the well being of the individual being assessed. Each organization may be behaving in an ethical manner within their functions and purposes but these can be in conflict and can impact on approved mental health practice in negative ways.

At times of economic austerity, with resources and performance being a central organization and structural focus, issues such as competing organizational priorities and the lack of appropriate resources are likely to have a direct impact on the decisions made in practice by approved mental health practitioners. Concerns such as the availability of inpatient beds, the willingness of the police to remain with a patient detained on Section 136, and professional debates about what constitutes appropriate treatment are all issues faced by practitioners, and likely to have an impact on day-to-day decision making. Ethical practice cannot ignore the structural pressures, and approved mental health practitioners will be called upon to make decisions within the context of economic pressures. Issues such as whether a hospital bed is available and delays resulting from arranging police support or an ambulance to transport the person may have a negative impact on the person or their family and community. There are no easy answers, but an ethical practitioner will need to consider all these circumstances in a transparent way and weigh the various options available.

Teleology and deontology

While ethics in mental health apply the basic principles of an ethical approach, they do so in the context of balancing an inexact scientific approach, social values and professional expectations. This has resulted in the emergence of two branches of ethics, both of which remain in evidence in current mental health services.

Teleology is a branch of ethics based on utilitarian approaches that prioritize final outcomes over the any negative impacts of the action (Bloch and Green, 2006; Robertson and Walter, 2007; Bogg, 2010b). This is clearly evident is interventions under mental health legislation where the management of risk to the individual, or to other people, becomes the primary consideration, as well as in some of the more invasive treatment options (e.g., electroconvulsive therapy). Deontology, on the other hand, maintains that the action is of equal importance to the outcome (Bloch and Green, 2006; Robertson and Walter, 2007; Bogg, 2010b). This is in evidence in the recovery approach, with the emphasis on personalization, choice and control being the current philosophy of health and social care services.

It is likely that, as an approved mental health practitioner, both teleological and deontological approaches will feature in day-to-day practice and a critical analysis of both the action and the outcome in each case will be needed to inform decisions. It is at this point that the practitioner's personal values are likely to interact with the ethical framework that they are applying. Risk to the individual and/or others appear to be the dominant factor that dictates whether interventions are carried out in accordance with deontological or teleological principles. However, there is also evidence to show that the assessment of risk has a significant subjective bias (Beck, 1992; Douglas, 1994; Lupton, 2000), with issues such as personal values, beliefs and experiences, in addition to the application of objective evidence, all impacting on what the practitioner views to be risky (Langan, 1999; Morgan, 2007b; Bogg, 2010b).

Neither the teleological nor deontological approach is without criticism. There are situations where the risk of not acting is far greater than the risk of acting, and there are situations where it is not. There are also situations in which the individual is unable to protect themselves or act in their own best interest as a result of mental ill health, and in these situations the skill of the practitioner in this context becomes the ability to identify the difference. Remaining critically reflective of decisions will help approved mental health practitioners to remain aware of the impact of their own value-base and identify the theoretical basis on which they are making decisions.

The work of authors such as Kinney (2009) and Yianni (2009) provides differing views of what can be considered ethical in mental health contexts. For example, Kinney (2009), maintains that formal detention cannot be ethically justified and remains a grey area for all those involved. This view however does not take account of the wider duty to society, nor does it recognize that the same decision can be judged as both ethical and unethical at the same time depending on perspective and the situation in which it occurs. Yianni (2009) on the other hand argues that care is sometimes only facilitated by the use of compulsory measures and as such can be considered as an ethical intervention in and of itself.

Ethics and approved mental health practice

Approved mental health practice is influenced by several different ethical perspectives, and practitioners are required to balance, at times, competing and conflicting demands. While there are common principles, different values and agendas can change the priorities of all those involved in compulsory treatment, for example service users, carers, practitioners and provider organizations, and these can influence the various decisions that are made.

One of the most fundamental decisions an approved mental health practitioner makes is the decision to admit an individual to hospital against their wishes. As well as being a deprivation of liberty, this decision also has significant ramifications for the person and their families (where relevant). A formal detention may affect the person's future, their employment and aspirations and their relationship with the wider community. Approved mental health practice occurs within a set of clear boundaries, which inform and underpin decisions, but the interpretations and judgements of the individual practitioner will determine whether an application for admission is made.

Case Study: Deciding to Detain

Simon is a 34 year old Black British man; he has a long history of contact with mental health and criminal justice services. He has an established diagnosis of schizophrenia, and a history of opiate and crack cocaine use leading to periods of acute psychosis, characterized by verbal aggression, command hallucinations and self-injurious behaviour. Simon has had numerous formal admissions, the most recent being four months ago. He is exhibiting an established relapse pattern which results in continued deterioration of his mental state and an increase in anti-social behaviours of various forms. In addition, he has been convicted for numerous offences and has spent a number of periods in custody for crimes ranging from shop theft to robbery.

Simon is currently homeless and has been residing in a night hostel, the staff and other residents have been increasingly concerned by his bizarre behaviour and an assessment is convened. He is convinced that mental health services are trying to control his life and harm him and will not accept an informal admission, and it is likely that physical force will be needed to be used to admit him to hospital if that is the decision made.

From this brief case synopsis a number of issues are highlighted. Not only does the approved mental health practitioner need to consider the legal framework, Codes of Practice and professional ethics, they also need to be able to recognize the impact of Simon's diverse needs and appreciate that a decision to admit Simon in this instance is likely to result in increased distress. All of these factors need to be balanced against Simon's current situation and what is likely to be the most effective option in his individual case. In Simon's case there is clear evidence of risk, to both himself and others, and this is likely to make the decision more straightforward with evidence, professional culture and expectations of ethical compulsory practice all guiding the practitioners decision making. However there are also situations where the balance is more difficult to determine.

As has been highlighted earlier in this chapter, and discussed in more detail in Chapters 2 and 3, mental health legislation applies an explicit set of ethical principles that should be used to underpin any decision or action. These principles were developed as a specific ethical framework on which decisions impacting on the liberty of individuals should be made, and while some argue treatment without consent can never be ethical (Kinney, 2009) they are designed as a guideline for ensuring that decisions take account of, and weigh, a range of complex information. These guiding principles should not be seen as hierarchal, each principle needs to be considered to a greater or lesser extent depending on the individual circumstances. The approved mental health practitioner will need to consider, not only the immediate situation with which they are presented, but also the risks of acting (or not acting) for both the individual and the community in which they live.

Each compulsory mental health assessment requires approved mental health practitioners to determine, not only what is in the best interests of the person, but also how best to deliver their duties to the wider community within the boundaries and systems of the health and social services and structures in their particular area of practice. The issue of capacity, and whether an individual is able to consent to treatment, is one example of how the guiding principles should be applied. Where capacity is determined the approved mental health practitioner has to decide whether formal admission is an appropriate response to the risks they are identifying, and whether detention is ethical in light of these risks. While this is a balancing act, the consent of the individual can be assessed and factored into the decision-making. However, where the individual lacks capacity there are additional factors to consider arising from the likelihood that the person is unable to object or protect their rights within the process. In these circumstances the approved mental health practitioner will need to consider not only the situation and risks they are assessing, but also whether to make an application to ensure that safeguards are in place for the individual. In this instance it may be that the individuals' circumstances outweigh the principle of applying the least restrictive alternative.

Ethical practice and Community Treatment Orders

While admission to hospital, and providing treatment without the person's consent, gives rise to a number of ethical debates, as already discussed, the introduction of Community Treatment Orders (CTOs) in England and Wales in 2008 created an additional dilemma for practitioners. CTOs are set out in Section 17a of the amended Mental Health Act 1983 and allow for a patient to be discharged from hospital but remain subject to certain conditions, which if not met could result in the individual being recalled to hospital and ultimately their inpatient detention being recommenced.

These powers are intended for those who are, so-called, 'revolving door patients' (Kisely and Campbell, 2007; Lawton-Smith et al., 2008) who have repeated inpatient admissions and identified patterns of relapse in their mental health condition. This legislative change means that compulsory treatment can be extended beyond a patient admitted to hospital, and can now also be applied to individuals in the community who meet the criteria (Section 17A).

Between 2008/9 and 2011/12 the use of CTOs doubled, from 2,134 to 4,220 (Care Quality Commission, 2012) however their use is not consistent across the country, with use varying between 4 per cent and 45 per cent of patients being discharged onto a CTO depending on local preferences and practices. As with other powers under the Act, the application of a CTO requires a pre-defined set of criteria to be met (see the Act and associated Codes of Practice (Department of Health, 2008, Welsh Assembly Government, 2008)) and has a number of safeguards in place to ensure the individual's rights are observed.

The decision to introduce CTOs was taken in the context of significant debate and it has been argued that the use of coercion in the community has particular ethical considerations that go beyond those that arise as a result of compulsory treatment in a hospital setting (Burns and Dawson, 2009; Dale, 2010). This is particularly the case with the conditions that Responsible Clinicians (RC) are able to place upon the person and their lifestyle, which can include restrictions that are deemed necessary to:

- ensure that patient receives medical treatment for mental disorder;

- prevent a risk of harm to the patients' health or safety; and

- protect other people. (Department of Health, 2008, paragraph 25.30, p. 226)

How this criterion is applied will depend on individual circumstances, and conditions may include restrictions on particular behaviours (for example use of substances, visiting particular areas or people, curfews and so on). While there is an expectation that conditions will be kept to a minimum, what is deemed necessary will be influenced by the knowledge, skills, values and ethics of the professionals involved. In this context the practitioner's role includes balancing concepts of necessity with the civil rights of the individual.

It has been argued that CTOs serve to blur the boundaries between treatment and social control, and that those no longer meeting the criteria for detention in hospital should be discharged rather than facing another layer of coercion (Fulop, 1995; Dale, 2010). In contrast to this view, other commentators (Blake, 2001; Dawson, 2007), argue that there are circumstances where state coercion is necessary to protect individuals and enable them to act autonomously, with CTOs being an example of this in practice. Additionally, questions are now also being asked about whether CTOs are effective for people with particular mental health difficulties (Mullen et al., 2006;

Gledhill, 2007; O'Brien et al., 2009). A recent study published in the Lancet by Burns and colleagues (Burns et al., 2013) used randomized controlled trials (RCTs) over a period of 5 years to determine the impact of CTOs on readmission rates for individuals diagnosed as experiencing psychosis. The study concluded that there was little difference in readmission between those subject to a CTO and those treated in hospital or in the community without any compulsion. This finding is also supported by previous studies (Kisely et al., 2005; Mullen et al., 2006; O'Brien et al., 2009; Johnson, 2013; Thornicroft et al., 2013). This emerging evidence has a significant impact on the debate about whether CTOs are an ethical use of power; if an intervention is considered ineffective it is unlikely to be an appropriate treatment option, which means it becomes increasingly difficult ethically to justify its use. Further research is needed and approved mental health practitioners will need to remain up to date with these developments as part of ethical practice.

Conclusion

Ethics and values play a significant role in mental health treatment, and compulsory treatment in mental health services is an area where issues such as the use of power, and ensuring decisions are based on ethical principles are central considerations. For approved mental health practitioners there is a continuous need to take a critical approach to practice, informed by a sound understanding of the various approaches that are considered common practice in mental health service settings. As such this chapter has discussed a range of theories, perspectives and practice issues, with the aim of supporting readers to understand the complexities associated with ethical practice in the context of mental health legislation.

Values and ethics, however determined, have an important role to play in approved mental health practice, and practitioners will need to reflect on, and incorporate, a whole range of frameworks and expectations to deliver their roles effectively. While there are clear commonalities in what is considered ethical, with the law providing a set of guiding principles to guide decision making, there remain stark differences relating to what is considered ethical and how this is interpreted in law.

Mental disorders are the one area of health and social care that includes civil powers that can be used to compel an individual to accept medical treatment, and the factors influencing such a decision need to be carefully balanced and weighed to ensure that individual restrictions are both appropriate and ethical within the current legal framework. Approved mental health practitioners serve as a counterbalance to a single dominant medical perspective and are required to provide a more holistic view, and account for the whole circumstances of an individual's situation before making a decision to apply for compulsory admission. An essential part of this is to consider the impact of their own, and others', values and ethics on their decision making, and remaining aware of how these can impact in practice.

Whether the use of compulsory powers in cases of mental health distress can ever really be ethical remains an ongoing debate and depends on the particular point of view. Approved mental health practitioners are charged with making decisions in line with the legislative framework and to do this in an ethical way means taking account of the varying perspectives and values, and drawing on the available evidence to inform decision making.

Reflective Questions

1. How do approved mental health practitioners define ethical practice?

2. What structural, economic or other influences might approved mental health practitioners consider to contribute to ethical or unethical practice?

3. What ethical dilemmas do approved mental practitioners regularly face?

4. What are the tensions and conflicts in ethics and values that approved mental health practitioners' experience, and how might these impact on the decisions made?

5. Consider whether without critical reflection of professional ethics and values approved mental health practice is ill-informed.

7

Diversity in Mental Health Assessment

Amanda Taylor and Jill Hemmington

Editors' Voice

This chapter recognizes that the concept of diversity is not always well understood or defined at either a theoretical or a practice level. A task for the author, and then the reader, is to find the middle ground between a hazy, theoretical or academic understanding of diversity that focuses on abstract concepts of identity, and a basic, crude, demographic classification system or mind-set around how individuals or groups behave by virtue of a specific characteristic. It is a particular viewpoint that deliberately does not aim to be definitive, but rather recognizes that diversity means different things in different contexts. This concept is introduced and explored, and then a case study – that of a young man who is deaf (or 'Deaf', from a cultural perspective) – is used to break down the many facets and components of who we are, and how our identity is formed. The learning around deafness is in many respects transferable. However, diversity is not just about individuals and their identity, as there is a social context and perspective whereby issues of power, oppression and inequality are evident. An approved mental health practitioner will need to bear in mind that their interpersonal encounters with service users have the potential to compound these factors within their assessments and choice of outcomes. Acting in a way that empowers service users, through collaborative and partnership working, can go some way to addressing this. Approved mental health practitioners must deconstruct the idea that issues of diversity or culture only affect a few people or minority groups, or that such groupings inevitably have the same experiences, beliefs or values and are affected in similar ways. Each assessment, and each individual service user is different – and it is this difference that needs to be explored.

When presented with the words 'diverse' and 'diversity' it is reasonable to assume that an individual would automatically think about something or someone who is different from the self. It is perplexing that professionals have been unable to consistently transfer or embed their theoretical knowledge of diversity into their practice. This is indicated by a range of mental health inquiries (Shepherd, 1996; McGrath and Oyebode, 2002), and by the recommendations of the Independent Inquiry into the Death of David Bennett (Norfolk, Suffolk and Cambridge Strategic Health Authority, 2003) which led to the five year mental health action plan Delivering Race Equality (Department of Health/NMHDU, 2009). Many of these inquiries evidence a clear deficit in the nature of practitioners' understanding that is required to successfully intervene with individuals from diverse backgrounds.

The aim of this chapter is to challenge notions of diversity being simply and solely located within traditional, fixed dimensions and to alternatively view it as being unique to the individual, group and community. Furthermore, it will, utilizing the content of an inquiry report, ask the reader to 'stop and think' at timely intervals to reflect on how the presenting issues are conceptualized and fit with the reader's own value base. There is a knowledge, values and skills-based theme underpinning much of this chapter that prompts reflection, concluding that it is within 'analytical pauses' that we can explore the complex and intricate nature of diversity in relation to approved mental health practice, and our subjective positions within it.

It could be anticipated that a book chapter entitled 'Diversity in Mental Health Assessment' would be premised on specific categories and attempts to define individuals or groups in tangible or observable ways. Payne (2006) refers to diversity in terms of the 'big three: race, class and gender'. It could also concentrate on the protected characteristic within the Equality Act 2010 (age; being or becoming a transsexual person; being married or in a civil partnership; being pregnant or having a child; disability; race including colour, nationality, ethnic or national origin; religion, belief or lack of religion/belief; sex; sexual orientation). Assessment in approved mental health practice could be influenced by a practitioner's fixed ideas about names, rituals, language, gender roles, custom, dress, beliefs, food/diet, non-verbal communication or religion. However, even though all these categories and elements of the person are completely and equally relevant, this chapter seeks to provide additional breadth to a mental health practitioner's reasoning when engaged in an assessment process; reasoning that will have a critical bearing on outcomes for service users.

Diversity can be conceptualized in different ways. For example, it could relate to subjective thoughts and feelings that a person holds around their identity. This could be formed around real or perceived differences about many things, such as the categories outlined above. An alternative objective approach would look at diversity as having a social context where social relationships or political and organizational processes are significant (Singh, 2012).

Diversity: As we know it

Diversity is a subject that requires persistent reappraisal. The accessibility and impact of migration, together with westernisation, intercultural marriage and reproduction, the ever changing construct of the family and variation in the fabric, composition and context of the lives of service-users stimulates us to review our understanding of individuals, groups and communities as fluid entities. Societies are becoming increasingly complex and the individual faces diversity in all areas of life. More and more, the idea of a stable or fixed identity is becoming less useful. Increasingly, there is a need to consider the intersecting effects of, for example, race, class and gender. The concept of intersectionality can be used to explain how multiple aspects of personal identity can affect understanding, assessment and outcomes (Seng et al., 2012). Similarly 'intersectionality of identity' is a reference to the way in which an 'individual embodies within the self, multiple, cultural, ethnic and group identities' (Mahalingam et al., 2008).

There is, therefore, a subjective quality to identity that cannot be categorized within simple demographic characteristics or definitions. Crenshaw (1989, p. 149) reflects on this complexity, where

> [Black women] sometimes experience discrimination in ways similar to white women's experiences; sometimes they share very similar experiences with Black men. Yet often they experience double discrimination – the combined effects of practices which discriminate on the basis of race, and on the basis of sex. And sometimes, they experience discrimination as Black women – not the sum of race and sex discrimination, but as Black women.

There are several levels at which the effects of intersectionality may have an influence on the individual. This is not new and it is consistent with earlier socio-ecological models of human development (e.g., Bronfenbrenner, 1979).

Here, individual psychological development takes place in interactions between five concentric circles of mutually influencing, social-ecological systems. The intrapsychic is central, moving outwards to the familial and broader social, political and organizational contexts (Seng et al., 2012).

Diversity is therefore multidimensional in nature, with the potential for resultant oppression if it is not understood on both structural and humanistic levels (Bronfenbrenner, 1979; Rogers, 2004; Ruch et al., 2011). Thompson (2001, p. 160) also cautions against the manner in which various elements within the 'dimensions of diversity' can evolve into oppression and discrimination.

Effective work with diversity rests on the approved mental health practitioner's level of cultural competence, which is always going to be an aspiration rather that something that we can say we possess entirely. For Campinha-Bacote, cultural competence is

> the ongoing process in which the healthcare professional continuously strives to achieve the ability and availability to work effectively within the cultural context of the patient (individual, family, community)...The process requires that [they] see themselves as *becoming* culturally competent rather than being culturally competent. (Campinha-Bacote, 2011, p. 42, emphasis added)

Dadlani et al. (2012) believe that awareness of clients' cultural experiences and worldviews has to be central to culturally informed practice, and yet culture is often only considered when a service user is a member of a marginalized group. While accepting that service users' identities develop from their unique cultural experiences and social dynamics, approved mental health practitioners need also to bear in mind that as professionals they belong to a 'dominant social group' that 'maintain systems of privilege and oppression' (Dadlani et al., 2012, p. 177). If these practitioners fail to recognize the effect of this privilege and oppression, they are less likely to be helpful. There is also a danger that they consider culture as something that refers only to service users who are different or in a minority group and, consequently, view these service users as a 'pathologised other' (Burman, 2004), inevitably devaluing their cultural norms.

There is a 'stop and think' point here in relation to identity. Identity could be conceived of as a conscious response to the question 'Who am I?' (Hoare, 2013). Engage with this for a moment, and ask yourself the question. Are your responses based on your roles or titles? Mother, father, nurse, doctor, social worker, son, daughter? Black, white, disabled?

Yet Erikson (1974) conceptualized identity processes as those that generally occur below the 'radar of conscious awareness' (Hoare, 2013). Erikson's view is that any responses to the 'Who am I' question portray

> a definition of identity I have never used and never would use, because the answer to the question 'Who am I?' (if there really were one) would end the process of becoming itself. (Erikson and Newton, 1973, p. 109)

Identity is not therefore largely conscious, and 'identity is never "established" as an "achievement"...or anything static or achievable' (Erikson, 1968, p. 24). Its development is a continuous process throughout all of the life course, and it relates to a person's wholeness (Hoare, 2013). For Adler (2012, p. 367), narrative identity is 'the internalised, evolving story of the self that each person crafts to provide his or her life with a sense of purpose and unity'. From adolescence, individuals begin to create the 'story' about their experiences that consolidates their past, perceived present, and anticipated future (McAdams et al., 2001). This then provides the self with a sense of purpose and meaning. These personal narratives reveal the ways in which the individual makes sense out of his or her experiences.

Authenticity and empathy

Bogg's (2010a, p. 61) definition of diversity: that it is 'whatever makes us different from each other' is effective in its simplicity. Using this as a starting point, the significance of what will then be termed authentic understanding of an individual's biography needs to be explored. Knowledge and understanding within the human professions lies within the subjective self and the subjective other (Milner and O'Byrne, 2009). Authentic understanding is the way in which we first recognize and then comprehend difference that is outside the range of our current experiences and perceptions; both personally and professionally.

So how does an approved mental health practitioner engage in meaningful assessment? How does one understand and interpret need? A further important concept here is that of empathy 'To sense the client's private world as if it were your own, but without ever losing the "as if" quality – this is empathy' (Rogers, 1957, p. 99). Empathy is often described as 'getting into the shoes of' or 'getting under the skin of' the other person in order to understand their individual, subjective world. To refine this, and to 'tune in', approved mental health practitioners must 'communicate their commitment to understanding their clients' worlds by frequently checking the accuracy of their understanding and showing their willingness to be corrected' (Nelson-Jones, 2006, p. 103).

Rogers (1986) suggested that the practitioner's responses should always be about testing understanding or checking perceptions until we understand exactly the others' feelings. This means never making assumptions, particularly based on what we think we might know about another person's cultural background.

There is an emotional (feeling) aspect to empathy, and also an intellectual (cognitive) element. *Becoming* empathic means acquiring knowledge (for example an examination of the stereotypes we may hold about others,

---

Reflective Task 1

Think

- Develop a picture in your mind's eye of a person who is not the same as you. The difference might be one of gender, race, sexuality, class, ethnicity, age, physical or sensory impairment or learning disability. Focus on this one person. What makes them different, and what ideas are you developing? Where did you get your ideas from? Childhood? Your parents' attitudes? The newspapers you read? Have your ideas changed over the course of your life?

- Now think about the same person in the way that your professional self might think. How comfortable are you undertaking a compulsory mental health assessment here? What do you see? Have you imposed any barriers to understanding this person? Would you feel nervous or threatened? Would you prepare? What would you prepare? Have you made any assumptions? What is your starting point to getting to know this person and how they got here?

Reflect

- Are you now thinking about interventions, practical tasks or ensuring that you use the right words? Can you reconcile your own values with your professional ones? What strategies do you employ first to understand and second to assess/engage with diversity and diverse service-user groups?

Practice Issues

- Have you encountered or do you foresee any difficulties when engaging with diversity and difference? Which cultural groupings are you aware of and which do you need to revise your knowledge of?

---

and the cultural and structural notions we have about a society) and developing the ability to feel 'with' someone else (Seden, 2005, p. 74). An approved mental health practitioner enters any interpersonal encounter with their own formulation and expectations and all practitioners will differ in terms of their own experiences, ideas and prejudices. It is then incumbent upon them to recognize any barriers to understanding that might be self-imposed.

The relationship between the practitioner and service user is seen as 'fundamental to the science and art of healing' (Ward et al., 2012, p. 34). The nature of any interpersonal interaction defines both the quality of the service user's experience and the type of outcome. Both these areas have significance within approved mental health practice – the former in relation to the likelihood of engagement, and the latter in terms of whether the service user is likely to lose his or her basic liberty. Ward et al. (2012, p. 34) refer to 'empathic interactions' and define these as 'those that involve an understanding of the experiences, concerns, and perspectives of another person, combined with a capacity to communicate this understanding'.

Peplau (1997) explored communication between nurse and patient and described human connectedness as being essential to good health. The importance of collaborative, partnership-based assessment cannot be over-emphasized and this is enshrined in the principles of the Codes of Practice to the Mental Health legislation. The Scottish Code makes clear 'the importance of the patient participating as fully as possible in any decisions being made' (Scottish Executive, 2005c, para. 3); in Northern Ireland 'all individuals should be as fully involved as practicable, consistent with their needs and wishes, in the formation and delivery of their care and treatment' (Department of Health and Social Services (Northern Ireland), 1992, para.1.9); in England 'Patients must be given the opportunity to be involved, as far as is practicable in the circumstances, in planning, developing and reviewing their own treatment and care' (Department of Health, 2008, para. 1.5) and in Wales 'patients should be involved in the planning, development and delivery of their care and treatment to the fullest extent possible' (Welsh Assembly Government, 2008 para. 1.10). However brief the time spent together, the significance of the nature of the relationship between approved mental health practitioner and the service user is clear.

Within the therapeutic relationship, Mall (2000, p. 242) explains that 'the willingness to understand and the wish to be understood go together and constitute the two sides of a hermeneutic coin'. So the approved mental health practitioner's capacity to carry out an assessment based on authentic understanding requires much more than the nominal amount of foundational knowledge in terms of what diversity as a core concept actually is. The notion of diversity as a fixed entity could lead to inaccurate conclusions being drawn, ones that do not speak to the fluidity of the composite parts of any relational system, let alone a human one. What is therefore significant and a prerequisite to potential engagement is accuracy and authenticity in terms of a professional's understanding of diversity in relation to the uniqueness of the life lived (Kelly, 1955; Ellis and Flaherty, 1992). For these reasons it is important from the outset that approved mental health practitioners pursue what is referred to as the 'professional conscience': a reflective curiosity that will creatively explore fluctuating ideas, attitudes and attributed meanings in terms of the notion of diversity while engaged with approved mental health practice. Dialogue, effective communication and empathy are part of this.

Being creative can offer a tool for unearthing or challenging fixed stereotypes or categories. Pilgrim (2009, p. 59) defines creativity as 'an act of imagination that leads to a solution to a problem or a novel form of artistic expression'. When examined from a practice position, ideas of imagination and artistry are relevant to the construction of knowledge and the application of skill. Explicitly locating these understandings within the context of approved mental health practice enables us to plan for innovation in terms of outcomes for those individuals who have little choice other than to engage. Subsequently, a number of questions arise. For example: How do approved mental health professionals engage with and assess diversity in a way that is innovative and unique, while simultaneously balancing the statutory role, duties, powers and legal processes that define the nature of the assessment? How inventive can approved mental health practitioners be with the skills they have developed for assessing and understanding diversity? Do the outcomes of compulsory mental health assessments reflect individual approved mental health practice or is resourcefulness, creativity and expression stifled by the framework of the statutory role? The nature of risk assessment, and how practitioners are informed as to what constitutes risk also needs to be carefully balanced.

Reflective analysis of a case study: Interpreting diversity

The Deaf Community, self-defined as a linguistic minority (Bramwell et al., 2000), has been chosen here to facilitate reflective analysis. As always there are hazards that exist in the over-simplification or generalization of this or any cultural group, but awareness should be drawn to the transferable nature of the relevant knowledge, learning, values and skills that lie at the heart of competent and ethical practice.

It is useful to 'stop and think' at this point. Imagine a scenario whereby you have received a referral for a compulsory mental health assessment. You learn that this person is deaf. What are you thinking? What do you need to know? Do you see them any differently? Have you been diverted to a different mindset that considers the biological aspects of the person? Have you been diverted into thinking about planning for practical arrangements?

Diversity: As it exists for a diverse population; locating the knowledge base

In order to engage in an authentic exploration of diversity within contemporary mental health practice, as previously explained, individuals who are deaf have been respectfully chosen as the platform for learning. Practitioners are asked to contemplate the potential transferability of their evolving understandings and recognize their relevance to various other distinct and diverse service-user groups.

For the purposes of this 'Deafness' will mean individuals who have little or no functional hearing: sign language users who, on the whole, view themselves as a linguistic minority and not disabled. In general, these are people who have a severe or profound hearing loss and who favour manual communication as their first language or language of choice. They are Deaf with a capital 'D'; with the capitalization used to demarcate a cultural as opposed to the lower case 'd' purely biological response to Deafness.

It is helpful to set some further context in relation to Deafness, beginning with findings that indicate that communication is fundamental to life stage development and the mental wellbeing of a Deaf person maturing within a hearing society (Du Feu and Ferguson, 2003). The stance taken here is that it is society and social systems that are disabling, not Deafness (Gregory and Hartley, 1991), and that Deafness is not something that requires correction, but significant forethought, informed decision making and sensitive management. Deaf people are not, as they are largely perceived, individuals with a hearing deficit who require medical intervention nor are they Deaf in their totality and not does the Deafness encapsulate all of who they are. A point illustrated by Diane Springford, a woman who is Deaf as opposed to a Deaf woman, explains that 'Deaf is not bad, Deaf is not wrong, Deaf does not need [to be] fixed. What is between the ears is a lot more important than what goes on in the ears' (Springford, 1997, p. 2).

All individuals are made up of composite and at times conflicting layers, and all layers must be seen and attempts made to engage with the entirety of who they are. The reality is that the Deaf population and the people within it are not easily defined or explained. Higgins (1980, p. 32), discussing the multifaceted nature of Deafness, asserts that 'hearing loss is an extremely complex matter, which varies from person to person'. There are three fairly broad categories of understanding that can be applied when attempting to locate the reality of an individual who is Deaf and these are situated within medical, social and cultural perspectives (Du Feu, 2010). The medical position aims to categorize and treat the audiological responses of the person who is Deaf; the social construction argument suggests that it is society which is restricting (and not the Deafness) and the cultural view of Deafness describes people who are Deaf as a linguistic minority group with their own norms, beliefs, values and language. As Denmark (1994, p. 1) suggests, 'Deafness is not visible' and therefore the danger is that it is often overlooked.

Furthermore, additional layers of 'difference' can and do co-exist. Examples are the person who is Deaf and Caucasian, the person who is Deaf and Asian, the person who is Deaf, female and black, the person who is Deaf and gay, the person who is Deaf and Irish, the person who is Deaf, blind and Caucasian and so on. The point here is that Deafness, like in other cultures, is an element or layer of the person and that the multiple parts of an individual and their lived experience should be fully considered within the assessment process. Therefore, the authentic understanding of an individual who is Deaf requires a significant level of knowledge in relation to what the terms Deaf, Deafness and diversity systemically mean. This knowledge should be reviewed from sociological (to include cultural), psychological and biological perspectives.

Assessment and diversity

It will be beneficial at this juncture to pause and reflect upon current understanding and awareness in relation to an approved mental health practitioner's assessment with an individual from the Deaf population. Utilizing the framework of Reflective Task 2 think about the mandatory assessment and report from a systemic position, which includes the biological, sociological and psychological components of the whole person. Incorporate that which you deem as relevant within each of the embedded and influencing systems.

Reflective Task 2

- *Knowledge* – What knowledge (include legislation) would you bring to an assessment of an individual who explains their identity as located within the Deaf population?
- *Values* – Which professional values will underpin the assessment process and why?
- *Skills* – Which skills are significant in terms of an assessment with an individual who is Deaf and why?

*Think of different cultural groups; can you locate the transferability of knowledge, values and skills to this grouping?

The following extract, taken from the Independent Inquiry into the Care and Treatment of Daniel Joseph (Mischon et al., 2000), provides preliminary insight into the complex nature of a statutory assessment with an individual who is Deaf. Mischon et al. (2000) begin their report by outlining the multifarious nature of the case content, explaining that

> this particular inquiry has been extremely complex because we found ourselves having to look at not only the issue of mental illness, but also mental illness in the context of the implications of Deafness and the complexities of communication. For those of us on the inquiry panel without specialist knowledge of working with

Deafness, the inquiry process has been a real 'eye-opener' in terms of learning about the difficulties encountered by Deaf people at almost every level of everyday living. Things that most of us take for granted simple things like going to the doctor and explaining how you feel pose major problems for those who are Deaf and use BSL [British Sign Language] as well as for those trying to care for them. (Mischon et al., 2000, p. 2)

Arising from these reported findings, practice knowledge, values and skills will be examined to demonstrate the inherent complexity when assessing people from this linguistic minority (Padden and Humphries, 1988, 2005). The Inquiry report (Mischon et al., 2000) will continue to form the framework for reflection and knowledge construction when evaluating the narrative of a diverse individual, group or community.

Daniel Joseph was 18 years of age at the time of an incident in 1998 that led to the death of Carla Thompson and serious injury to Agnes Erume who had been in periodic receipt of various educational, social and mental health services throughout her lifetime (Mischon et al., 2000). In relation to diversity, Daniel is recorded as being from an 'Afro-Caribbean' family. However, it is significant also to note that Daniel is Deaf, the ethnicity of his father is unknown, he was born into a hearing family, moved between Trinidad and the UK in the early years of his life and was educated and lived within western society from the age of three. The subtext within this biographical detail raises a number of issues that relate directly to the actuality of Daniel's identity (Stephan and Stephan, 2000). The relevance of actual and perceived life stage development and individuation, the impact of this content on presentation and, in total, an authentic understanding of all of these features is pertinent to the overall professional assessment. For these purposes it is vital that the construction of meanings is explored.

The Inquiry report provides a chronological account of Daniel's life up until the time of the incident and goes as far as to source handwritten evidence completed by Daniel himself. This level of detail is not readily accessible when a referral for assessment is received, and so this report affords us with the ability to consider its complexity and to have time to reflect on the detail.

Assessment considerations

Gambrill (2006, p. xiii) explains the role of knowledge, values and skills in terms of 'critical thinking' and states that they will ultimately assist with 'sound decision making'. Utilizing a knowledge, values and skills (KVS) framework to explore engagement before, during and after an event creates

Reflective Task 3

Assessment: Put yourself in the position of the approved mental health practitioner preparing to engage in an assessment with Daniel. Begin by constructing meanings in terms of life stage (present and previous); understanding in relation to how you might define culture (shared meanings, beliefs, attitudes) and 'ethnicity' (origins); citing any issues or difficulties you consider are relevant. In addition to these considerations couple this with the Deafness and continue to formulate a cultural picture that is inclusive of these dimensions and that provides understanding and direction in terms of how you might actively engage in the assessment process.

Think again within the Knowledge, Values and Skills (KVS) assessment framework:

- *Knowledge* – What knowledge (include legislation) do you have or what knowledge will you need to develop to enable you to acquire an authentic understanding of Daniel and his lived experience?
- *Values* – Which professional values will be required?
- *Skills* – Which skills are significant in terms of an assessment with a person who is Deaf? Why and how might you creatively utilize them?

*Ask yourself what you 'see' when you imagine yourself in face to face proximity with Daniel. Can you see past his reported large gait, the colour of his skin, or his Deafness? How can you engage with him to ascertain who and how he is?

the potential for accuracy in future practice and makes available the opportunity for the development of the practitioner's evidence base. Trevithick (2012, pp. 33, 154) goes further, breaking the knowledge component into three groupings, namely 'theoretical knowledge, factual knowledge and practice knowledge'. It is important to recognize that preparatory understandings can be consolidated throughout the assessment and that an ongoing review of the overall process is essential to enable continued progressive development of the practice approach.

Case analysis: Outlining the reality; appreciating the complexity

Knowledge

In order to acquire an authentic understanding of Daniel a concise synopsis of his life is offered from the content recorded in the Inquiry Report. This

Reflective Task 4

The following reflective analysis aims to pose questions, explore values and define skills that will provide a framework from which authentic understanding can be achieved when preparing for and engaging with diversity. Again, it is significant to pause and consider the transferable content within this information that can be adapted when engaging across the range of diversity.

Age/life stage development/ theoretical understandings

- Who is Daniel and how does he fit into the world?
- How has he progressed or not through the life stages?
  What are the attachment patterns?

Culture/Diversity

- How would Daniel define his identity? Does he understand these concepts?
- How might you define this layer of his identity?

Education

- Where was Daniel educated and how would this information inform the assessment process?
- Is Daniel's level of understanding age appropriate?

Family construct

- Who are the key people in Daniel's life?
- How would he explain these relationships?
- Does he have any issues in this respect?

Legislation

- What are the core pieces of legislation that will guide the practice approach?

Diagnosis

- Is there a history or diagnosis?
- Are there any indicators that further assessment is required?

Previous involvement

- Is there any previous service involvement?

Spirituality

- Does Daniel understand and or have any defined spiritual needs?

Reflective Task 4 (*cont'd*)

Risk factors

- What are the factors that cause concern in terms of risk?
- Which strategies will you need to employ?

*Think of a different cultural group; can you locate the transferability of knowledge, values and skills to this grouping?

---

is substantiated by research, literature and theory pertaining to life stage development and Deafness. Consideration will be given to practice values and core practice skills; ones that pay attention and respond to the multiple layers of diversity. This begins with the knowledge that Daniel, at the time of the event, was an 18-year-old male of Afro-Caribbean descent and that the origins of his biological father are not known. Therefore, in terms of diversity, clarification of heritage is something that would require further thought at the point of assessment if for no other reason than Daniel himself may have introjected notions of a father figure that could have shaped his understanding of the self (Segal, 2004). Daniel's age, subsequent life stage(s) and maturation should be defined (Walker and Crawford 2010); gender perspectives should also be contextualized at this stage of the assessment; alongside any possible impacts of westernization.

Another significant factor is the Deafness, and reported content, which explains that the family were never encouraged to learn signed communication. This failing subsequently led to Daniel having delayed access to language, an issue that will have impacted upon the development of his cognitive capacities (Marschark, 1997; Pinker, 2007). This is explained further by Knight and Swanwick (1999, p. 60) in their transcript pertaining to the parents of Deaf children, who conclude that

> it is considered that language development and cognitive development are linked in many ways, this reiterates the importance of families developing comfortable and appropriate ways of communicating with their child.

Therefore, language and understanding, in terms of acquisition and overall development, will require careful consideration.

There are conflicting accounts within the Inquiry report in relation to Daniel's family construct, location and resultant influences. Daniel is reported to have had a secure attachment with his mother however, intermittent residency between Trinidad and England, with and without his mother's accompaniment, makes this suggestion difficult to reason (Mischon et al., 2000, p. 3). This information, coupled with the fact that Daniel was eventually brought back to England by a stranger to live with his maternal grandmother, a woman who would 'shut Daniel in a darkened room and remove all his toys', (Mischon et al., 2000, p. 12) cannot possibly equate to circumstances that are conducive to the development of secure attachments (Bowlby, 1998). Daniel also apparently demonstrated ambivalent behaviours when his mother would return to visit him while in the care of the state. This further validates the aforementioned sporadic separations as causation for historic difficulties with self-expression and the communication of the distress he must have been feeling associated with a possible lack of trust in the world (Winnicott, 1964). Spiritual beliefs, alongside child rearing patterns and physical ill health assist with making sense of the maternal grandmother's behaviours towards Daniel. However, in no way did this dissolve or repair the damage that evidently occurred and that consistently appeared to impact upon his ability to feel safe and secure (Mischon et al., 2000, pp. 14–15). Locating these understandings with other detailed accounts of similar behaviours, those evident when Daniel appears to feel threatened or insecure, clearly link with the content of the circumstances prior to the incident where he is reported to have been in a state of flux due to relationship difficulties and an assumed pregnancy (Mischon et al., 2000, p. 94). Additional consideration of this content will provide practitioners with greater understanding in terms of how they may be perceived by Daniel while attempting to engage with him.

As we can see from this brief analysis there is clear evidence of the immense complexity that diversity and difference have upon the lived experience of Daniel Joseph. The biological, psychological and sociological contexts and resultant shaping influences appear confusing at best and restricting and harmful at worst. This poses questions regarding how this young man negotiated his way in, and understood, the world around him. It provides further background when considering his experience both from an intra- and interpersonal perspective. It is, therefore, vital that as practitioners we can seek that which is outside of the self and consider not only the diversity relating to the other but go some way to working within their 'internal frame of reference' to understand the layers that exist (Nelson-Jones, 2008, p. 45).

Values

Numerous, if not all, practice values are relevant to each person in every case. Nevertheless, in this circumstance particular values have distinct relevance and meaning. Given the historic, perceived or otherwise, imbalance of power between the hearing and Deaf populations in terms of discrimination and oppression Marschark (1997, p. 4) suggests that 'it often seems that the hearing majority thinks (rightly or wrongly) that it knows what is best for the Deaf minority, and the Deaf minority believes (rightly or wrongly) that it is powerless to change the establishment'. It is within the conscious application of professional values that the capacity to eradicate any reciprocal prejudice might exist. It can be understood from the inquiry that Daniel's level of self-worth may be an issue given the disparate nature of his early relationships and the relationship patterns that appear to have been repeated throughout his life. His experiences in the organizations within which he was placed, on the whole, offered him security, safety, and an opportunity to self-actualize. However, given his language deficit and its likely impact we need to consider to what extent this could reasonably be achieved.

It has been, and remains difficult to understand why 'understanding difference' (Figure 7.1) is not seen as a core practice value. It is the basis of who each of us are if we are to accept notions of uniqueness and individuality.

Skills

There exist comprehensive considerations of culture and difference but sadly these tend to generalize and provide little specific direction concerning the Deaf and many other diverse populations.

Simon (1999, p. 8) reflects on the significance of communication and explains that people's own identity and meaningful existence depend on finding a place in the social world. The ability to achieve this 'place', in turn, depends to a very large extent on one's interactive skills.

Hargie and Dickson (2004, p. 2) speak of the contentment that can be found through human interaction, and discuss it as being 'the very essence of the human condition' and that 'the self emerges through social

Figure 7.1   Understanding difference

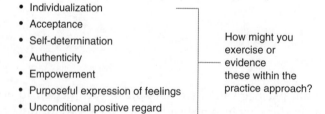

interaction'. Placing this knowledge together with Daniel's life experiences and interpersonal capacities is a sobering event, particularly when reflecting on Freeman's summary of the impact of Deafness on individual maturation within the hearing world, where

> the greatest barrier for any person with Deafness is the inability to communicate in a deep and meaningful manner with hearing individuals. Without appropriate accommodations, those with Deafness are often inadvertently excluded from virtually all communication. This can affect a Deaf person's social, educational and emotional environments. (Freeman, 2005, p. 1)

An approved mental health practitioner will need to consider how engagement could be achieved, and how to connect interpersonally with a person who is Deaf – and indeed with any other from a diverse cultural group. It is essential that a significant degree of 'tuning-in' is completed when preparing to intervene with a culture that is different to that of the practitioner's (Shulman, 1999). This process will be crucial if engagement is to be effective, meaningful, authentic and achievable.

The Deaf population require and are fully entitled to access their first language (manual communication) under what is termed 'reasonable adjustment' (Disability Discrimination Act, 1995). Attention must to be paid to which sign language the person uses as, again, there can be distinct differences in this respect. For example, if you are attempting to engage with a person who is Irish and Deaf you will need to either have a recognized sign language qualification to establish understanding and interaction in Irish Sign Language (ISL) or be aware of how to access an appropriate (ISL) interpreter. A person in England, Scotland or Wales is likely to use British Sign Language (BSL) and the same parameters exist for engagement. However, a further consideration that practitioners must be aware of, one that speaks to the aforementioned 'layers' of diversity, is that there is also regional variation. An example, from my own practice where this went very badly wrong was an occasion when I spent an entire assessment calling (in sign language) a service-user's auntie a 'pig'! This did not, as you would imagine, encourage engagement, establish trust or demonstrate core practice values on any level. Accuracy and attention to detail is clearly essential.

Even though we can and do believe ourselves to be efficient and competent in the application of practice skills, engaging with a person whose first language is different from our own, unless we are bi- or multilingual, requires sophisticated levels of understanding and the ability, and/or access, to a communication medium that can effectively bridge any interpersonal gap. It should also be noted that working through an interpreter is a skilled activity and one that demands awareness of the complexities that can be a hindrance in this process; such as the interpreter not being aware of practice terminology and approaches that could affect the therapeutic dynamic. It cannot be assumed that a relative, friend or any available other can be employed as a substitute for a qualified interpreter. In fact, if you proceed in this way you risk breaching a person's basic human right to privacy and freedom of expression (Department of Health, 2009). Similarly, within the clear confines of approved mental health practice the respective Codes of Practice to the legislation advise the same (Department of Health, 2008; Department of Health and Social Services (Northern Ireland) 1992; Scottish Executive, 2005b; Welsh Assembly Government, 2008).

Diversity: As we now own it

The evidence offered through the exploration of the Independent Inquiry into the Care and Treatment of Daniel Joseph (Mischon et al., 2000), as with many other reports, clearly indicates the need for change and suggests numerous ways to secure this. As illustrated throughout this discussion diversity is not about categories or mindsets but, rather, it exists uniquely for those it relates to. This needs to be understood and embraced by approved mental health practitioners. Considering this core concept through the lived experience of the Deaf population has demonstrated the multifaceted, fluid and complex nature of diversity. Furthermore, it has shown that a core sense of humanity is required when endeavouring to conceptualize the diverse lived experience of the other in an authentic manner. It has highlighted the practitioner's responsibility towards the requirement for authenticity and the demands for a creative practice approach. Practitioners need to challenge their understandings constantly to, progress their knowledge. They must get comfortable with difference and excited about diversity and from this basis develop practice that is as innovative and imaginative as it can be. Singh (2010, p. 341) suggests that dialogues about differences generally are hindered when we are 'developmentally unprepared to handle them'. Tensions are often present where difference is apparent. Within approved mental health practice, difference is often the 'elephant in the room'. Uncertainty and inexperience in relation to understanding others is both natural and common. Empathy, 'tuning in' and constantly asking oneself questions are the starting points to a thorough, effective assessment that has honesty and collaborative work at its core. Individuals' outcomes, no matter which layers of diversity are present, depend upon it.

Reflective Questions

1. How might approved mental health practitioners define diversity?

2. Who is affected by diversity?

3. What is your answer to the question 'Who am I?' What categories have you used?

4. Which specific skills does an approved mental health practitioner need to undertake a thorough, culturally competent assessment?

8

The Impact of Space and Place

Anthea Murr and Tamsin Waterhouse

Editors' Voice

Consideration of approved mental health practice, as this chapter highlights, tends to have the urban context as its default. Here the authors challenge this default by asking the reader to contemplate what constitutes mental health in a rural context, and also the psychological, physical and practical impact of delivering services in such environments. The chapter echoes an earlier thread in this book which seeks to understand the influence of evidence and of research, here the notion that proximation and remoteness are key concepts and underpin approved mental health practice. Of particular note is the way in which default concepts need to be challenged. Notions of communities and boundedness, confidentiality and anonymity, and an understanding of what constitutes normal behaviour are reconsidered. For us as editors it felt important to look anew at how these concepts are considered and in particular to consider evidence outside of the usual. This chapter does both and as a result helps its readers to reconsider received wisdom, confront value stances and challenge any default. Lastly, this chapter echoes the challenges that working across borders bring; another important consideration in light of the increased divergence resulting from devolution.

It is important that approved mental health practitioners, undertaking assessments in rural areas and communities understand mental disorder as experienced in such places and are aware of the particularly rural practicalities to be negotiated in delivering services there. One of the key reasons why we think it is important to understand mental disorder in a rural context is because of a concern that, in the absence of good knowledge of rural communities, the default position for understanding mental disorder is urban (Pugh, 2000; Lobley et al., 2004). Furthermore, the policies providing the templates for service provision are often written at a distance in urban administrative centres without consideration for the implications of delivery in rural areas, that is the policies are not routinely 'rural proofed' (British Medical Association, 2005; Pugh, 2009).

This chapter will begin by considering the different methods for defining 'rural' which result it in being a contested term. It will then consider areas of particular expertise and knowledge for working in rural contexts.

The Meaning of Rural

Many popular understandings of rural come from it being in binary opposition to urban which may lead to a presumption that both urban and rural areas are homogenous. We dispute this homogeneity, preferring instead a view that, 'the differences between rural areas in terms of social, environment and economic challenges are arguably as great as the differences between urban and rural areas' (British Medical Association, 2005, p. 2). Approximately 86 per cent of the land mass of the UK is designated as rural by the Department for the Environment, Food and Rural Affairs (Department of the Environment, Food and Rural Affairs), and approximately 25 per cent of the population is deemed to be distributed across those rural areas (Department of the Environment, Food and rural Affairs, 2012). A number of ways to define and measure rural have been designed by policy-makers as a prerequisite to measuring and alleviating need. Calculating population density and scarcity is the method most widely used for determining whether an area is rural. In 2005 a unifying population density definition was created enabling more reliable distinctions to be made both between urban and rural, and between different rural areas (Department of the Environment, Food and Rural Affairs, 2005).

Remoteness is as much a measure of difference between rural areas as it is a means of measuring whether a place is rural. In this method what counts as rural is measured by its distance from an urban centre. This may be measured by spatial distance, such as kilometres, or it may be measured by temporal distance, that is, the amount of time it takes to reach that place from a given urban centre, commonly called 'drive-time'. For example, an approved mental health practitioner might measure whether the location of a particular mental health assessment is rural by working out how much time it will take the ambulance to reach them once deployed. Places which are deemed to be rural on a measure of population density may not be remote because of their proximity to an accessible urban centre. However, some locations are described as remote rural areas because they are sparsely populated and not within accessible reach of an urban settlement.

Other factors used to define rural include the balance of particular economic sectors within the area, and land use. The former measure considers principally the percentage of the population which is engaged in agriculture, namely farming and fisheries, and land management. Many of the mental health research projects carried out in the first decade of this millennium were described as rural studies but essentially conflated rural into farming and were as much studies of occupational (farmer) stress as they were studies of stress in a rural context (Lobbley et al., 2004, Boys, 2007). The latter factor considers not the employment of the population but the patterns of land use including agriculture, tourism and leisure. Frequently these measures are not used in isolation but in clusters to create multi-variable ways of understanding the meaning of rural and to differentiate between different kinds of rural, for example accessible rural or remote rural.

The above attempts at defining rural are largely premised on place or space, but such 'spatial determinism' can be rejected in favour of definitions more rooted in understanding rural communities rather than rural areas (Parr et al., 2004; Blackstock et al., 2006). Pugh (2000) has drawn attention to the bounded nature of place; the territory on which people feel comfortable and which they may think of as their 'neighbourhood' or 'home'. He suggests that this notion of boundedness extends beyond the physical terrain to include those thought of as 'neighbours' and as being part of the same community. Pugh argues that, in rural communities, this physical and social 'home territory' is spatially larger than for people who do not live in rural communities and he discusses the way people in rural areas seek to place each other socially through greater self-disclosure than might be anticipated or welcome in less rural environments. Parr et al. (2004), who refer to these ideas as 'social geographies', assert that understanding the meaning of rural involves understanding that the people who live there, while spatially remote, are socially proximate, in contrast to a perception that in urban areas people are spatially proximate but socially remote.

Developing Expertise for Working in Rural Areas

This section aims to outline some of the issues for consideration when undertaking assessments under mental health legislation in rural areas. It draws on the experience of the authors who have both undertaken such assessments. The discussion below aims to be instructive, not exhaustive. Following this the evidence base for service provision in rural areas will be discussed, with a focus on areas of practice for both the professional and their employing organization to consider. While many of the factors are relevant to mental health practitioners in urban areas it is the influence of the rural context which is of note here.

First, the practicalities; finding a rural address can be difficult. Roads often are not named, and some houses or farms are deep down rural tracks. The advent of satellite navigation systems has helped with this considerably, but many approved mental health practitioners still carry both road atlases and ordinance survey maps in their cars. Mobile phone signals in rural areas can be patchy, and in some places non-existent. It may be that the mobile provider that the Local Authority subscribes to does not provide appropriate cover in rural areas. Both approved mental health practitioners and their employers therefore need to ensure that they have access to a phone which will provide them with the best cover. Access to some locations can be compromised in poor weather. An approved mental health practitioner colleague, for example, once made an application to detain someone but was not able to arrange conveyance for three days, as snow delayed the ambulance. Consideration needs to be given to responding to such eventualities, perhaps through the provision of a suitable vehicle or trying to ensure that local approved mental health practitioners respond to local calls, rather than relying on a centralized rota from which approved mental health practitioners could be required to travel some distance.

Approved mental health practitioners covering large rural areas will require more time to arrive at the assessment and more time to convey the individual to hospital if admission is considered appropriate. The impact of distance and time taken to travel needs to be recognized when devising approved mental health practitioner rotas. In rural areas which are also tourist destinations additional time needs to be factored in during peak tourist periods. Rural workers therefore need to develop more advanced skills at dealing with travel difficulties and distance from care, in timekeeping, and in effective team working (British Medical Association, 2005).

Time, distance, and difficulties locating the address will all have bearings on conveyance. It is likely that it will take longer for ambulances and/or the police to arrive at a rural address, and, in turn that the length of time that the individual spends being conveyed will also be longer. Some rural areas present particular issues around conveyance; for example assessing those who live on islands. A ferry may be appropriate for conveyance, but this is dependent on weather and time-tables. Other forms of transportation therefore need to be available, which may include helicopter/air ambulance. The British Medical Association (2005) recognizes that air ambulances must be considered for emergency situations in rural areas. While addressing distance as a practicality a further impact of it that needs to be understood by approved mental health practitioners is 'distance decay'. Distance decay states that the further someone lives from key healthcare facilities the less likely they are to be diagnosed and treated for a range of illnesses, and the greater the risk in emergency and acute situations (British Medical Association, 2005).

Both approved mental health practitioners and their employers have a legal responsibility to ensure their health and safety (Health and Safety at Work Act, 1974). Approved mental health practitioners need to develop an awareness of the specific influence of the rural context on the risk assessment process, which can impact on both the likelihood and seriousness of any assessed harm. There are particular risk factors for approved mental health practitioners, and those being assessed, associated with rural assessments. For approved mental health practitioners, risk factors include fatigue (associated with long travel time), managing delay (for example conveyance), isolation (related to poor phone signals, and the lack of immediate neighbours) and stress. Approved mental health practitioners also have to manage the risk to others, for example it is known that farmers and those in sparsely populated areas are at a particularly high risk of suicide (Boys, 2007). This may be related to their social isolation, the availability of tools on the farm through which to kill themselves (largely drugs and guns), and their familiarity with death (Lobley et al., 2004). In addition they are more likely to have been exposed to suicide; a known risk factor. Any risk management plan needs to take into account these factors.

An approved mental health practitioner deciding that compulsory admission to hospital is appropriate may find themselves in the unenviable position of taking responsibility for the property and animals of the person who has been detained. For some this may include farm animals. To give an example a colleague once detained a farmer, and found that she had a herd of cattle that required milking twice a day. On that occasion assistance was provided by the National Farmers Union. This example highlights the benefits of working with the community, and of utilizing the knowledge and assistance of third sector organizations.

Many rural areas are not borders, but most borders fall in rural areas. In order to illustrate this we will focus on the Welsh/English border. For approved mental health practitioners there are a number of considerations to be made when assessing people across the border (or admitting them to a hospital across the border). In particular:

- Wales and England have different Mental Health Act Codes of Practice (Welsh Assembly Government (2008) Department of Health (2008)). The approved mental health practitioner who works on the borders must be aware of both Codes, and follow the Code for the country in which the assessment is taking place.

- Wales and England also have different statutory forms. When detaining someone the Doctors must fill in the statutory forms relating to the country in which the assessment is taking place, and the approved mental health practitioner must fill in the statutory application of the country where the hospital is based to which the patient is being admitted.

- In 2010 the Welsh Assembly introduced the Mental Health (Wales) Measure (Welsh Assembly Government 2010). This places additional expectations on primary and secondary mental health services. Although the Measure is far reaching, of particular relevance to Welsh/English border approved mental health practitioners is that the entitlement to an Independent Mental Health Advocate (IMHA) is extended to more categories of inpatients being held for assessment than is the case in England.

Even when practitioners are not working across borders they will be working across agencies. In most areas partnership agreements are in place between key players (health, the local authority, police and ambulance service), supported by policies (for example around conveyance). Both the Welsh and the English Codes of Practice (Welsh Assembly Government, 2008, Department of Health, 2008) recommend that policies should be in place to cover police assistance for people undertaking assessments, Section 135, Section 136 and Conveyance. Employers need to recognize the difficulties that approved mental health practitioners face; they have the unenviable task of coordinating Mental Health Act assessments, and yet certain parts of the assessment (such as the speediness of the police's response, the availability of an ambulance, identifying an appropriate bed) are not within their gift. It is therefore imperative that operational difficulties are recorded, monitored, and fed into partnership meetings in which clear action plans can be devised (and monitored) to address them. The potential difficulties of assessing people in rural locations place additional emphasis on the need for good partnership working.

Recruiting and developing a workforce with key skills and knowledge can be problematic. From experience it has proved difficult to recruit trained approved mental health practitioners into rural teams. Employers therefore need to give emphasis to training existing staff to become approved mental health practitioners, and, once qualified, to retaining them through appropriate support, supervision and training. This will provide opportunity for approved mental health practitioners to develop their understanding of the nature of rural areas, communities and cultures. Boys (2007) highlights the need for professionals to develop expertise on stress in rural contexts, ideally from those with practical experience themselves of living and working in a rural community. It is to this expertise and knowledge that we will now turn.

Confidentiality and anonymity are considerable challenges for rural mental health practice. Perhaps it is helpful to consider confidentiality as a continuum rather than an absolute. Neighbours (in both a rural and an urban setting) are likely to notice ambulances but in the high visibility context of rural places news may circulate differently, as will be considered later. In managing confidentiality we would, however, offer the following rules of thumb:

- Discuss confidentiality with the individual being assessed. She/he may know their community better than the approved practitioner and should have the opportunity to offer advice on how they wish to proceed, especially if assistance is required from other organizations or the larger community.

- Be clear about who needs to know what, and what they need to know. In specific practice known to us the National Farmers Union, whose assistance was being sought, were informed that someone had been admitted to hospital and that there was a herd of cattle which needed milking, but they were not informed of the details of the hospital admission.

- Discuss confidentiality and boundaries at the beginning of the assessment. It may be that the approved practitioner also lives and works in the local area. Discussions need to take place about how informally meeting each other in the community outside of work will be managed.

Pugh (2000) recognizes that workers in rural areas have a higher social visibility. This creates challenges for confidentiality both for the worker and the service user. Workers themselves may be part of the community which they serve. They therefore need to develop ways of managing the complexities of dual and multiple relationships. A common example is workers whose children are at school with the children of their service users. As a result confidentiality in relation to rural mental health practice can be seen as 'messier' than that in urban practice (Lobley et al., 2004). Given the stigma associated with mental disorder confidentiality is all the more important. A literature review by Jacobs et al., in Lobley (2004) concluded that 'the glare of rural familiarity can feed into the often quite acute under-utilisation of local mental health services' (p. 273).

In a study of people with dementia and their carers in rural Scotland, Blackstock et al. (2006) found that 50 per cent of carers thought that their bounded communities resulted in more person-centred care from formal providers because they were known to them in informal capacities as friends, neighbours or acquaintances. They argue that rural services compensate for limitations in those services through strong interpersonal networks. The personalized relationships help with access to services because they know that when the formal appointment is over they are likely to still bump into workers at the shops, school gate or in the street.

What carers in the above study identified as 'personalized care', is also referred to as the 'dual relationship' which workers have with those to whom they offer services and support (Pugh, 2007; Turbett, 2009). Pragmatic elements of this have been noted above in relation to confidentiality. But underpinning this is also a significant values perspective. In a recent classroom exercise on an approved mental health practitioner course many trainees declared that they would not carry out an assessment for compulsory detention under mental health legislation on any service user known to them personally. They stated that this would be awkward for them and would conflict with the interests of the service user. There was an uncritical assumption that assessment by strangers, or people with simply a 'service provider' relationship, was best. We would argue that this should not be accepted as a 'given' as it may reflect an urban presumption which may not fit well into a rural psyche which often likes to 'place' people in terms of who they are, who they relate to and where they fit in the community. It is largely accepted that a skilled worker in a rural area has adapted to a level of careful self-disclosure in order to build trust which is not necessarily shared by those working outside rural contexts (Turbett, 2009).

Developing an expertise in managing confidentiality is allied to developing expertise in understanding and managing higher visibility in rural areas. Parr et al. (2004) argued that people are more visible in a rural landscape because of the relative sparseness. Thus it is not easy to maintain privacy while being mentally disordered in a rural community because people see the comings and goings of family members and mental health practitioners, many of whom are recognizable. Such visibility means that the decisions of practitioners can become subject to significant public scrutiny if friends and neighbours are of the view that not enough is being done to either 'remove' a distressed person from the community or give more support and services that would enable that person to stay at home (Turbett, 2009).

Thus, Parr et al. (2004) argue, the activities of the service user, their family and friends and practitioners become the subject of conversation which makes rural lives more visible. Whether this conversation (gossip) is malicious or benign is itself dependent on the role and status of the person in the community, including whether or not the person is a local or an incomer. Local people may initially be more accepted and tolerated and the gossip may be more benign, not just because they come from the area (are local) but because being local often means being part of a dense overlapping network of friendships and families.

Parr et al. (2004) make a distinction between inclusionary or exclusionary acts, and understanding and managing these is also a part of rural expertise. Inclusionary acts by community members were described by recipients of mental health services as the provision of opportunities for positive involvement in and mattering to a local setting. Exclusion was perceived to be about rejection, avoidance and distancing by other community members and being made to feel different as a result of experiencing mental disorder. The kind of community behaviours that participants identified as promoting inclusion were people asking them how they were, people offering assistance and people commenting positively on how they were doing. However, these are the very acts which were also identified as excluding. For example, one person experiencing mental health difficulties who is asked by a neighbour how they are may interpret this as an act of caring and inclusion. Another person may interpret it as a desire to fuel gossip and to provide an early alert to others if they behave 'strangely' again. They, therefore, experience being asked how they are as distancing and controlling. Parr et al. (2004) also note that not asking after someone's welfare could be differentially interpreted as avoidance and rejection; avoidance based on social awkwardness in talking about mental illness; or as acceptance and tolerance which required no specific attention being drawn to those difficulties. For these reasons our earlier suggestion for managing confidentiality, that a worker seek advice from a service user about whether they wish to be greeted or 'ignored' should they meet, is important.

Social status is a key factor identified by Parr et al. (2004) which influences the way social interactions are interpreted. People who live in rural areas will inevitably become bound up in certain kinds of social relations and will have status assigned to them which is derived from, and contributes to, the evolving nature of those relations. A central determining status is that of 'local' or 'incomer' (Pugh, 2000). Parr et al. (2004) argue that the 'eccentricity' of local people is more likely to be tolerated and less likely to be stigmatized than the 'eccentricity' of incomers. This is largely because the local person's family and friends are known and people may share overlaps in relations within a close knit or dense social network. The incomer, being less well known, is not protected by membership of the network in the same way, and additionally may be regarded as having brought their troubles with them. However, an incomer may be freer to be themselves and express their emotional distress as they are potentially perceived as 'outsiders' anyway and do not have an 'insider' status to lose. Being local may pose a dilemma to distressed people as they feel unable to truly express their emotions and thoughts as they fear the loss of their protected status if they are perceived to move from 'eccentric' to 'deviant'.

This complexity of perceptions leads us to propose that people working in rural areas also need to get to know a community and develop expertise in finding appropriate responses to the presenting difficulties.

Hughes and Keady in Lobley et al. (2004) recognized the importance of mental health workers understanding the context in which they work and concluded that immersion in, and engagement with, a community was an important precursor to effective intervention. Examples of the difficulties of reaching into a community in crisis with little prior engagement are found in research following the foot and mouth disease outbreak. One study (Peck et al. in Lobley et al., 2004) showed that farmers' main source of support came from family, friends, other farmers and vets. Only 2 per cent of farmers interviewed sought help from specialist or other sources. When farmers were given five types of support to choose (telephone support line, visits from health and social care, internet help line, farmer's self-help group, or written advice) only 13 per cent said that they would use visits from health or social work (the lowest number for any group), and 26 per cent thought that it would be not helpful or harmful (the highest number of any group). Health and social care were not perceived as being relevant to farmers, some of whom thought that services may be harmful.

Thus, approved mental health practitioners need to be aware of the particular issues that face people in rural life. There may be a number of causes contributing to stress and, in order to negotiate a solution, the practitioner needs to understand the problem. A farmer presenting with depression, for example, may not find hospital admission helpful as a contributory factor for the stress/depression may relate to financial worries, and his/her need to farm the land. Removing a farmer at lambing time from his/her flock may cause more pressure and stress than working with him/her at home. Likewise it is difficult to see how respite could be arranged when the farm still needs to be run. The provision of services in rural areas is at best patchy. One of the key messages is that good service provision in rural areas is dependent upon them being grounded in the community, and upon workers having a good working knowledge of the key issues facing rural people, including farmers (Lobley et al., 2004). Approved mental health practitioners, therefore, in order to explore the least restrictive options, need to have a well-developed understanding of the resources and strengths within the community. There is an argument that working in a rural area takes additional time; time which is not associated with travel. Professionals cannot be simply 'parachuted in' with the expectation that they will achieve results; this is less likely to work (Turbett, 2009). In order to develop understanding of the community practitioners are encouraged to understand the increased costs of service delivery and take a whole system approach.

There is a failure to both recognize and fund the additional costs of providing services in rural areas (Pugh et al., 2007). This is exacerbated for some service users by the lack of social or financial resources which they could access to meet their needs. The increased costs of rural service provision relate not just to travel and increased time, but also to the lack of opportunity for economies of scale and the poor infrastructure in relation to formal and informal welfare agencies from which services can be sourced.

Additionally population 'thresholds' may mitigate against the development of some services such as supporting self-help groups or day services. As a result services may not be developed in a local area, instead being delivered from a central base. Overall people in rural areas are less likely to receive services comparable in quality and cost to those in urban areas (Pugh, 2000).

A whole system approach recognizes the interplay between a range of service provisions within rural areas. Thus changes made to transport, for example, can have a significant impact on the delivery of other services, such as health and social care (McDonald and Heath, 2008). In recognition of this the government in 2000 introduced the requirement to rural-proof policies. Rural proofing requires policy makers, when developing and implementing policy, to consider whether there will be any significant differential impact in rural areas; to identify the impacts; and to give consideration to adjustments or compensations which may be required (Countryside Agency in Pugh, 2009).

Barry et al. (2000) state that the use of mental health services within a rural area is likely to be low, and they recommend the use of local papers, radio and media to promote services. Pugh et al. (2007) suggest utilizing a range of methods to publicize services, such as through post offices, General Practitioners, schools and churches. Boys (2007) suggests that mental health services in rural areas need to be precisely targeted through the use of Assertive Outreach Teams, help lines and case work. It may also be appropriate to recruit and train key local people such as shop-keepers, the clergy and the police (McDonald and Heath, 2008). Links need to be made with third sector organizations that are active within the community (such as the National Farmers Union) and with General Practitioners, who are often the first point of contact in rural communities (Barry et al., 2000). In addition to this there are those who argue that inter-professional working is an important aspect of service provision (British Medical Association, 2005). This allows professionals the opportunity to develop their roles beyond traditional boundaries; of particular benefit in rural settings in which a range of professionals may be lacking. Workers in a rural setting may be asked to undertake dual roles or tasks which are not part of their job description. A good example of this is the rural postal service. The post van may also provide transport for people and the person who delivers post may also collect it from some homes as well keeping an eye on isolated people. In the same way Pugh (2000) states that social workers in rural areas require a 'repertoire of generalist skills to meet a diverse range of local needs', something which he argues is not covered within their training.

Having considered some of the areas of particular expertise we move to consider areas of knowledge which rural mental health workers require.

Understanding Social Perspectives of Mental Disorder in Rural Contexts

The kinds of difficulties that exacerbate mental disorder for people in urban areas also have similar affects for people in rural areas since poverty, stress, discrimination and loneliness are recognized as universal determinants of mental ill health (Rogers and Pilgrim, 2003; Tew, 2011). However, it is the context in which these difficulties, or stressors, are experienced that shapes their impact and patterns how people respond to those affected (Pugh, 2000). It is, therefore, preferable to think about mental health in rural contexts rather than to think about some separate entity called 'rural mental health' (Lobley et al., 2004). In reviewing literature on mental health in rural communities it is apparent that the definition of rural most commonly used at the turn of the millennium was that of 'economic sectors' with a resultant employment bias towards stress in farming communities (Lobley et al., 2004). This bias is understandable given the historical context of research in rural affairs conducted at the time to inform the Rural Stress Action Plan policy initiative to reduce stress and suicide in farming communities (Ministry for Agriculture, Farming and Fisheries in Boys, 2007).

With this bias in mind we now turn to consider the rural context of the social and sociological factors associated with the development of mental disorder. Of particular note is that deprivation in many rural areas clusters in small pockets in the midst of relative affluence and is therefore often not identified (British Medical Association, 2005). Economic difficulties and unemployment in rural areas are strongly related to changes in farming practices with the consequent loss of traditional rural labour through increasing use of machinery and technology. Although new employment sectors have entered rural areas, for local unemployed people there remains a mismatch of the traditional rural jobs being lost (manual labour in farming, forestry and fisheries) and the new employment opportunities available with the arrival of 'high tech' industries (Pugh, 2000). There is concern about the effect of European migrant workers on local rural economies and employment opportunities (Gilpen and Henty in Pugh, 2009). Competition for work and a mismatch in the labour market potentially leads to increases in lone working from home, job insecurity and unemployment; each with their own source of worry and stress. Worries about financial uncertainty and debt are frequently cited as stressors in studies of health in rural areas (Phelps in Lobley et al., 2004).

Lobley et al. (2004) and Boys (2007) have reviewed studies identifying other key sources of stress for people in rural areas and summarize these as follows. The constant changes in policy governing business and commerce which result in increasing regulation, bureaucracy and forms, have been found to add considerably to the stress of people attempting to run businesses and farms. Difficulties understanding the forms and negative attitudes towards the impact of the regulations also add to people's stress. Within the farming sector occupational stress shows some particular patterns with livestock farmers experiencing more ill effects from stress than arable farmers and women farmers more ill effects than men. However, older farmers are found to have fewer ill effects than middle or younger aged farmers. While the fear of losing a job or a business is an acute stressor for anyone, for farmers the fear of losing a farm carries additional burdens as it may not be seen as just a business but an embodiment of themselves, their family and their history. Additionally farm workers cite the hazards and unpredictability of farm work as stressful and they report certain seasons being more stressful than others, for example, lambing, planting, and harvest. When ranking the severity of these factors, agricultural workers have stated that poor weather, form filling and adjusting to rapid changes in bureaucracy (policy and regulation) caused the most severe stress and that machinery breakdown, not enough time and compliance with environmental regulations caused moderate-to-severe stress (Deary in Lobley et al., 2004). Farm work remains physical (if not as labour intensive) and becoming unwell and being unable to work generates stress through fear of losing a whole annual cycle of production because a specific season is lost.

While people in rural areas identify universally recognized stressors such as crises in personal relationships as a source of significant stress, along with other normative life-events such as births and deaths, changing jobs or losing jobs, there is recognition of particular concerns with retirement, succession and inheritance in rural areas.

Boys (2007) identified a range of groups at risk of adverse reactions to stress associated with isolation. These include farmers, older women, women with young children in poverty and isolated, and home-based workers who experience some of the same difficulties faced by farmers of isolation and lone working. Lone working itself is identified as a vulnerability factor even where the individual reports being in a family and supportive social network. Also included in those at risk are carers and people with disabilities who are isolated and unable to access facilities and support; young people who find achieving meaningful independence difficult, and people in minority groups who experience discrimination, abuse and negative attitudes that are not effectively tackled.

What seems apparent is that the vulnerabilities identified above refer to different kinds of isolations including:

- *Physical isolation* refers to rural areas being less populace, having a lower population density.

- *Social isolation* refers to a decline in the number of places in which rural people would have routinely met and been sociable, for example the closure of pubs, shops, post offices, markets, auction yards, churches.

- *Cultural isolation* refers to the marginalization of 'rural life' through incursion by incomers who are thought to have different values and are perceived to be a threat as they fragment kin networks and the rural way of life. Cultural isolation also refers to the changing employment patterns and changing patterns of social networking created by internet technologies.

- *Psychological isolation* refers to self-generated isolation through maintenance of cultural mores and values of self-sufficiency, self-reliance and strength of (independent) character.

- *Geographical isolation* refers to distance from services, although as stated earlier, this may be measured temporally (drive time) or spatially (distance in length).

People may experience various forms of isolation simultaneously. For those with low income and lacking a private means of transport the difficulties of isolation are compounded by not being able to access the services that may alleviate the problems or distress and exacerbates aforementioned distance decay (British Medical Association, 2005; Pugh et al., 2007).

Homelessness, arising from inadequate housing and lack of affordable housing, is considered a hidden stressor in rural areas because homeless people cannot stay and, therefore, leave to go to urban centres where services may be available.

Arguably this discussion is as much about an identification of the 'disadvantaged' in rural communities as it is an identification of stressors. This deprivation is created and perpetuated through combinations of factors noted above including low income, poor social circumstances, difficulties in personal relationships, absence of services or difficulties in accessing available services and limited life choices. The relationship between stress and disadvantage is not simple and is understood to be an interactive, transactional process taking account of the source of the stress, the perception of the situation and the resources available to cope (Lobley et al., 2004; Boys, 2007; Tew, 2011). The resources available to people for coping are drawn from a variety of sources including cultural expectations, values and psychological attitudes and disposition.

In addition to understanding the sociological factors associated with mental disorder in rural areas it is useful to consider whether there is a particularly rural psychosocial context to the experience of mental disorder.

Rural people are regarded within the literature as having particular values in which self-worth is derived from rural characteristics of stoicism and self-reliance. It is argued that these characteristics are a bedrock of rural culture which influence the experience of mental health difficulties (Parr et al., 2004; Blackstock et al., 2006, Nicholson, 2011).

There is evidence that farming people think that the countryside and country people are misunderstood and that this exacerbates the effects of stress (Lobley, 2005). This mindset is thought to underpin some feelings of hopelessness that the countryside, farming and rural life have no future and there are feelings of powerlessness to change this. These thoughts become reflected for some people in reports of low self-esteem.

McGregor (in Lobley et al., 2004) found that those reporting being stressed in rural areas were also more likely to be self-blaming emotionally when difficulties arose and that this impeded ability to cope. So, although the general evidence is that there are lower stress ratings in rural areas compared with the national average (Lobley, 2005), and a lower incidence of deliberate self-harm (Harris and Hawton, 2011), once a person has become stressed it seems there are personality traits, perhaps related to rural cultural mores of independence and self-reliance, that caused them to be emotionally less well equipped to cope with their difficulties. Evidence for this preference for 'self-reliance' is implicit in the recognition earlier in this chapter about which services were found helpful during the foot and mouth crisis. However, the discussion concerning dual relationships should be noted also in order to understand that 'self-reliance' does not exclude formal services where the services are perceived to be part of the community, or understood to be delivered by members of the community.

Conclusion

Within this chapter we have argued that the meaning of rural is contested and in our exploration of the definitions of rural we have considered spatial and cultural meanings. We have highlighted the danger of rural being considered to be merely the opposite of urban, and have argued for a more holistic understanding that can challenge urban presumptions about mental health. We have focused on the particular expertise practitioners working in a rural context need to develop in terms of managing both the practicalities of being in rural areas and adapting to a rural culture of social relations. We have highlighted the expertise specifically pertinent to approved mental health practitioners. Finally we have considered a knowledge base from which to develop an understanding of the rural context for the normative stresses and strains of life that are associated with mental ill health. This knowledge base is valuable when considering social perspectives in mental health assessments in rural areas. Throughout the chapter we have drawn attention to considerations for employers.

We recognize that some of the issues which we have highlighted are true for all mental health practitioners. However we believe that the rural context throws a different light on the experience of mental disorder, the provision of services and their accessibility.

Reflective Questions

1. Consider whether the physical environment in which approved mental health practitioners work impacts both on the way in which mental health is perceived and how services are delivered.

2. Consider whether as a mental health practitioner is it important to understand and challenge the accepted norms around key concepts underpinning practice?

3. To what extent do key issues such as isolation, confidentiality and community belonging, differ depending on the context in which approved mental health practitioners practice?

4. To what extent does increasing divergence as a result of devolution impact on approved mental health practice, and does this matter?

9

The Experiences of Service Users

Julie Ridley

Editors' Voice

To reflect upon the experience of service users who have been formally detained is clearly important for any approved mental health practitioner; ultimately the final responsibility for such an outcome rests with them. In the light of increased numbers of detained patients, such reflection continues to be paramount. This chapter draws on the evidence collected in a participatory research study undertaken in the wake of the implementation of the Mental Health Act in Scotland; an Act which heralded high expectations among all stakeholders, including service users. The research reveals the experience of detention as a non-linear journey and is vividly illustrated with the use of direct quotes. These we suggest are essential reading for any practitioner providing a powerful insight into the process and reality of detention from the most important perspective, that of the affected person. In particular the feeling of powerlessness, lack of understanding about what was happening and loss of control are fundamental considerations. Building on the questions raised in preceding chapters it is clear that approved mental health practitioners do not have easy decisions to make. Of particular relevance to the reader will be the views expressed about approved mental health practitioners not least because the evidence mirrors the debates to which this book continually returns namely what is the role of the approved mental health practitioner? This chapter rightly urges the need to guard against complacency.

This chapter analyses an extensive research project which recorded service user, carers' and health and social care professionals' experiences of compulsory care and treatment in Scotland following the implementation of the Mental Health (Care and Treatment) Scotland Act 2003 (the MHCT Act). It is important that an approved mental health practitioner, known in Scotland as a Mental Health Officer (MHO, is able to hear and reflect on service users' experiences. In this chapter, conflicts and dilemmas in relation to mental health legislation, policy and service user self-determination are discussed. The chapter presents key findings and conclusions from the cohort study commissioned by the Scottish Government in 2007, which have important messages and learning material for all practitioners working in approved mental health practice (Ridley et al., 2009). Following on from the discussion in Chapter 6, this chapter asks the reader to contemplate crucial ethical challenges when undertaking approved mental health practice.

Background and context

Although those treated under compulsion comprise the minority of mental health service users, they nonetheless represent a growing, and increasingly significant group of service users. Official statistics for England and Wales show the number of people subject to restrictions under the 1983 Mental Health Act continues to rise (Health and Social Care Information Centre, 2011). Although the total number of formal admissions to hospitals and the number of new community treatment orders decreased between 2009/10 and 2010/11, annual figures show a 5 per cent increase in those subject to the 1983 Act. The use of supervised community treatment or CTOs has, some claim, 'rocketed beyond expectation', and has resulted in individuals being obliged to stick to medication regimes they believe they no longer need (Gould, 2011). In contrast, the number of people detained under the 2003 Act in Scotland has fallen since implementation. However in the same reporting period, the Mental Welfare Commission for Scotland reported a 6 per cent increase in overall compulsory admissions, and a continued increase in the use of community-based CTOs.

The legislative context considered here is the Mental Health (Care and Treatment) (Scotland) Act 2003, which came into force on 5 October 2005, and has been described as 'visionary and revisionary' (Atkinson et al., 2005), bringing the legislation for Scotland into the twenty-first century: placing emphasis on treatment and care in the community, on safeguarding patients' rights and on participation of patients and all those supporting them in their treatment and ongoing care. The new legislation was drafted following extensive consultation and a root and branch review of the 1984 Act (Scottish Executive, 2001). This articulated recognition of service users' rights as citizens and consumers to equitable, participatory and least restrictive services. Implementation of this legislation heralded high expectations among all stakeholders including service users.

The drafting of Scottish mental health law preceded that in England and Wales and there were some important differences in emphasis. For example, while the principle of reciprocity in the Scottish Act obliges service providers to give quality services as a precondition of compulsion, the neglect of this principle at the time in the proposed reforms of mental health legislation in England and Wales influenced concerted opposition from the Mental Health Alliance (Pilgrim, 2007a). Additionally, in Scotland the law focuses on mental health as well as control of mental disorder, so offering more balanced messages about patients' rights and needs in terms of health promotion as well as compulsion.

The MHCT Act contained a number of innovations and new provisions which are examined in detail in McManus and Thomson (2005), and Patrick (2006). In brief these included:

- Compulsory powers enforced in the community in addition to hospital compulsory care and treatment

- Reciprocity as part of the principled framework

- New rights and safeguards, including a right to access independent advocacy services, and Advance Statements (Directives)

- A new Mental Health Tribunal – which considers the case for proposed compulsory interventions under the Act

- New powers invested in the Mental Welfare Commission for Scotland

- New duties on Health Boards and local authorities in relation to social opportunities and the development of well-being

- The creation or enhancement of specific professional and supportive roles (that is Responsible Medical Officer (RMO) who is a psychiatrist, Approved Medical Practitioner (AMP) designated Medical Practitioners who can be psychiatrists or GPs, enhanced role for the Mental Health Officer (MHOs), a specialist social worker; and Named Person replacing next of kin).

The Act also covered those who enter into the mental health system through the criminal justice system. An additional right of appeal was introduced for patients who believe that they are being detained through use of 'excessive security' at the State Hospital (Scotland High Security Hospital), and may require their local Health Board to identify alternative accommodation.

The research study

The research reported on here (Ridley et al., 2009) was commissioned by the Scottish Government as part of a national research programme to review developments in mental health law (Rushmer and Hallam, 2004). Essentially, this qualitative study evaluated different stakeholder experiences and perspectives, including those of service users, informal carers (Ridley et al., 2010), health and social care professionals and independent advocates working with the new Act, and considered this alongside different stakeholder expectations expressed prior to implementation.

From the outset, Ridley et al. aimed to make the research participatory believing that people have the right to be involved in research about aspects of their lives and that better quality mental health research is produced when people are involved in the process (Rose, 2004; Turner and Beresford, 2005). The researchers were keen that service user perspectives would inform their approach and its implementation, and particularly that they paid attention to the rights of service users throughout the research process. The initial research proposal was developed in partnership with service users from one organization. The research team comprised eight mental health service users who worked alongside professional researchers with backgrounds mainly in social work, social policy and housing research. Some of the professional researchers also had direct experience of mental health services or as carers. Co-researchers undertook interviews with service users in partnership with a professional researcher.

The involvement of service users in the research team directly influenced the approach taken to assessing individuals' capacity to participate in the research interview. Service user researchers contributed to protocols for gaining informed consent from potential participants, commented on the content and format of questions, and were involved in deciding how the paired interviewing should be conducted. As team members, service users participated in the reflection and analysis of themes emerging from the data transcripts of the service user interviews, and commented on draft reports.

Methodology

Drawing on recent narrative approaches (Brown and Kandirikirira, 2007; Scottish Recovery Network, 2007) the study investigated aspects of compulsion predetermined by the research objectives while also seeking to discover themes and issues emerging from participants' accounts. Semi-structured qualitative interviews with service users enabled exploration of consistent themes while also engaging with unanticipated issues that had been raised by individual participants. Focus groups and one-to-one interviews (either face-to-face or by telephone) gathered data from informal carers on key topics addressing similar areas. Interviews with a range of national and local health and social care professionals and advocates were also carried out.

The study was conducted in two main stages with an interval of between 6 to 12 months dependent upon when service users were recruited to the study as this had to be flexible. While service users and carers were interviewed at both stages, professionals were only interviewed during Stage 1. Unrelated samples of 49 service users, 33 informal carers and 38 professionals and advocates were drawn from four Health Board areas in Scotland, chosen purposively to reflect rural, urban and mixed geographical areas and the State Hospital. Service users were asked to provide contact details for a professional of their choice (psychiatrist, social worker, nurse, and so on) who they agreed could be contacted prior to interview. The professionals thus nominated supported participation of the majority of people with only 11 per cent being considered too unwell to participate. Data generated from service user interviews were analysed by the whole team using standard qualitative analysis methods to identify themes and patterns, and ensuring the interpretive process incorporated different perspectives, that is, those of service user, carer, professional and researcher.

This chapter now focuses primarily on findings from the service user interviews and is organized under the following key headings: being detained and reasons for compulsion; experiences of compulsion; participation; care and treatment; and finally some reflections on the MHO role.

Understandings of detention

People interviewed for this study were not a homogenous group and came from all walks of life. Some recounted the trauma of being detained for the first time, others referred to multiple in-patient stays, some as detained patients. The study sample included a mix of men and women with twice as many men participating. The average age of interviewees was 40.5 years and the youngest person interviewed was 21 years and the oldest 63 years. Just a small minority came from black and minority ethnic background and a few individuals with learning disabilities who were subject to the MHCT Act participated.

Using the Scottish Executive pathways through compulsion model (Scottish Executive Social Research, 2005) as our conceptual starting point, interviews with service users began by asking about the period prior to, and leading up to compulsion, their experience of detention and aftercare. The model or ideal type envisaged a period of 'non-compulsion/stability', an 'episode leading to compulsion', Tribunal, care and treatment, discharge and returning to 'non-compulsion/stability'. From people's accounts the reality of this 'journey' was clearly more complex, less linear than this suggested. In the period of 'non-compulsion', many interviewees described less than stable circumstances that in some cases were prolonged over months, possibly years. For several, this was not the first time they had experienced compulsion, and many were at various stages of recovery finding ways to live with the impact of having a severe mental illness.

A stressful or traumatic event might trigger a period of worsening health. For some, the severity of their mental health problems escalated over time, precipitating a crisis, followed by treatment under the MHCT Act. Some described living with serious mental illness for several years without ever coming into contact with mental health services until recently, whereas others had been in and out of hospital (not necessarily under compulsion) for most of their adult lives. Yet others had been in a period of relative stability, which had changed unexpectedly. Some had been voluntary patients and through non-compliance with treatment had been detained.

While a variety of factors led up to a period of compulsion, for some a key factor had either been the onset, or escalation, of serious and enduring mental health issues. Others could identify and describe in vivid detail, stressful or traumatic past or present events which were the main reason why they believed they had been detained. The impact of social and environmental issues on their mental health was explained as the cause for other people. Compulsion had been at the instigation of families, friends, neighbours, police, or housing agencies after becoming concerned about the person's behaviour or outward signs of personal neglect:

> Well somebody tried to break into my flat and I stayed awake for about a month without any sleep and I didn't eat and I lost a lot of weight and then I started getting delusional and then my brothers took me into hospital and had me committed...

Not complying with medication regimes and experiencing deterioration in mental health had led to some people being involuntarily admitted to hospital. In such cases, the pathway typically involved converting from voluntary patient to compulsory order, for example:

> I was feeling quite low and suicidal... I got sent into hospital to get checked over and that's how it started. I stopped taking medication, I thought I was fine and I relapsed and was put back in. At the time I wasn't eating or drinking very well. I was hearing voices that told me not to. They sectioned me because I wasn't looking after myself... When I first went into hospital it wasn't under compulsory. I escaped three times so I was put on a short term detention order.

For a few, the route into compulsion had been through the criminal justice system. Some of these individuals had been living on secure or locked wards for a number of years. These included individuals with additional and complex needs, for example, people with learning disabilities or autistic spectrum condition, or dual diagnosis. There were also those who, during a period of imprisonment for an offence, had been assessed by a psychiatrist and subsequently transferred to the State Hospital. Descriptions of failed asylum applications and becoming a refugee were how a few explained why they had been subject to compulsion. The decision to admit some people to hospital involuntarily was understood to have been taken because they were considered to pose a risk to themselves or others, which generally they did not agree with:

> because I had this label suddenly applied to me that I would do some of the crazy things that people with the label might do but I know I wasn't going to do that, but they didn't ask me. I just feel so offended by it. I'm the one inside here, I know what I will or will not do and just because you've decided to put a label on me it doesn't make me that.

In summary, individuals' accounts of the state of 'non-compulsion' and the 'episode' leading to compulsion, suggested that in reality so called 'stability' was for many a highly fraught and uncertain time, and that the pre-compulsion 'episode' might be better represented in terms of the interplay of personal or health crises with carers' and professionals' responses, rather than as a specific event.

Experiences of compulsion

The people interviewed experienced different compulsory measures with around a third reporting being under a community CTO, although for some of these an original hospital CTO was still in force during a long period of community leave. Service users' understanding of the compulsory measures they were under was mixed. Some said they had been told about the compulsory treatment order and what it meant for them by their MHO, or by hospital staff, or a CPN. Many reflected that they had not understood compulsion at the time they were admitted. Even when they were clear about what compulsory measure they were under and its implications, they might be vague about its duration and of their rights. Some had experience of renewal or extension of original orders, and others were subject to orders that did not last as long as expected. Such uncertainty is illustrated by the following response at second interview:

> I was appealing the section which to my knowledge I got a letter back to say that it had been rescinded, so I'm not on a section anymore, but I'm not very sure. I couldn't be certain of that...

Often given limited or no information about compulsion from professionals involved in their care, service users had happened upon information from television or radio programmes. At the other extreme, some felt they had too much information about new drugs they had to take, some describing alarming side effects. Others only received information when they asked. Timing was critical as some did remember receiving information but had been unable to absorb it:

> I'm sure I had enough information but I don't think you take it in. I maybe should have asked but I think you really need somebody to sit down with you and just go through it in basic detail what all this means....

How service users felt about compulsion differed, although it was universally unwelcome. The experience was commonly associated with an overwhelming sense of loss and powerlessness:

> They just basically said that that's what they have the power to do, that they believe that I still need compulsory care and treatment and I'm sectioned... it's like I've got absolutely no powers whatsoever to change the system, it doesn't matter what I say or do.

Although looking back, compulsion was felt by over half the interviewees to have been the 'right thing' for them, others were of the opinion that it represented an unjustified loss of civil liberty and infringement of their human rights, with no benefits that they could perceive. This was particularly the case for those who had been detained because of anticipated or future risks to themselves or others. Other studies report between 33 and 90 per cent of service users agreeing that compulsion was justified. In previous research, service users' experiences present a mixed picture: that is, both negative and unhelpful experiences, as well as experiences of compulsion that are supportive and helpful (Johansson and Lundman, 2002; Jones et al., 2009).

A common dissatisfaction was with formal detention. Instead of supporting recovery, many service users claimed the experience in hospital had set them back. At one extreme of the spectrum of views were participants whose experience had been 'like going to hell', while at the other a few emphasized the strong camaraderie among patients and the helpfulness of hospital staff. For example, one person who had been under a Short Term Order described the experience as 'great fun, like being in college', and another that his/her experience had been like 'home from home'. Some felt it had been a 'safe environment' where they needed to be when unwell and others that it compared favourably with prison.

In contrast, many described this experience in negative terms and as far from beneficial to recovery:

> I wasn't really getting any better in the wards. It wasn't actually, anything to do with the section, it was the ward, I just couldn't get better in there. I was just slowly really going off my head. It was the ward, the environment in there that was making me really, really ill.

Inflexible and impersonal regimes contributed to detention as a 'nightmare' experience. On the other hand, there were those who welcomed having 'responsibility taken away' and a structure to daily life imposed. Strict regimentation, coupled with close observation and the restriction of so-called privileges was 'the norm' for those residing in high security facilities. For the most part, days in psychiatric hospitals were boring and monotonous. There was nothing to do and plenty of time to do nothing according to many people interviewed. One young man likened life on the IPCU to a 'retirement home'. Recreational and leisure activities tended to be limited to smoking, watching TV/DVDs, the gym, playing pool or computer games. Staffing levels significantly impacted on this, particularly in respect of access to facilities and day leave. Interviewees were positive about having open access and the freedom to walk in the hospital grounds.

Quality of staff support was critical and also variable, not only between hospitals, but also between shifts and between individual nurses. Participants acknowledged that their perceptions of staff were affected by their mental health at the time, recognizing that they and other patients had 'not been easy' to interact with. All the same, in most people's experience, there were some members of the clinical team who attempted to build better relationships with patients than others:

> I always went to him, he was just helpful and pleasant... his manners were top class, he didn't talk down to you... just a friendly guy.

Nurses could have a 'life changing' impact on patients and their recovery. Such nurses were said to have a good understanding of people, were enthusiastic and engaging and responded flexibly to individual circumstances. This was the difference between 'the A team and the B team'. The biggest issue highlighted was that the quality of relationship was inconsistent. Shift changes could signify a drastic change in patient treatment and ambience of the entire ward. Blame for some of the issues with staff attitudes was laid at the door of inadequate resources. Nursing staff were further limited by the system in which they operated:

A lot of the nurses recognize that drug therapy is not the be all and end all, and a lot have studied other therapies but don't get the chance to use them because of this top heavy dogmatic psychiatric approach that seems to be current right across the world really.

Of concern were experiences of violence and abuse at the hands of professionals: unwanted 'forceful interventions' and bodily harm as a result of direct violence – 'getting a beating from staff'. While some of the incidences were clearly historic, disturbingly some occurred post MHCT Act. It was not only some staff but other patients who contributed to hospital as unsafe environments:

> Well one day I'm living by myself and then you're in a ward with six people all from different backgrounds and you don't know anybody, and you're sharing a toilet, and it's just that hospitals are horrible no matter where you go.

The above quotation was typical of what many participants said in relation to their overall feelings about periods of compulsory detention. Other patients could be unpredictable or volatile. Their accounts highlight issues of violence, sexual, physical and racial abuse among patients in some hospitals. Several commented on what they perceived as an unhealthy mix of patients with serious mental health problems with others who they perceived to be criminals and/or patients with serious drug and alcohol problems. Upsetting to service users was that violent attacks seemed to be regarded by some nurses as part of the 'culture of mental health hospitals'. An individual from BME background commented on his experience of racial abuse

> Such common terms as 'black bastard', 'nigger', would be common place in daily confrontations as well as physical assault, at times quite violent physical assault. It made me very insecure...A blind eye was taken and in fact on one occasion where there was quite clear racial intimidation present, a nurse said 'not in here, take that outside, sort yourselves out outside'.

Women reported sexual harassment on mixed and segregated wards:

> Sometimes you get the males wandering up and just hanging outside your door tapping and knocking on your door and you're trying to relax.

In contrast, some service users felt they had gained most insight about their situation and mental health problems from talking to other patients. For one participant, being in hospital was about 'building a community', which she still valued. Some friendships formed while in hospital had continued beyond compulsory care, and as the following quotation illustrates, were clearly an important component of people's recovery:

> The good things are meeting people that have got mental health problems. I've made a few friends ... and we'll all meet up now and again sometimes here or at P's flat, and it's good because you can relate with each other and you're going through the same experiences.

The majority of those under a community CTO, had experienced conversion of an existing hospital CTO rather than entering directly onto a community-based order. This included some individuals who had initially been voluntary patients, under a hospital CTO, then transferred to a community CTO. Some had been in hospital six months prior to the community-based order, but for others it had been a matter of weeks when the order had been varied. Among those under community CTOs were some individuals who were required to live in nursing or residential homes or in supported accommodation, as well as those returning to ordinary housing.

Experience of community CTOs at the time of the research was still new and it was clear that there were two camps of opinion: those who considered community compulsion to be a draconian and those for whom it provided a comforting safety net allowing a smoother transition to hospital should the need arise. The only downfall identified was that the community CTO might end after six to 12 months, thus the safety net for someone who was bi-polar was short lived:

> Just basically restricting because I've got to keep to rules and regulations under it ... I normally like to do things at my leisure ... I don't like emotional threat of 'you'll be re-called into hospital if you don't'.

> They're more likely to say, 'well we'll bring him in ' ... It keeps me within the system and maybe being compelled to stay with it has benefited me because it made me sort of get into a habit of taking my prescription drugs as opposed to being mentally ill.

In principle, the idea of being treated in the community was welcomed on account of being more 'family friendly' and being preferable to detention when in the past this had been a negative experience. Nevertheless, while community CTOs were for some preferable to being treated in hospital, they were not welcomed by everyone. Early indications were that community CTOs were limited in scope, often equating with CPN visits to check compliance with medication only. Service users had been disappointed with this, as they had understood it would mean access to more comprehensive support packages.

Participation

Enhanced participation especially in decision making was to be achieved through a number of new provisions under the MHCT Act: the Mental Health Tribunals (MHT), a more 'informal' forum intended to replace the legalistic Sheriff Courts to deliberate on proposals to enforce compulsion; encouragement to draw up an Advance Statement to plan for future treatment; the new role of Named Person replacing an assumption about nearest relatives; and increased access to independent advocacy, particularly for those facing Tribunals.

Interviewees' descriptions of MHTs encompassed both positive and negative viewpoints. On the one hand they were 'relaxed', 'fair', and 'informal', while on the other they continued to be depicted as adversarial settings. Many believed that the decision to section them had all been made prior to the Hearing. Without asking them directly, half of the service users interviewed said the decision made by the MHT had been a foregone conclusion and that it had been a waste of time. Some felt that professionals did all the talking at the meeting, that Panel members made little effort to understand their perspective, or to adapt to meet additional communication needs such as sensory impairment or autistic spectrum condition. Consensus was however that the MHT afforded a better opportunity for participation than the previous system, and was an opportunity to influence decision making around treatment, even if it did not always result in the desired outcome.

Unlike other parts of the UK, those under the MHCT Act have a right to make an Advance Statement, and MHT Panels are obliged to take such statements into account in their decision making. Despite being two years into implementation, just half had heard of Advance Statements and only 7 out of 39 service users interviewed at the second stage had chosen to make one, and at this stage not everyone understood them. A minority were completely satisfied with their treatment and could not envisage a reason to make one. Many others were simply sceptical. Even though some recognized potential benefits, the general consensus was that in practice, Advance Statements would be over-ruled:

> I've not made an Advance Statement because every time I try to they keep on blocking it...They've got the powers to overthrow it, so what's the point really?

Indeed, some had had their prior wishes explicitly ignored:

> I said, 'I wrote down that I didn't want that again', and I got it anyway...I said in my Advance Statement I didn't want C or D and they piled on the full dose...

Unlike Advance Statements, most service users had heard of the role of Named Person, and most had nominated one, commonly a close relative or friend. Views were mixed about its value however: while some were positive, others were undecided, and some felt that having a Named Person made no difference at all. Notably by the time of the second interview, around a quarter of service users had changed their Named Person to someone they considered more sympathetic to them, which indicates a shift in the balance of power between service users and carers through introduction of this role.

Service users generally knew about their right to independent advocacy, and several had an advocate supporting them at Tribunals. Whether or not the advocate was useful however varied with length of time they were known to the service user. Advocates provided important support to prepare for, help with attending and participating, and debriefing after the Tribunal. They were most effective when known prior to the Tribunal rather than in situations where they met the service user on the day of the Hearing. Not all interviewees chose to exercise their right to have an advocate, some expressing the belief that it was unnecessary when they had a lawyer to represent their views. Interestingly lawyers interviewed for this study were strongly in favour of independent advocacy, stressing that advocates were complementary to their own distinct role (Ridley et al., 2009, p. 99).

Care and treatment

The MHCT Act states that the MHO must prepare a care plan to accompany the application for compulsion, which should set out the person's needs for care and how the planned treatment will meet these needs (Patrick, 2006). The Code of Practice indicates that this plan should be participatory and drawn up in partnership not only with other relevant services, but also with service users and carers. In theory, an individual assessment of needs is carried out in a holistic way involving the multi-disciplinary team. In most people's experience, this was rarely the case. The only participants who were affirmative about having a care plan were those who were also under the CPA. Typically, participants said, 'I think I've got one but I've never seen it.' Care plans were a professionally driven concept, used by professionals to record service users' deficits (rather than capacities), and detail of the services it had been decided the person should receive. On a positive note, in some people's experience, they could be used to provide a handy checklist to remember what should be happening, and could be used in reviews and CPA meetings for this purpose.

There was little experience of MHOs drafting care plans with service users and what service users understood to be 'care plans' were often the individual plans drawn up by the key nurse when the person was in hospital. This response was fairly typical:

> I had to ask the social worker about the care plan and he said, 'I'm very sorry because I should have given you one a long time ago and haven't', and then he made one up and put it in the post to me. There probably was a care plan in the hospital. I was never asked to contribute to it.

In most people's experience, care and treatment under compulsion equated with drug therapies, especially in hospital, and was less focused on non-clinical, social, psychological and other support required for supporting recovery and enabling a good quality of life. Non-clinical aspects of care and treatment were not receiving as much attention as might be expected given the ethos of the MHCT Act and the thrust of mental health service development towards social inclusion and recovery. Few had accessed psychological therapies or counselling and, in relation to addressing wellbeing and social agendas, support for employment was rarely, if ever, addressed in individuals' care plans. Although there were positive examples of active support received with leisure, training, education, and employment, there was a distinct lack of strategic change in addressing these agendas. Also, although the interviews did not specifically focus on people's housing circumstances and views, a number of participants highlighted the significant role of housing in planning for successful discharge and resettlement, and in care in the community. Those who were dissatisfied with their care and treatment under compulsion wanted more holistic assessment of their needs and the support they needed for recovery.

Despite recognizing some benefits from drug therapies, or at least that the drugs they were taking did them no harm, a common complaint concerned the catalogue of negative effects often experienced from some of the more commonly used drugs. In many cases, potential effects had not been explained and when they did experience them it felt as if no one was listening to their concerns. As one person said, 'nothing seems to be getting done' when they complained, even when, as another participant said, such side effects were 'horrific'. This is a similar finding to that of Rose et al. (1998), who found that service users frequently felt they were over-medicated and were distressed by the side effects, despite recognizing some benefits. Side effects included being excessively tired and lethargic, which as this account vividly illustrates, can have a major impact on quality of life:

> I'll get up in the morning, have my breakfast, take my pills, go to my bed an hour and a half after taking the pills for a lie down...and I have a doze. Lunchtime, about an hour after lunchtime, have another doze, that takes me through to about

three or four o'clock in the afternoon, go out to the shop, have tea, have another doze then finally go to bed at half past 11 at night... It's no much of a life really.

Effects experienced from anti-psychotic and other drugs were major weight gain, headaches, cramps, shaking, dizzy spells, hallucinations, suicidal thoughts and sexual impotence. One person described himself as 'a drooling cabbage', and another related how the Depot injections he was on 'tend to cloud my brain up'. Another described 'a mad rush that goes to my head' after his fortnightly injection, which made him take to his bed for two to three days for the full side effects to wear off. Unwanted weight gain caused depression and affected people's ability to participate in leisure pursuits they had previously enjoyed. The unknown effects of the medication on hormones and the reproductive system were also of concern for young men and women. Some had never received a satisfactory diagnosis and were perturbed by the use of powerful drugs to treat something that had not yet been diagnosed. One young woman prescribed drugs to treat schizophrenia during a short stay in hospital said her condition had never been explained to her.

Various accounts were given of changes in medication and of finding options that worked better for them as an individual. Participants had mixed experiences of being involved in the decision to stop, to increase/decrease or change their drugs. A change of medication or treatment had been negotiated in partnership with some psychiatrists, reflecting the movement towards there being better dialogue between clinicians and patients emphasized by the Concordance approach that has been favoured since the mid 1990s. Whereas a compliance-based approach refers to the medical professionals' role as ensuring that patients comply with prescribed treatments, concordance stresses that treatment should be developed through dialogue where patients' experiences, values and aspirations about their illness and its treatment are at the centre (Royal Pharmaceutical Society, 1997; Horne et al., 2005). Many people's experience indicated that a more traditional, paternalistic emphasis on gaining compliance persisted. Many felt powerless to influence their treatment even when they had highlighted detrimental side effects.

Service users' views of MHOs

In their role as the coordinator of doctors' reports and paperwork to the Tribunal, MHOs were often perceived as being in cahoots with psychiatrists, especially when there was disagreement. The ambivalence felt by many service users was typified in this comment:

He was my first point of contact but when it came to the Tribunal he was the on the side of the psychiatrist. So he had two hats and you never knew who you were dealing with. Were you dealing with a social worker who was there to help you or were you dealing with the guys who were trying to have you sectioned?

When MHOs acted as social workers, they were perceived to have been helpful, for instance, supporting applications for disability living allowance, helping find suitable housing, dealing with debt problems and so on. In this role, they could be 'responsive and really listen'. Some service users expected MHOs to act more as advocates and a few did give examples of MHOs visiting them in hospital to ensure their rights were upheld regarding treatment, and had at times challenged psychiatrist's decisions thus moving from adversary to ally. MHOs interviewed for this study drew attention to the tension between the enhancement of their role under the MHCT Act and the reality of the responsibility involved in coordinating applications.

There has been a dramatic increase in preparing paperwork, both in terms of the application and the amount of liaison needed, which was done more informally before ... (MHO)

As McCollam et al. (2003) highlighted prior to implementation, the workforce implications arising from the MHCT Act need to be addressed.

Conclusions

Although this qualitative study has limitations, it was important that the accounts of those directed affected by compulsion are told alongside those of carers and professionals. Although some degree of bias was inevitable in a self-selecting sample, account was taken of the wider service user experience than is often the case. Additionally, the participatory research approach helped to ensure that service-user perspectives and interpretations were central to the study design, its conduct and analysis of findings. Moreover, its findings do resonate with those of other research.

In conclusion, the study indicates room for improvement in respect of shifting the balance of control in decision making about care and treatment under compulsion. If being detained under compulsion is like 'going to hell', approved mental health practitioners need not be complacent and unthinking in terms of detaining people. In particular, indications were that many people's care and treatment regimes were more often than not based on the medical model, with little regard paid to psychosocial explanations or offering alternative treatment responses. Less attention seemed to be paid to broader issues and strategies that have been shown to enable and assist recovery. The importance of holistic care planning that takes into account service users' views is underlined.

While the voice of service users was beginning to be heard through implementation of more deliberately inclusive processes implemented under the MHCT Act, service user participation remains a complex aspiration in the context of compulsory care and treatment. Some might argue that participation and compulsion are incompatible making self-determination in this context illusory. However, a significant proportion of people felt that some form of treatment was necessary for them. Key ingredients to success lie in the approved mental health practitioner's willingness to listen actively and to communicate openly; and, essentially, in achieving a balance between professional expertise alongside service users' expertise.

Acknowledgements

In writing this chapter I acknowledge the work of the research team: Dr Ann Rosengard, Susan Hunter, Simon Little, Lea Cummings, Vincent Edkins, Francis Fallan, Tracy Laird, Anne McLaughlin, Jen Muir, Agnes Thomson, and Janette Whitelaw.

Reflective Questions

1. How can approved mental health practitioners really understand the experience of detention?

2. To what extent do the decisions made by approved mental health practitioners take into account the feelings associated with the process and accounts of detention as recounted by those whom it affects?

3. How effective is an approved mental health practitioner in undertaking their role in such a way that the service user understands what is happening and has control where possible?

4. How powerful is approved mental health practice?

5. How can approved mental health practitioners guard against complacency?

10

The Role of the Nearest Relative

Philip O'Hare and Gavin Davidson

Editors' Voice

The particular focus of this chapter concerns the Nearest Relative, a legally defined role in mental health law and a controversial one which all approved mental health practitioners need to be aware of and understand. Underpinned by a dispute as to whether the use of a relative was, or ever has been, an appropriate way to provide a check on decisions made under mental health law, this chapter offers a necessary précis of the role's progression. A historical account provides the reader with a vivid insight into the deliberations. Moreover the reader is alerted to the gradual development of social work's role and the increasing influence of it especially in relation to how a relative should be viewed and in what respect they retain involvement. Emerging from the blurring of these roles, approved mental health practitioners nonetheless are obliged to be mindful of the Nearest Relative and engage with them, but this can cause confusion. This chapter weaves its way through this confusion by discussing the individual review and differing outcomes by each of the nations of the United Kingdom. Lastly case law developments while aiming also to help clear this confusion provide not only a real sense of the fluidity, but also as the authors put it the 'sharpness' which any contemporary effective approved mental health practitioner needs.

The Nearest Relative (NR), as a legally defined role in mental health law with a range of powers and duties, was first established in the Mental Health Act 1959 for England and Wales, the Mental Health (Scotland) Act 1960 and the Mental Health (Northern Ireland) Act 1961. However, historically a relative has always played an important part in the care and control of family members. It was understood to be significant due to kinship and the principle of blood relationships but continues to be the cause of much debate

151

and disagreement (Bean, 1980). BASW (British Association of Social Workers, 1977) have always contested that it is not appropriate for relatives to make decisions regarding a patient's mental health and advocated for a more professional approach to safeguarding patient's rights. Proponents of the role reinforce the value of their function as one of safeguarding the patient's rights (Gregor, 1999; Rapaport, 2003). This chapter reflects on the historical origins of the role and explores some of the problems that have arisen with respect to civil rights and the practicability of the function.

Since it became a mandatory part of approved mental health practice to consult and work alongside the NR during assessments for compulsory detention, the task has become increasingly burdensome. In particular it has been hampered by an inflexible definition and the prospect of litigation awaiting any incorrect legal interpretation. The experiences of ASWs in England and Wales will provide the main focus for this chapter and in particular the case law referred to in the latter part of the chapter relates to the English perspective. The chapter will consider the situation in Northern Ireland which is reviewing the NR function (Bamford Review of Mental Health and Learning Disability, 2007) and Scotland which has taken a different route to resolving some of these difficulties with the introduction of the named person in the Mental Health (Care and Treatment) (Scotland) Act 2003.

History of the Nearest Relative

The development of the role of the NR only has meaning when considered in the historical context of mental health services and the framework of mental health law. Prior to a legal structure or formal services specifically for mental disorder, the responsibility fell upon relatives to make decisions about care and treatment for their ill family member. Poor families could choose between keeping them at home with restrictions and sending them away – sometimes referred to as single lunatics (Jones, 1972). For the wealthy their route was organizing admission for their family member into the private madhouses: legislation to license and control the admission to these institutions introduced the relative to the legal process alongside the medical assessment (Hewitt, 2009). The Act for Regulating Private Madhouses 1774 introduced a certification process for admission requiring the identification of the committing person (usually the relative) and The Madhouse Act 1828 required the confinement to be authorized by the relative (Porter, 1987).

However, in these early years there were a number of problems in terms of monitoring the appropriateness of some of the admissions: there were no records kept of the private madhouse in-patients or the single lunatics. The extent and nature of the problems that these people presented with in order to receive such treatment was never recorded. Inevitably, there were a number of wrongful detentions and the use of the habeas corpus writ, the legal redress to have you case reviewed and to be freed, was rarely used (Unsworth, 1987; Burrows, 1998).

It is significant that at this period in history when the concerns over false imprisonment were first raised publicly, it was not just the owners of mad-houses and corrupt physicians who were singled out but the relatives also. In an anonymous article in the Gentleman's Magazine in 1763 the writer makes reference to the ulterior motives of some relatives:

> When a person is forcibly taken or artfully decoyed into a private madhouse he is, without any authority or any further charge than that of an impatient heir, a mer-cenary relation, or a pretended friend, instantly seized upon by a set of inhuman ruffians trained up to this barbarous profession, stripped naked and conveyed to a dark-room. (Jones, 1955, p. 32)

There followed a period between the end of the eighteenth century and the mid twentieth century, when successive pieces of legislation were passed by Parliament in attempts to protect the rights of the insane and tighten the procedures for incarceration. One example included the establishment of the Lunacy Commission in 1845 which was tasked with monitoring and inspecting the new asylums (Jones, 1972). This period was also significant in that the asylum promoted the newly established psychiatric profession to be the main gatekeeper for these institutions (Scull, 1979) and the numbers of people detained in hospital increased dramatically (Raftery, 1996). These were stark reminders for the need to strengthen safeguarding measures for in-patients and avoid public fears of collusion between relatives and doctors (Hargreaves, 2000).

The Lunacy Act 1890 introduced for the first time a legal definition of rel-ative although at this time no hierarchy was used (Hewitt, 2009). However, the law regarding relatives begins to take shape and reveals a likeness to the future NR. The Act preserved a role for the relative in petitioning for the admission and discharge of their family member. The Reception Order was granted on petition from a 'near relative' accompanied by two medical rec-ommendations; an Emergency Order was similarly granted on petition from a relative along with just one medical recommendation. The relative also had powers of discharge though this could be barred by the medical officer if there were significant dangers. Additional powers for the relative to object to a patient's detention were introduced some years later with the Mental Treatment Act 1930.

There has been a view that the relative was the best positioned to be guardian of the patient's liberty:

> The closer, in kinship terms, that he or she is to the patient, the more zealous would be the relative expected to be. (Bean, 1980, p. 60)

In the absence of a robust rights-based approach to law and the lack of advocacy as a concept perhaps family should take on some protective role? However, Bartlett and Sandland (2007) suggest that maintaining the involvement of family in a legal capacity has been justified on the basis of their caring role at home and the 'vestige of Victorian values about public and private life' (p. 165). They argue that both of these assumptions are problematic in that families are not always caring and incidents of exploitation or abuse have raised questions about the appropriateness of involving relatives in decisions.

The Percy Commission and the Nearest Relative

The Mental Health Act 1959 introduced the role of the 'nearest relative' and for the first time the law defined the NR and provided a priority order of the relatives. Compulsory admission for an emergency, observation or treatment required an application by a NR or Mental Welfare Officer (MWO in England and Wales). The Percy Commission (1957), which had guided the implementation of the new 1959 Act, had intended the role of the NR to be protective and had accepted that relatives should play a key role in monitoring the patient's detention and in safeguarding their access to after-care. It did acknowledge the potential for abusive relatives but concluded that this would be rare (Hewitt, 2009).

At the time there were a few critical voices with respect to the NR. During the reading of the Bill, the lone voice of MP Edith Summerskill raised some concern:

> it is quite conceivable that the nearest relative is not necessarily the person most concerned to promote the welfare of the patient...No doubt we are all thinking of our nearest relatives and that 'But by the grace of God there goes...' some of us. We should be quite content that our nearest relative should be there to look after our welfare, but can that be said about all people? (Summerskill, 1959)

Larry Gostin, who became the first legal director of MIND, provided some extensive reflections on the 1959 Act but it was interesting to note that he did not challenge the NR being nominated as one of the applicants for compulsory admission. For example, Gostin (1975) was critical of the misuse of the Emergency Order, and focused on the problems relating to finding a suitably qualified doctor, with expertise in mental illness, to provide the solitary recommendation. He raised concerns about the ease of application of this section and the possibility of unfair decisions. The ability of the relative to perform their function was not questioned or connected to the misuse of this section. Gostin (1975) seemed more preoccupied with the appropriateness of the NR to be able to discharge the patient. He reflected on difficulties in the relationship between patient and NR such as the part it plays in the patient's symptoms, the family problems being a cause of the hospitalization and the fall out after the admission of family blaming each other. However, these points were made in the context of discharge rather than the process leading to admission. It is exactly these issues that could make it inappropriate for a NR to be involved in the process at all. The focus on patient's rights deflected attention away from the role of the NR and probably helped to maintain their role as concerned advocates (Prior, 1992). Others have argued that NRs retained their powers mainly due to unsatisfactory alternatives and the under-developed role of social work (Rapaport and Manthorpe, 2008).

The 1959 Act was also a defining moment for the social worker's role in the admission process. The historical problem of compulsory admission balanced against the civil liberties of the patient, was at what point and to whom was the effective decision-making power vested (Unsworth, 1987). The Percy Commission recommended that access to treatment and care for the mentally ill should be on the basis of an undisputed medical recommendation and it was clear that medical expertise would be dominant. But a door was left ajar for the MWO who was required to make an application for compulsory admission if such action was necessary and the patient's relative had been consulted. This was viewed in part as a quasi-judicial perspective during the admission of a patient but also secured an opportunity for greater influence in the decision-making process (Unsworth, 1979). Initially there was no requirement for MWOs to be a social worker but over time social workers began to populate the role and integrate their developing social work value base.

In comparison to the clarity of the doctor's role, there were ambiguities about the MWO roles, for example their right to refuse medical advice was never supposed to be a lay review of medical expertise and they were also considered more of a substitute for the relative (Fisher et al., 1984). They secured an independence from their employers in assessing for compulsory admission, which offered the potential for a wider scope to interpret their role. On the other hand Hargreaves (2000, p. 138) argued that this was mainly a 'conscience clause rather than a licence to defend the patient's civil rights'. It also raised an important question about whether they were really independent or, as some saw them, just a junior member of the team influenced by the status of the psychiatrist and having merely a procedural role:

> It does not seem to have occurred to the Commission that trained and experienced social workers might not be content to see themselves as errand boys for the family or doctors. (Hoggett, 1996, p. 53)

Gostin (1975) observed that the 1959 Act made it difficult for the MWO to influence the situation since they were given little legal standing, their opinion was given similar weight to that of an NR and it restricted their ability to supervise the admission process. The MWO often felt disadvantaged because of a lack of confidence and expertise thus applications were commonly inevitable (Barnes et al., 1990).

It appears that neither the relative nor the MWO had the ability, professional power or skills to provide the role of a truly independent reviewer in the process. The important aspect of the 1959 Act was the fact that the ultimate decision making power did not lie solely in the hands of doctors; the MWO at least had a foot in the door along with a limited recognition of their expertise and need to be involved in the assessment process. Of equal importance in relation to the NR was that it continued to receive fairly widespread support but the evidence from practice was that it became increasingly rare for them to be the applicant (Fisher et al., 1984).

Mental Health Act 1983 and the Nearest Relative

In the consultations prior to the Mental Health Act 1983 there were diverse views about the future role of the NR and the MWO which had become more closely aligned to the social work profession. Nevertheless the review of the 1959 Act concluded that no change in the law was needed with respect to their roles (Department of Health and Social Security, 1976). The argument for retaining the NR as applicant was summarized in the subsequent White Paper (Department of Health and Social Security, 1978, p. 32): relatives are 'unlikely to know the legal requirements or to have the necessary forms' but 'some relatives may prefer to feel that they are in control of the situation, and they will be in the best position to judge when they are unable to cope any longer with the patient'. It became evident that advances in social work education and training and the local authority organizational changes had provided a more professional workforce than what had appeared during the reform of the 1959 Act. MIND and BASW were keen for the role of social workers to be enhanced to provide a balance to the dominance of psychiatry and the MWOs had evolved to become the primary applicant challenging 'the assumption that medical and social goals are necessarily identical' (Fisher et al., 1984, p. 177). However, Bean (1980, p. 215) was more dismissive of these views and argued that there was an inherent ambiguity about the social workers role: 'the obscurity is compounded by linking the social worker to the relative and then ascribing additional duties to the social worker'. Bean's difficulty was that he did not believe that social workers had the skills for complex decision making. He went further to accuse BASW of being disrespectful of relative's experiences and questioned why the very person who has intimate knowledge of the patient's condition and behaviour should be ignored (Bean, 1986).

In many ways the conflict between medical and social perspectives inherent in the legislation, the need for independence during the assessment process to protect patient's rights and the requirement that all alternatives should be exhausted before detention is considered, focused mostly on the social work and psychiatric professions and deflected from any debate about the role of the NR. Prior to the 1983 Act and in the years that followed there were calls for the applicant to be better trained and more knowledgeable about mental illness. This should have called into question the ability of the NR to make an application. Although the review considered the possibility of removing this power, the 1983 Act still incorporated it. Barnes et al. (1990) believed this was influenced by the more conservative lobby including the carer's organization, the National Schizophrenia Fellowship, which was concerned about patchy 24-hour social work services. Submissions to the review also wanted the NR to be kept as a counterweight to professional authority and maybe more significantly the Association of Directors of Social Services was also concerned about imminent strike action by social workers (Rapaport and Manthorpe, 2008).

The Mental Health Act 1983 created a new title of the Approved Social Worker (ASW) with new duties and powers. The NR was now defined more rigorously and Section 26(1) provided a hierarchy of relatives:

(a) Husband or wife

(b) Son or daughter;

(c) Father or mother;

(d) Brother or sister;

(e) Grandparent;

(f) Grandchild;

(g) Uncle or aunt;

(h) Nephew or niece.

The choice of NR would usually be the highest on the list and the older of two competing relatives. There were also ways of leapfrogging others on the list on the basis of caring for, or ordinary residing with; along with a range of exclusion and inclusion sub-sections. The complex nature of this extensive and at times complicated definition has been the subject of an extensive handbook (Hewitt, 2009) which has often been a welcome aid for confused approved mental health practitioners.

The NR continued to have powers such as the right to object to some sections, to make an application for admission and to request discharge; there were requirements to be consulted and to receive information from the hospital about the patient's detention. It was noted by the Mental Health Act Commission that these powers were second only to those of the psychiatrist and even exceeded those of the ASW (Mental Health Act Commission, 1999). However, the ASW was now seen as the person who would be the preferred applicant for admission and there is no doubt that in the early days of the 1983 Act the Government intended the ASW to have an increasingly more influential role in the admission process (Local Authority Circular, 1986).

This did create the potential for some confusion and blurring of the respective duties and rights of NR and ASW. For example, one of the anomalies of the 1983 Act was the duty of the ASW to inform the NR when they do not make an application so that the NR may consider their power to make the application instead (Section 13[40]). Bean (1986, p. 22) referred to these 'curious tandem-like qualities' as contradictory because the social workers were duty bound to seek the least restrictive alternative and only make an application when appropriate, whereas a NR can make an application regardless of the ASW's opinion. This scenario also had the potential for an NR being asked to resolve a dispute between social worker and psychiatrist where professional relationships were tense. However, in a large scale study of the early implementation of the 1983 Act, Barnes et al. (1990) found only 1.6 per cent of applications were made by NRs. The reasons given for the NR making the application were the lack of ASWs immediately after the Act (probably due to strike action) and also the recommending doctors by-passing an ASW particularly where relationships were strained. The next detailed study of ASW activity made no reference at all to applications by NRs (Social Services Inspectorate, 2001). This has been reaffirmed within the Code of Practice which states:

> The ASW is usually the right applicant, bearing in mind professional training, knowledge of the legislation and of local resources, together with the potential adverse side effect that a nearest relative application might have on the relationship with the patient. The doctor should therefore advise the nearest relative that it is preferable for an ASW to make an assessment of the need to be admitted under

the Act and for the ASW to make the application where necessary. (Department of Health and the Welsh Office, 1999, paragraph 2.30)

The 1983 Act firmly established the ASW's complex and challenging role as applicant in meeting a range of demands from practical logistics through to difficult decisions and potential conflict with colleagues, service users and their families. However, the role of NR continued to be a resilient feature of mental health law for the next 20 years across all of the UK. Criticisms remained about its inability to reflect social change and an arbitrariness of identification which often militated against the best person being defined as NR (Rapaport and Manthorpe, 2008). ASWs began to report about some of their difficult experiences with the role of the NR, for example the removal of an inappropriate NR by changing the displacement criteria (Mental Health Act Commission, 1991). The Government ignored this until other legislation, such as the Human Rights Act 1998 and the European Convention on Human Rights, began to impact on the identification of the NR with some significant cases which eventually influenced legal reform (Rapaport, 2012).

R (SSG) *v* Liverpool City Council (2002) EWHC 4000 (Admin.) was a landmark case in which the NR of the patient SSG should have been her mother but the relationship between them was difficult and SSG requested that the ASW take her same-sex partner to be the NR. At this time there was no provision for gay and lesbian couples to have any status other than a five-year rule of ordinary residence. On the basis of an infringement of the right to respect for private and family life (Article 8: The European Convention on Human Rights), the judgment clarified that section 26 should give equal status to gay unmarried couples and heterosexual unmarried couples.

Article 8 was the motivation behind the case of FC *v* UK (1999) 37344/97 ECHR 184, where the NR of FC had been identified as her adoptive father. She alleged that he had sexually abused her in the past and there was no contact between the two. An application to the county court for displacement had failed due to insufficient powers to make a change. A similar case JT *v* UK 26494/95 (2000) ECHR 133, also appeared before the courts at around the same time and in this case the patient had been abused by her step-father who was living with the NR (mother). In both cases the Government agreed that they would make changes to the law to allow a patient to change their NR under reasonable circumstances. Unfortunately, this met with delays mainly due to the protracted review of mental health law reform in England and Wales.

R (E) *v* Bristol City Council 2005 EWHC 74 (Admin.) 2005 MHLR 83 arose mainly due to the sluggishness of legal reform reacting to JT and FC. The patient objected to their NR, the sister, being consulted due to a poor relationship and the psychiatrist's view regarding the potential for further damage to her mental health. The ASW decided it was not reasonable or practicable to consult the NR and this was supported by the ruling which deemed any consultation would breach Article 8:

> Is the approved social worker really bound to inform/consult the nearest relative of a patient who may intensely dislike a patient and/or who would, or might, not act in the patient's best interest? The answer in my judgment is, of course not and particularly so where the patient, as here, is competent and has strongly expressed her wish that her nearest relative, Mrs S, is not informed or consulted. (paragraph 28)

The case reinforces the autonomy of the patient and the ability of an approved mental health practitioner to interpret the law (for example practicability) so as to take account of a patient's wishes, health and well-being. This has since been built into the Code of Practice where AMHPs should consider consulting as 'not reasonably practicable' where there may be a detrimental impact:

> Detrimental impact may include cases where patients are likely to suffer emotional distress, deterioration in their mental health, physical harm or financial or other exploitation as a result of the consultation. (Department of Health, 2008, paragraph 4.60)

Some additional case law that has arisen as a result of judicial review will be considered in more detail later in the chapter. The importance of these legal challenges is that they marked a period of law reform where once again the role of the NR would be reviewed. Some argue that it signposted a decline in the standing of the NR (Rapaport, 2004) and across each UK jurisdiction the NR has subsequently taken significantly different pathways.

Reforming the role of the Nearest Relative

Scotland and the Nearest Relative

In Scotland, the Millan Committee (Scottish Executive, 2001), which reviewed the Mental Health (Scotland) Act 1984, recommended that the NR should no longer be able to consent to emergency or short-term detention, or apply for long-term detention as they had been under the Mental Health (Scotland) 1984 Act. They suggested this role was potentially burdensome for NRs, damaging for the relationships involved and could bypass the important safeguarding role of the Mental Health Officer (MHO in Scotland).

It was also asserted though that this was not intended to lessen the involvement of people's family and carers. The subsequent Mental Health (Care and Treatment) (Scotland) Act 2003 introduced the role of the 'named person' and ended the role of the NR as applicant for detention in Scotland. People aged 16 and over can nominate their named person through a signed declaration that is witnessed to confirm that the person understood the effect of nominating that person and was not unduly influenced to do so. The witness must be one of a prescribed list of professionals. The named person must then be informed and consulted about some aspects of compulsory care and can also make certain applications, such as to Mental Health Tribunal for Scotland (Scottish Executive, 2005b). If there is no named person in place then the person's main adult carer is involved and, if there is no adult carer, then the default is the person's NR.

An early study of the implementation of the 2003 Act, which came into force in 2005, found that 'The nomination of a named person did not seem widespread at this stage. There was no consistent method of recording the details of the named person, nor was access to the named person's details standardized' (Atkinson et al., 2007, p. 1). Dawson et al. (2009, p. 1) found that the 'majority of Named Persons were default, comprising mainly carers and/or nearest relatives. Default Named Persons were seen as less active within the role. Named Persons were involved at the point of orders being made but were less so, on an ongoing basis'.

Berzins and Atkinson (2009) interviewed services users (20) and carers (10) about their experiences of the relatively new role of named person in Scotland. They reported that everybody welcomed the introduction of the role of named person and that although only one service user had their named person formally identified in their medical records most had taken some steps to identify their named person. In deciding who to name the main considerations were identified as whether the person would be aware of the service user's wishes and, whether they would carry them out. They concluded that 'all professionals take proactive measures to discuss the relationship with the Nearest Relative with all service users at risk of exposure to compulsory treatment to ensure that unsuitable Nearest Relatives do not become involved in compulsory measures by default. This is straightforward for Scottish service users who now have a clear process allowing them to choose a Named Person' (Berzins and Atkinson, 2009, p. 214).

England and Wales and the Nearest Relative

In England and Wales the Richardson Report (1999) began a protracted period of review of the Mental Health Act 1983. Up until 2006 proposed changes in the role of the NR had reflected the Scottish reforms in that a nominated person would be introduced and appointed by the patient. Their powers, alongside more prominent carer rights, would reflect some but not all of those of the NR and if this had been imposed it would have been 'an end to the interlocking functions of the nearest relative and the ASW... reflecting trends in mainstream social policy' (Rapaport and Manthorpe, 2008, p. 1122). It appears that ultimately in the later stages of the Parliamentary debate, the Government became more anxious about the possibility of patients being able to nominate someone who may not be appropriate and removing what they saw as the safeguards of the NR (Spencer-Lane, 2011). This also reflects their attitude to the reform generally which has been criticized for ignoring the rights of patients and the lack of focus on patient autonomy in favour of a more safety first approach (Pilgrim, 2007a; Mackay, 2012).

The outcome was that in the amended legislation of Mental Health Act 2007, the powers of the NR remained mainly intact with changes to the identification of NR and displacement arrangements reflecting the outcome of case law from previous years. Section 26(1) hierarchy was unchanged except that civil partners were given equal status with spouses and with cohabitants of more than 6 months. The displacement criteria of section 29 introduced the possibility of patients applying to the county court for displacement of their NR and a new ground for displacement based on unsuitability; courts were also given new powers to appoint an acting NR for an indefinite period. These changes reflected the rulings in the cases JT, FC and SSG which were discussed earlier.

Rapaport and Manthorpe (2008) argued that there was no guarantee that a nominated person would have been any less challenging for AMHPs, for example, a patient being admitted for the first time would be unlikely to have any person nominated which limited their safeguards or a carer as a nominated person may end up with too many conflicting roles or none at all if displaced. They concluded that the recognition of the NR role:

> will largely depend on the political strength of the AMHP workforce to form alliances with carers and service users, gather information about safeguard's effectiveness... it will depend on professional discernment and skills to respond to the needs of individuals and their families. The AMHP will need to give thorough consideration to what constitutes damage to the patient's health and well-being, and ineffective relationships. (Rapaport and Manthorpe, 2008, p. 1127)

The end result of reform was that England and Wales still have an NR function still intact albeit slightly altered from previous incarnations and now compatible with Human Rights legislation.

Northern Ireland and the Nearest Relative

In Northern Ireland under the current Mental Health (Northern Ireland) Order 1986, the NR, identified in the same way as in England and Wales, or the ASW can act as applicant for compulsory admission (Article 5.1). The application has to be accompanied by a medical recommendation completed by a doctor, preferably but increasingly less often, the person's own GP. If the ASW acts as applicant they must identify and consult the NR unless, as with the 1983 Act in England and Wales, 'not reasonably practicable or would involve unreasonable delay' (Article 5.3). If it is not possible to consult the NR and the person is admitted then the ASW has to inform the NR 'as soon as may be practicable' (Article 5.5). If the NR objects to the decision to admit then a second ASW must be consulted and the NR's objection recorded. If the NR acts as applicant then, as soon as practicable, a social worker has 'to interview the patient and provide the responsible medical officer with a report on his social circumstances' (Article 5.6). Once a person is admitted the NR can both request discharge and appeal to a Mental Health Review Tribunal.

The ability to overrule the objection of the NR, without displacing them, in the 1986 Order is a clear difference from the 1983 Act in England and Wales. The rationale was provided by the MacDermott Committee (1981) who reviewed the Mental Health Act (Northern Ireland) Act 1961. They argued that under the previous law:

> if the nearest relative objects to a social worker making an application for admission, no responsibility is vested in anyone to process with the application and a state of impasse results... We think that inaction following such deadlock is unsatisfactory. It is desirable that in the event of disagreement, ultimate authority for deciding whether to process should be clearly allocated. We consider that this is a decision which should be taken by the social work profession. (p. 10).

Prior (1992) viewed this emphasis on the professional role of social work as evidence of an emerging professional model of mental health care in Northern Ireland.

There is some guidance in the Mental Health (Northern Ireland) Order 1986 Code of Practice (Department of Health and Social Services, 1992) on the process to decide whether the NR or an ASW acts as applicant. It states that the 'doctor should ensure that the nearest relative is aware that he can ask for an ASW to consider making the application' (paragraph 2.9) and it is acknowledged that there will be 'occasions when the nearest relative does not wish, or is unable, to make the application. Applying for admission at a time of crisis can be a stressful experience. On occasions an application by the nearest relative may be regarded by the patient as rejection by his family' (paragraph 2.10).

The relative proportion of applications for admission completed by NRs and ASWs has changed over time. Initially the majority were completed by the NR and it was not until 1996/7 that applications by ASWs outnumbered those by NRs. This trend has continued with NRs completing 488/1,599 (31 per cent) of applications in 2000/1 (Mental Health Commission, 2009) and by 2010/11 this had continued to decrease to 109/1259 (9 percent) (Regulation and Quality Improvement Authority, 2012).

Prior (1992) in an early commentary on the role of the ASW included discussion of the NR and argued that

> the social work application is now seen as containing a professional opinion and recommendation requiring a certain level of training and expertise in mental health work... the problem lies in the fact that the legislation gives similar powers in applying for hospital admission to the nearest relative, who has no expertise, no training and who is not expected to be objective about what is best for the patient. (Prior, 1992, p. 107)

Davidson et al. (2003), in a report for the Northern Ireland Human Rights Commission have also highlighted some concerns about the role of NR as applicant. They reinforced that the NR is unlikely to know the detail of the law and so if the grounds for admission are met. They are also unlikely to be able to provide a relatively objective assessment of the person's rights and needs and/or have a full appreciation of the possible impact on their future relationship. They therefore recommended that the role of NR as applicant should end but a person, nominated by the assessed person, should be consulted. This perspective was considered to be sufficiently important to introduce this new role.

The Bamford Review of Mental Health and Learning Disability which considered law, policy and practice in Northern Ireland also recommended changes to the role of NR. It also concluded that:

> the special status accorded to the nearest relative of a patient in the 1986 Order and, in particular, the right of that person to make an application for assessment... should be repealed. On the other hand it is essential that full recognition be given to relevant views expressed by attorneys, nominated persons, carers and, where appropriate, the NR. (Bamford Review of Mental Health and Learning Disability, 2007, p. 20)

In response to the Bamford Review and the other drivers for change, including the developing European Court of Human Rights case law, the Department of Health, Social Services and Public Safety are developing a new law, the Mental Capacity (Health, Welfare and Finance) Bill, that will replace the current Order and end the role of NR as applicant and introduce a role of nominated person to be consulted and involved when serious interventions are being considered. It is proposed that where a nominated person isn't available an independent advocate would be involved, and for serious interventions that are resisted or objected to, both a nominated person and an advocate would be appointed and consulted (Department of Health, Social Services and Public Safety, 2010). It remains to be seen how these proposals will be developed in the draft Bill which has not yet been published.

Case law and the Nearest Relative

The fundamental problem of negotiating and consulting with the NR became, for the ASW in England and Wales, one of the most demanding aspects of the role. In particular the ambiguities inherent within the rigid hierarchic definition of the NR have created significant legal challenges in the High Court in Westminster. We have already discussed some of the ECHR cases (SSG, FC and JT) that eventually impacted directly on the reforms in England and Wales. The focus of this section will be judicial reviews in London that have attempted to clarify the continuing complexities of the NR function. For Scotland the shift to a named person has resolved many of these complications and thus this case law is not so significant. Although Northern Ireland has its own statute making Assembly, it still complies with relevant English case law rulings as well as the case law made in the Northern Ireland courts. However, the pending changes to introduce a nominated person will also resolve many of the complexities. But for England and Wales there remain considerable questions about the future of the NR arising from the following case law.

Identifying and consulting with the Nearest Relative

Problems have arisen in the identification of and consultation with the correct NR. In some circumstances a relative can leapfrog another on the hierarchy of section 26 on the basis of caring for or residing with the person being assessed. However, the Act does not define either of these terms and unfortunately, case law has provided little clarity either. Re D (mental patient: habeas corpus) [2000] 2 FLR 848 essentially defined care as being more than minimal for example assisting with financial concerns, cooking, washing and cleaning. While this may be a matter of common-sense, not all caring relationships are clearly defined, for example, fluctuating mental ill health can result in sporadic care, care is not always physical help so how can emotional care be quantified and what does minimal mean.

R *v* Liverpool City Council, ex parte F. CO/2744/96,16 April 1997 was a complex case, which involved a choice of NR between a mother and grandmother. The man being assessed had left home to live with his grandmother following a family argument and on the basis of information from the grandmother, the ASW decided that she was caring for him and was declared the NR. It subsequently turned out that details had been missing from the relatives accounts and the actual period of caring was only a matter of days, in the meantime the man had been homeless. The court ruled that the ASW should 'take into account the duration, continuity and quality of care...and also the intention of the patient himself' (Hewitt, 2009, p. 59). This raises a number of questions for the approved mental health practitioner about how you quantify continuous and how do you assess the capacity of a person to decide what they really want, particularly if they are unwell. Carers are often faced with the possibility of their relative being unwilling to accept their help during crisis periods: does caring also include an element of imposition, in other words what if the person does not want to be cared for? In this case the court also considered the issue of ordinary residence and suggested that this may also depend on the stability of the person's situation, their itinerant lifestyle and thus ordinary residence may not exist. For the approved mental health practitioner this case could introduce some doubt about how NRs are consulted where there are difficult family dynamics and only partial information is available: 'The court clearly had some sympathy with the ASW, who had to choose between different versions of past history from the mother and grandmother, who had fallen out' (Jones, 1998, p. 7).

The case of R (WC) *v* South London & Maudsley NHS Trust [2001] EWHC 1025 (Admin.) appears to throw further confusion on how to decide. In this case WC lived with his wife but when his marriage was going through difficulties he moved in with his mother: prior to his current admission he had been living with his mother. The court ruled that the NR was the wife and it would not interfere with the approved mental health practitioner's decision unless they failed to apply the test under Section 26, or acted in bad faith or in some other way reached a conclusion that was plainly wrong (Hewitt, 2009). The judge clarified that there is no requirement for the AMHP 'to don the mantle of Sherlock Holmes' and the Court cannot query the reasonableness of an AMHP's decision, it can only inquire into the honesty of their contention that it appeared that the relative was the NR.

Once identified, the duty on the AMHP to consult can sometimes present practical and timing issues in terms of assessing someone who may be at risk and fulfilling their legal duties. So how often do you try to contact them, how much information to do you offer and when is the best time to contact them? The quality of the consultation was an issue in the case of R *v* Secretary of State for Social Services, ex parte Association of Metropolitan Authorities 1986 in which the court ruled:

The essence of consultation is the communication of a genuine invitation to give advice and a genuine receipt of that advice; to achieve consultation, sufficient information must be supplied by the consulting to the consulted party to enable it to tender helpful advice. (p. 2)

Therefore, merely informing the NR of the application will not suffice and the judge in the case went further to say that the AMHP is required to consider the appropriate timing of any consultation so that the NR is able to comprehend the information and advice. Last minute consultation where decisions by the clinical team have already been made may not necessarily fulfil this duty. This has been further tested in GD *v* the Managers of the Dennis Scott Unit at Edgeware Community Hospital and the London Borough of Barnet, QBD (Admin.) 27 June 2008. The ASW attempted to contact the NR, GD's father, but was only able to leave a message. When the NR contacted the ASW only a short time later, to object to the section 3, GD had already been admitted. The ASW had delayed contacting the NR because they had been concerned that if alerted the NR would take GD away from the home as in previous crises but as a consequence of the delay the NR had no effective contribution. The judge summed up by saying that: 'The consultation must be a real exercise and not a token one. If an objection is raised it does not have to be a reasonable one. It does not have to be one which judged objectively is sensible'. Davidson (2009, p. 80) argues that the changes to the NR in the Mental Health Act 2007 amendments may mean some patients 'may acquire nearest relatives more in tune with their own thinking' with a subsequent rise in objections and displacements. The AMHP's role is to consult with all NRs in spite of their objections and obstructiveness.

BB *v* Cygnet Healthcare 2008 EWHC 1259 (Admin.) was a case were the nearest relative was unable to speak or understand English and so the sister was contacted. The AMHP submitted that she did not object and understood this to be on behalf of her family though they were unhappy about the admission. The judge granted a writ of habeas corpus and the patient was discharged but he was critical of the AMHP:

- A nearest relative does not have to use the word object but the fact that the family were unhappy should have alerted the AMHP to the possibility that the NR objected.

- An intermediary who has been nominated by the NR could be used if an appropriate consultation is undertaken with that person but the burden of proof to show that proper consultation has taken place falls on the AMHP.

Barber et al. (2012) argue that, while approved mental health practitioners may have been less vigorous in their pursuit of the NR in the past, this case should nurture a more rigorous approach to their work with NRs.

In circumstances where the delay in consulting would cause an unreasonable delay the AMHP is not required to consult but so far unreasonable has not been defined. The closest came with the case of R (V) *v* South London and Maudsley NHS Foundation Trust & Croydon LBC QBD (Admin.) (8/2/2010). The AMHP was assessing a patient subject to a section 5(2) which was due to expire at 7.30 in the evening; the AMHP completed an application for section 3 at 12.15 but did not consult with the NR as she thought it would cause unreasonable delay. The judge in this case did not agree and believed this was sufficient time. Another factor in this judgment was the assumption by the AMHP that the NR would consent as they had previously given consent; in summary the judge said that for a well-known patient who may have had multiple detentions it will not be acceptable to assume that the NR will consent based on previous history.

This has been further explored in the case of M *v* East London NHS Foundation and Hackney London Borough Council 11/2/2009 which concerned a man who had been discharged by his NR and within days he was assessed for admission again. The AMHP, who knew about the previous history, consulted the NR in a series of telephone calls and in one of the calls the NR objected. However, in the final phone call the NR began to ask questions about the section and what would happen which the AMHP had interpreted as a withdrawal of their objection. This was deemed unlawful as there appeared to be no reasonable grounds for the decision. The judge went further and suggested that the AMHP's duties to consider all the circumstances of the case, may in fact need to consider previous actions by the NR so for example a previous request for discharge may be considered an objection in the future. Hewitt (2010) argues that some controversial questions should emerge from this in terms of the AMHPs duty to investigate historical details to ascertain what an NR wishes: 'must a nearest relative who has once objected to detention be taken, in the absence of an express change-of-heart, to do so forever in the future?' (Hewitt, 2010, p. 39). What if an AMHP decides not consult in the future for valid reasons, are they then bound by a historical objection – the NR may lose not the right to object but 'the right to concur' (Hewitt, 2010, p. 39).

In some extreme situations the AMHP is required to make decisions based on what may not appear lawful but is only reasonable. In the case of DP *v* (1) South Tyneside District Council (2) Northumberland, Tyne & Wear NHS Foundation Trust (2011) DP had made allegations against her family including that she was at risk of forced marriage and death. During their assessment for admission under section 3, the AMHP decided not to consult with the NR, the father, as the consultation would have included informing him of DP's whereabouts. The judge refused the application of habeas corpus and explained that the AMHP dealt with the dilemma as a reasonable and responsible mental health professional would have done and thus it was not practicable to consult NR reflecting the earlier findings of R (E) v Bristol City Council.

Conclusion

The previous case law highlights the continuing difficulties and complex family dynamics faced by approved mental health practitioners in working alongside the NR. The Mental Health Alliance had called for more detailed changes in the identification process of the NR (Mental Health Alliance 2012) and the process has since been described as a 'lottery' and 'a burdensome imposition for some carers' (Spencer-Lane, 2011, p. 50). Section 26 takes no account of the global arena where families often live apart in different countries or separate due to the need for asylum (relatives living abroad are excluded from being the NR); long term friends may know each other better than family but are excluded unless they have resided together for more than five years; where no relatives exist or contact is lost, the patient can often be left without any NR (Spencer-Lane, 2011). The law appears to be quite out-dated and reflects values of a bygone time.

Questions remain as to who is the best person to safeguard the patient's rights particularly where there are difficult and complex relationships within the family. Is it always appropriate for NR to be so closely involved? Early indications from Scotland appear to have received the named person favourably and with Northern Ireland about to take a similar route is it time that England and Wales need to consider a role for substitute decision makers to provide or withhold approval for detention based on the perceived best interests of the person? Perhaps a more radical but common-sense approach would be to support patients to be involved in the decision-making processes about their own care/lives so that the need for substitute decision making by NRs or anybody else is prevented?

Where is the evidence of effectiveness of the role? 'In spite of the importance of the NR, the potential for bias and the length of its existence, its research and literature base is meagre' (Rapaport, 2003, p. 52). The nature of evidence is considered by O'Hare in Chapter 11, but some considered evaluation may be needed to offer some direction for the future of the NR. Spencer-Lane (2011) is concerned that without a reasonable debate the danger is that the NR will continue to be effected by judges on an ad hoc basis.

There has been a persistent theme in the history of mental health legal powers about the jostling for authority between doctors, lawyers and social workers. Usually this has been decided on the basis of expertise or at least a perception of skill and proficiency. Also, carers and service users have begun to identify their own status as experts by experience. The problem for each of these 'expert' contributions in the process of sectioning is that they each have vested interests and, as explained throughout this chapter, the capability to protect patient's rights in compulsory mental health care has remained elusive and contested. Until the NR law is reviewed again, the role of the AMHP will remain central to the preservation of fairness and justice for detained patients and this chapter should offer a sound warning of the need for sharpness in their legal deliberations over consulting the NR.

Reflective Questions

1. What impact does the historical evolution of the role of the Nearest Relative have on my current approved mental health practice?

2. In what way does an effective approved mental health practitioner need to understand why the role of the Nearest Relative has come about?

3. Different nations have responded in different ways to reviewing the role of the Nearest Relative. Why does this matter for my practice?

4. The Nearest Relative is clearly defined in mental health law, but there remains confusion about the relationship with approved mental health practice. How does this affect my practice?

11

Evidence-Based Practice

Philip O'Hare

Editors' Voice

The penultimate chapter picks up on the influence of research; a theme which the reader was first asked to consider in Chapter 1. Evidence-based practice is a contemporary phrase that began life among medical circles but has since been adopted more widely. In this chapter the reader is asked to consider evidence; is it, put simply those facts that are found in research upon which approved mental health practitioners base decisions, or is this description too simplistic? In order to explore further, the author uses evidence arising from research relevant to approved mental health practice. Initially, as in Chapter 1, the reform of mental health legislation highlighted the limited availability of research, or evidence, about approved mental health practice. In turn its use resulted in different outcomes in each nation; such divergence a recurrent strand in this book. The reader is encouraged to reflect upon what evidence is and question whether approved mental health practitioners make decisions based upon evidence made available from research or rather is the process a more pragmatic one based on circumstance? Ultimately practitioners do make decisions but are these based on any certainty arising from the evidence or are other factors also important. The author in this chapter suggests that evidence even if used does not bring certainty and in so doing produces a platform for the final chapter.

This chapter explores evidence-based practice (EBP) in the context of approved mental health practice and considers some important issues for decisions regarding compulsory care. Approved mental health practitioners across all UK jurisdictions are the main 'applicant' within their respective legal frameworks. They ultimately have the decision-making power to detain a patient based on a range of evidence and taking into consideration the total circumstances of each case. The chapter begins with a deliberation of the contested nature of EBP in health and social care and examines the relevance of this concept for approved mental health practice. The discussion is developed with reference to the principle of least or minimum restriction now embedded as a guiding principle within the respective UK Codes of Practice (Department of Health and Social Services (Northern Ireland), 1992; Scottish Executive, 2005c; Department of Health, 2008; Welsh Assembly Government, 2008). Some of the inherent dilemmas and conflicts of approved mental health practice will be explored to demonstrate that basing decisions upon the evidence-base is not as straightforward as might appear.

Mental health social work has focused increasingly more attention on the subject of EBP in recent years. Notably the dominant driving force for this influence has been national policy across the UK as applied to practice, training and education (Department of Health, 1998b; Northern Ireland Social Care Council, 2002; Scottish Executive, 2003b). This may in some part be playing catch up to the other mental health professions such as psychiatry and psychology, which have a longer history of investigation and scientific research to support their interventions. Morago (2010) contends that there is still some doubt about the extent to which EBP is transforming social work practice mainly due to the lengthy timeframe to create relevant evidence but also, ironically, the poor reporting of its application. But it could be argued that the very ethical and moral basis for social work interventions where liberty and rights are at risk should be informed by a robust examination of evidence (Crawford and Mathews, 2011). This is most poignant in the actions of approved mental health practitioners in enforcing mental health law and their use of compulsory powers. There have been limited qualitative evaluations in relation to the process and the quality of decision making by approved mental health practitioners at the point of assessment. In England and Wales the most detailed studies were in the early stages of the introduction of the Mental Health Act 1983 (Olsen, 1984; Barnes et al., 1990; Sheppard, 1990). Since then studies mainly focused on the quantifiable nature of the work such as the social characteristics of the detained patients (Huxley and Kerfoot, 1994; Hatfield et al., 1997), or the broader reviews of detained in-patients in the biennial Mental Health Act Commission Reports (for example Mental Health Act Commission 1999; 2009). The Department of Health (2000b) acknowledged this during the consultations of the reform of the 1983 Act in England and Wales and commissioned research to fill gaps in knowledge specifically around the assessment and decision-making processes (Quirk et al., 2000; Roberts et al., 2002). Scotland has produced even less evidence of the administration of the Mental Health Officer role with only dated studies (Smith, 1991; Ulas et al., 1994). Northern Ireland has probably produced the most in-depth recent studies of approved mental health practice as the authorities begin the process of mental health law reform; this research has tended to focus more on the experience of ASWs during their assessments and qualifies the dilemmas and challenges for the role (Britton et al., 1999; Campbell et al., 2001; Wilson et al., 2005; Davidson and Campbell, 2010).

Approved mental health practice, therefore, has limited evidence to consider in relation to the actual assessment process and what influences the decisions that are made. Munro (2002) has been critical of the paucity of evidence and gaps in our knowledge of social work interventions and suggests that this will inevitably undermine the profession. The practitioner is required to make sense of a range of disparate and conflicting information, often in chaotic environments, balancing numerous roles and requirements and abiding by complex law and Codes of Practice. Where do approved mental health practitioners find relevant evidence and how is it applicable in such fraught situations? How is evidence interpreted to influence crisis situations?

Scotland and Northern Ireland have maintained the applicant role in their mental health law, narrowly contained in the social work domain and this may further confuse the basis on which evidence is used to support or oppose compulsory powers. For example Mackay (2012) argues that Scotland reformed their Mental Health Act in 2003 on the basis of improving safeguards and developing a rights-based approach to compulsion while in England and Wales reforms were deemed to be driven by a safety and risk focused goal (see Pilgrim, Chapter 4); Northern Ireland is moving towards a single capacity-based mental health legislation following the Bamford Review (Bamford Review of Mental Health and Learning Disability (Northern Ireland), 2007). Across each of these jurisdictions decisions could vary quite immeasurably dependent on the interpretation of evidence within different ethical and legal frameworks.

In England and Wales the applicant role has been extended to other professions namely mental health nurses, chartered psychologists and occupational therapists. This raises some interesting issues about how each profession may approach the dilemmas of EBP; their different traditions with respect to research may be an opportunity to evaluate practice with more rigorous research methods. It may also create tensions around research preferences and the validity and applicability of findings. However, there is an intrinsic danger in polarizing the ideals of each profession, for example, nurses allegedly being deferential to a medical model and social workers being the 'crusaders' for the social model. But this may be too simplistic and in the early years of nurses taking on the role of the Approved Mental Health Professional (AMHP) in England and Wales there was sufficient evidence to indicate that, despite scepticism from some quarters, they were able to consider social perspectives and share the values of their social work colleagues (Hunter, 2009; Jackson, 2009):

> If properly supported by training...community mental health nurses possess and value the very contributing factors that could promote positive user-centred outcomes. (Hurley and Linsley, 2006, p. 52)

The nursing profession also mirrors the social work inadequacies around research; some consider their profession to have a less developed evidence base and consequently a less effective profession. Newell and Gournay (2011) advocate the development of a more robust evidence base for nursing echoing many of the commentaries around the need for an evidence base in social work. This does raise some important questions about what sort of evidence does this mean? Is there a shared understanding of what EBP means for approved mental health practitioners? What is the value of research in crisis work? The next section begins to tease out some of the tensions around the nature of EBP.

What is evidence-based practice?

There has been a fairly consistent message in mental health and social care policy over a number of years that interventions need to be supported by evidence which is usually driven by a need to find out what works best. So for example, most of the current alternatives to hospital care such as crisis and home treatment teams, assertive outreach and early intervention work are all products of an evidence base that suggested they have favourable outcomes (Department of Health, 1999c; Care Services Improvement Partnership, 2007; HM Government, 2011). While EBP is nothing new its resurgence may be explained in part by the integration of health and social care services and the coming together of two different philosophical positions with respect to evidence, that is, the medical and social perspectives. Social work has been particularly concerned that the profession is not disadvantaged in terms of their knowledge base or expertise within the new configuration of services (Gould, 2006). However, EBP may also be a consequence of a more 'technocratic culture' within caring services and for some this plays into the hands of a managerialistic approach that emphasizes better value for money and efficiency over and above professional wisdom and practice (Webb, 2001, p. 58). Other critics such as Kane (2002, p. 221) argues that the application of evidence is driven by: 'Political, professional and ethical values; availability and constraint of resources; failures and crises; canvassed views from selected focus groups; [and] representation from pressure group'. Needless to say, there is an ongoing debate about what EBP means and more relevant to approved mental health practice, how does it inform decision-making processes.

A widely quoted definition of EBP is: 'the conscientious, explicit, and judicious use of current best evidence in making decisions about the care of individual patients. The practice of evidence based medicine means integrating individual clinical expertise with the best available external clinical evidence from systematic research' (Sackett et al., 1996, p. 71). This emerged from the discipline of medicine and is an indication of the strength of the relationship between the medical model and EBP which in some way explains the reluctance of social work to engage with EBP. Furthermore there has been an emphasis on a research hierarchy where evidence collected by a more scientific method of a randomized control trial (RCT) or systematic review are seen to be more valid than case studies and qualitative research. Gould (2006) argues that this has caused a number of problems for social work in that the voices of service users are minimized and practice informed research is relegated to a selection of opinions. The problem is that EBP is not uniformly accepted to be unbiased, rational or valid in the scrutiny of decision making. EBP can be narrowly focused, positivist and irrelevant, often pandering to the need to ration resources and missing opportunities to consider the experience of practitioners and the narrative of service users (Zayas et al., 2011). A relevant example of this is the Government implementation of Cognitive Behavioural Therapy as a standard intervention (HM Government, 2011). Pilgrim (2011) is critical that this is a simplistic approach based on some supportive scientific evidence without considering other interventions. In other words evidence is interpreted to inform a rationalist-based policy and convenient treatment at the expense of solutions for the more complex determinants such as social inequalities and the fostering of social capital. Another example is the appeal of risk assessment and management toolkits where there is often a tendency to measure short-term interventions which provide an allusion of certainty and meet the managerial goals of services (Brophy and Savy, 2011).

Social workers will often construct their identity around an anti-medical model of practice in favour of a social perspective. But in separating their position in this way it also separates them in relation to evidence; shifting away from a positivist empirical research focus to a less rigorous evidence base within the field of social science and ethnographical study. McCrae et al. (2004, p. 317) support the need for social workers to both challenge the 'scientific-bureaucratic reductionism on the grounds that it fails to account for the complexities of social care' and to develop a way of measuring the effectiveness of their interventions.

There are similar dangers in the rather simplistic and reductionist view of drawing a dividing line between evidence from social and medical perspectives in terms of qualitative and quantitative methods. Walters et al. (2004)

reflect on the promotion of research to inform social care and improve practice; the paper developed a model for practitioners focused on embedded research, organizational excellence and research-based practitioners. Other examples of understanding research in social work include a human rights and social justice framework (Maschi and Youdin, 2011) or emancipatory research (Orme and Shemmings, 2010). These disparate models would all aspire to use research to significantly change situations and are driven by both the ideology and values of social work. In this short chapter there is insufficient space to provide further evaluation of the broad range of approaches. However, the point is that the theoretical position of social work research is developing momentum and perhaps gaining the credibility it has lacked in previous times.

Mental health social work has often struggled with the concept of evidencing the efficacy of what it does on a daily basis (Morago, 2010). Social work has also been more comfortable as a profession represented by theoretical constructs to explain its 'raison d'etre' rather than being reinforced by empirical research (Webber, 2011). Moreover, social work training also focuses on the process of connecting theory to practice, consolidating values such as anti-oppressive practice and developing people skills to facilitate the day-to-day interactions (General Social Care Council, 2002). Generally the training at pre- and post-qualifying levels directs social work students and practitioners to a process of reflexivity and using supervision to consider these issues. In contrast Webber (2011, p. 4) insists that:

> Evidence-based practice is about considered rather than reflexive action. It requires practitioners to consider evidence before making decisions rather than acting first and reflecting after the event. This involves a critical appraisal of research findings to inform judgements about possible courses of action.

As the new Professional Capabilities Framework (PCF) is introduced to Social Work in England there are welcome signs of research and research-mindedness becoming central to social work practice through the Curriculum guides and the Knowledge and Critical Reflection and Analysis domains of the PCF (The College of Social Work, 2012).

Increasing focus on social-work evidence can be traced back and attributed to researchers such as MacDonald and Sheldon (1992) as they began reviewing the efficacy of social work. Sheldon was eventually to head the Centre for Evidence-Based Social Services in 1996 which was a significant step for the advancement of EBP in social work. Sheldon and Chilvers (2000, p. 5) adapted the previous definition of Sackett et al. to refer to evidence in relation to decisions about the 'welfare of those in need of social services' thus expanding the concept of EBP to a broader range of values. This is relevant in terms of timing because the Government was also beginning to consider the importance of EBP (Department of Health, 1999c) and the Social Care Institute for Excellence (2003) was flying the flag for an increased influence of research and EBP in social care. Recently there have been more robust evaluations of concepts such as practice-based research, which are critical of the limitations of RCTs and call for a flattening of research hierarchies: 'There's too much social work research to be done to be wasting time carping about whose research is superior' (Dodd and Epstein, 2012, p. 20). Others have argued for evidence-informed practice which is a more flexible approach to complex interventions where EBP and empirical evidence are only part of the picture and where there is less reliance on hierarchies (Nevo and Slonim-Nevo, 2011).

Mental health social work is usually constrained by the statutory framework imposed by legal processes and requirements of Codes of Practice which often dictate how a case will progress. Interventions are also increasingly prescribed by the eligibility and availability of suitable resources. In this context it is easy to see that evidence-based practice becomes less significant than procedural and resource-driven practice. I would argue that where evidence is required to support an application for detention under mental health legislation, the nature of the evidence upon which this is based is more about legal criteria and cataloguing risky behaviour of an individual than drawing on the outcomes of RCTs or systematic reviews. But the question therefore remains about whether EBP is relevant to approved mental health practice. How do approved mental health practitioners make sense of their legal roles being informed by evidence?

Least restriction and EBP

Approved mental health practitioners balance a wide range of complex dilemmas and situations when making a decision. One central question is whether the circumstances require compulsory detention in hospital or can a less restrictive course of action be considered. What evidence may impact on this decision? What knowledge and research can an approved mental health practitioner draw upon to make an informed decision about using alternative resources? How is effectiveness evaluated in deciding between alternative interventions?

The principle of least restriction was introduced in England and Wales with the Mental Health Act 1983 and supported the powers of the new ASW role within a wider social context (Department of Health and the Welsh Office, 1999). It was, to some extent, a reflection of the increasing evidence of the efficacy of psychosocial interventions in the community as opposed to hospital-based care and also a counter balance to the dominance of the medical model. In England and Wales the recent Mental Health Act 2007 amendments have maintained this principle within the separate Codes of Practice:

> People taking action without a patient's consent must attempt to keep to a minimum the restrictions they impose on the patient's liberty, having regard to the purpose for which the restrictions are imposed. (Department of Health 2008, p. 5)

While it remains a significant part of the current AMHP function, the Codes are guidance only, open to interpretation. In contrast to England and Wales, the principle of least restriction has been included within statute in the Mental Health (Care and Treatment) (Scotland) Act 2003 and The Bamford Review (Department of Health and Social Services and Public Safety (Northern Ireland), 2007) in Northern Ireland is also recommending that it is incorporated in future statute. Mackay (2012) suggests that this provides greater clarity for professionals and more accountability for their decisions. It would also support the view of a safety-first approach to mental health care in England which is quite different to the move towards rights-based mental health law in Scotland and Northern Ireland (Pilgrim, 2007a). There is currently insufficient evidence to evaluate the impact in practice of such a difference in application of the least restriction principle. A recent small scale qualitative study of approved mental health practice across the three jurisdictions found a fairly consistent approach and commitment to seeking alternatives to compulsion (O'Hare et al., 2013). Despite the different rhetoric between jurisdictions it remains a central focus for approved mental health practice and, some would argue, that social work has played a significant role in embedding the principle even within day-to-day activity of mental health services and practitioners (Webber, 2011).

The English and Welsh Codes also included a requirement that AMHPs need to use resources 'in the most effective, efficient and equitable way' (Department of Health, 2008, p. 6). Though the implications of this may be unclear, it could be interpreted as a way of limiting resources and thus compromising the nature of least restriction (Barber et al., 2012). Thus in practice the least restrictive option is often a restriction of resources but, moreover, the Code is directing practitioners to consider the efficacy of their interventions and brings into play the interpretation of evidence at the point of decision making. I will develop this further in considering the evidence for Crisis Resolution and Home Treatment (CRHT) but this raises difficult questions about who is defining efficacy and what is driving the need for efficiency? Do practitioners evaluate efficient interventions in the same way as managers, policy makers, service users and carers? Consider an example where a carer is experiencing high levels of stress while looking after a relapsing family member: this could be resolved by a compulsory hospital admission (assuming the legal criterion are sufficient) but will not fit comfortably with either the service user's aspirations or the national policy to use CRHT to avoid admission (HM Government, 2011). The more controversial area of the right of nearest relative to make an application for admission also raises important questions about how principles within the Codes are interpreted by the nearest relative; how would a nearest relative approach the least restrictive principle in terms of their knowledge of alternatives and decide on the basis of efficacy? This may be most significant for Northern Ireland where nearest relative applications still account for nearly 10 per cent of all compulsory admissions (Regulation and Quality Improvement Authority, 2012) and arguably adds weight to the contention that ASWs and AMHPs should be the preferred applicant as discussed by O'Hare and Davidson in Chapter 10.

A more significant concern has been the complication of actually finding alternatives that may be appropriate to manage levels of risk within community settings (Manktelow et al., 2002). This is hampered by approved mental health practitioners' limited decision-making powers for accessing resources particularly where funding is required (Parker, 1994). Previous studies have shown that, in general, community-based alternatives are used only rarely in approved mental health practice. Hatfield (2008) in a large study of nearly 15,000 assessments in England 1996-2004, found only 7.2 per cent resulted in alternative care; Davidson and Campbell (2010) found similar results in their smaller cohort study in Northern Ireland. In both studies accessing resources was a considerable hurdle to using alternatives though they had yet to see the impact of new resources such as Crisis Resolution and Home Treatment teams.

It would be too simplistic to conclude that more resources should make a difference to these figures. Alternative resources such as crisis houses, adult placements and small community-based therapeutic wards have been established for some time and increasing in numbers as new models of care appear within both the remit of Health Trusts and Local Authorities and more innovative projects in the voluntary sector. A systematic review by Lloyd-Evans et al. (2009) found that alternative residential options such as crisis beds and short stay admission wards account for 10 per cent of the total number of acute inpatient beds and yet the evidence about their effectiveness has been limited. They found that there was some evidence of increased satisfaction for patients compared to standard acute wards and concluded:

> More research is needed to establish the effectiveness of service models and target populations for residential alternatives to standard acute wards. Community-based residential crisis services may provide a feasible and acceptable alternative to hospital admission for some people with acute mental illness. (Lloyd-Evans et al., 2009, p. 109)

Another account of the low figures for diversion to alternatives may be explained in some part by the use of alternatives prior to the assessments for compulsory mental health legal interventions. So, in situations where alternatives have been exhausted, the focus for practitioners should be more about the best interest of the patient rather than the least restriction (Webber 2011). The Mental Health Act Commission (2009) speculated that patients were being managed more intensively by services in the community and consequently at the point of admission to hospital they were experiencing increased levels of acuity accounting for higher rates of detention. Risk averse and defensive practice in mental health policy particularly in England (Pilgrim, 2007a) has been an increasing influence on practitioners and subsequent decisions regarding compulsory care. Where effectiveness is unclear or levels of risk are increasing there will be a subsequent impact on 'safe' decisions being made to admit to hospital rather than consider alternatives. Is hospital a safe decision? Is there any evidence of the effectiveness of hospital care? Are decisions based on evidence or have practitioners come to see acute care as the default, risk-averse decision without challenging the notion that in-patient care may not be effective?

Least restriction and Crisis Resolution and Home Treatment (CRHT) teams

The evaluation of CRHT teams is typical of the intricate and problematic nature of applying evidence to approved mental health practice. The context and rationale for introducing CRHT in the UK has been well documented elsewhere and followed similar developments in USA, Canada and Australia (Department of Health, 1999c; Sainsbury Centre for Mental Health, 2006). The upsurge of interest and development of crisis intervention projects was supported by evidence of reduced hospital in-patient days, cost effectiveness and reduced stigma (Stein and Test, 1980; Hoult et al., 1983; Muijen et al., 1992). Clearly this fitted well with the move to deinstitutionalization and policies to reduce bed capacities, as well as meeting the service-user agenda of more recovery-focused care at home or at least outside the hospital institution. Thus it was only a matter of time before the model was interpreted for the UK and was rolled out as part of New Labour's Modernization Agenda and a cornerstone of mental health delivery (Department of Health, 2000c). Across the UK it is now standard practice to have potential admissions to psychiatric hospitals including those for compulsory care, assessed for CRHT intervention.

However, there are concerns at a number of levels about the interpretation of evidence in supporting policy and interventions. In the 1990s the widespread use of crisis teams raised questions about the quality of empirical evidence to support their extensive use (Geller et al., 1995) and since then a range of key documents have maintained that most of the evidence is still inconclusive (Sainsbury Centre for Mental Health, 2006). The Cochrane Review (Joy et al., 2006), which was considered to be influential on the thinking of the Department of Health, evaluated many studies of CRHT interventions and found that the evidence for crisis intervention in its pure form was limited and inadequate. Many of the studies were small scale, out of date with current provision, data was poorly recorded and most interventions involved 'packages' of care. The review concluded that:

> Home care crisis treatment, coupled with an ongoing home care package, is a viable and acceptable way of treating people with serious mental illnesses. If this approach is to be widely implemented it would seem that more evaluative studies are still needed. (Joy et al., 2006, p. 1)

Of course more evaluative studies have emerged over the last few years as CRHT has been embedded into the makeup of UK policy and services. But these studies raise further questions about how the efficacy of CRHT can be more clearly measured, for example, Glover et al. (2006) found that the introduction of crisis resolution teams was associated with reductions in admissions but concluded that other factors such as the policy of bed closures must have influenced the results. Jacobs and Barrenho (2011) have questioned the reliability of CRHT evidence because of a lack of robust methodology and found no significant difference between PCTs with and without CRHT teams. Johnson et al. (2005) produced a before and after study of a crisis resolution team in Islington which is widely quoted as supporting the use of this intervention and found that there were convincing reductions in admission rates and inpatient days. However, they found no effect on reducing compulsory admissions and suggest that crisis resolution teams may be more effective in preventing voluntary admissions:

> The poor social circumstances of many of our service users and the large numbers with a history of violence or involuntary admission may be inimical to home treatment. (Johnson et al., 2005, p. 73)

So is the evidence in relation to an alternative to compulsory admission any clearer? It is almost impossible to tease out differences that are occurring as a result of the national policy to close beds and the introduction of CRHT. Keown et al. (2011) analysed admission rates between 1998 and 2008 concluding that there was an association between the reduction in psychiatric beds and increases in compulsory admissions. They identified a consequence of reducing beds could lead to: a) delays in admission and deteriorating mental health; b) delays in planned admission leading to crises and compulsion; c) as shorter admissions become forced by demand for beds they may result in more frequent relapse; and d) wards may be becoming more disturbed and less attractive for patients to be admitted voluntarily.

Tyrer et al. (2010) analysed the data for compulsory admissions in Cardiff as CRHT teams were being introduced and found significant increases in the use of the Mental Health Act 1983 alongside decreases in voluntary admissions. This was explained as being a consequence of using CRHT for patients who initially may be more willing to engage or might have been admitted voluntarily but after time become more unwell and require compulsion. This of course does not show a successful intervention as this scenario may be more stressful for all involved including patients and family/carers. In contrast Barker et al. (2011) in their Edinburgh study found that informal and formal admissions were both reduced with the introduction of CRHT showing that 'crisis care in the community maintains patients in a stable condition without requiring later compulsory hospital admission' (p. 109). However, they also noted that variations in the implementation of guidelines 'makes consistent and effective implementation of evidence based interventions such as CRHT in different areas extremely difficult and differences in implementation may account for differences in outcomes...' (p. 109).

In many ways the decision to use CRHT is often taken out of the hands of approved mental health practitioners as it is national policy across all UK jurisdictions to use CRHTs at the point of crisis where admission to hospital is being considered (National Audit Office, 2007). The gate keeping role of the CRHT questions the independence of the approved mental health practitioner role and at the same time offers support during the fraught assessment process (Furminger and Webber, 2009). Morgan (2007a) indicates that there are generally good working relationships between approved mental health practitioners and the CRHT teams but also suggests that CRHT teams should develop their gate keeping role and become more involved in the assessment process. Further evaluation may be needed to consider the conflict between approved mental health practitioner's statutory roles and CRHT policy.

Approved mental health practitioners are faced with a considerable dilemma where the evidence to support CRHT is so inconclusive and disputed. This raises a number of questions for practice. Most mental health crises do not have the luxury of time so how is the evidence for CRHT analysed in the decision-making process? Are approved mental health practitioners aware of the contested evidence about the efficacy of CRHT? Which evidence do they use and does it exist for their locality? How is the evidence disseminated in a format which is accessible for busy teams? Is the use of CRHT a genuine attempt to consider LRA or is it a way of managing decreasing numbers of acute beds? I would argue that these questions are rarely explored by approved mental health practitioners whereas more often decisions are made based on eligibility criteria, bed availability and levels of risk.

Least restriction and Community Treatment Orders

Another aspect of approved mental health practice which has received considerable attention in recent years is the use of community treatment orders in England and Wales and community-based compulsory treatment orders in Scotland (both referred to as CTOs). Northern Ireland is planning a similar form of CTO in the future amendments to their mental health law. Essentially CTOs legislate for patients to comply with a range of conditions in the community including enforced treatment and imposing a range of health/social care services. The CTO in England and Wales was presented as a less restrictive way of managing 'revolving door' patients, preventing their deterioration and targeting those posing the highest risk to themselves and others. It offers approved mental health practitioners an alternative to admission or opportunities for earlier discharge. However, it challenges the nature and principles of the statutory functions of approved mental health practice which has usually been only concerned with compulsory admission to hospital. The introduction of the CTO was heralded by a range of critical voices questioning the ethics of extending compulsory powers into community-based care. Pilgrim (2007a) argues that the new CTO received less opposition in Scotland due to the greater safeguards to protect patients' rights and also the shorter consultancy period whereas in England and Wales the Government's dominant discourse of risk and safety ensured a more critical reaction from groups such as The Mental Health Alliance. Their concerns focused on the potential for defensive practice and overuse of the powers, dominance of drug treatment in patient's care plans and discharging patients too early with inadequate support services (Mental Health Alliance, 2010b). In the early stages of CTO implementation the vice-chair of the Alliance, Rosena Daw, warned that:

> There is more coercion without adequate safeguards, to the detriment of individual patients... It will lead to widespread use of this coercive regime in the community. That puts extra pressure on services and means that individuals and their families are put under unnecessary restrictions in how they live their lives. (Daw, 2009)

From the outset there have been criticisms that the powers of CTO have been introduced without any convincing evidence of their effectiveness. Burns and Dawson (2009, p. 1586) suggest that the evaluation of CTOs has been 'left as an afterthought to the imagination of academics'. The weakness of evidence has often been reported as problems with methodologies, for example, a lack of RCTs and a reliance on more observational, exploratory and qualitative studies which tend to be less applicable globally (Dawson, 2005). Churchill et al. (2007) reviewed 72 empirical studies across six countries and found:

> there is currently no robust evidence about either the positive or negative effects of CTOs on key outcomes, including hospital readmission, length of hospital stay, improved medication compliance, or patients' quality of life. (Churchill et al., 2007, p. 7).

Their findings do indicate some convergence of agreement for example those subject to CTOs have tended to be 40-year-old males, with repeated admissions, non-compliance with medication and a history of schizophrenia. Some of the studies in this review have shown that a positive impact on patients tends to be linked to better quality service provision (reinforcing the reciprocity principle within the Codes of Practice across the UK jurisdictions). But other findings such as an increased compliance with medication can be interpreted both positively for the service, achieving one of the aims of CTOs, and negatively for the patient as it reinforces the overdependence on anti-psychotic medication as opposed to other forms of intervention. The findings in some studies of decreased in-patient hospital days for CTO patients may also be viewed positively but closer scrutiny seems to indicate the selective prolonging of CTOs (Octet, 2012). Churchill et al. (2007) suggest that the ethical positions for or against the CTO will never be satisfied by the current evidence available because of the lack of consensus about the meaning of some findings and different views of stakeholders with respect to the effectiveness. The Department of Health commissioned a Randomized Control Trial by the Department of Psychiatry at the University of Oxford (Burns et al., 2013) which claims to have achieved the first authoritative evidence about the efficacy of CTOs in England and Wales. As reported by Bogg in Chapter 6 the study found that the use of CTOs does not reduce the rate of readmission of psychotic patients and they found no evidence to support the view that CTOs reduce overall hospital admissions. These findings do question the value of restricting a patient's autonomy and freedom.

What is the evidence for the use of CTOs in England and Wales indicating so far? The most recent statistics for CTOs in England reported that the number of patients subject to a CTO by March 2011 increased by 29 per cent to 4,291 (Health and Social Care Information Centre, 2011). Consequently the overall numbers of patients detained under the Mental Health

Act 1983 continues to rise. Of some interest has been the decrease in the admissions for treatment under Section 3 though the Information Centre does speculate that these figures may be a result of an increase in recalls to hospital (the Section 3 remains in place during the CTOs) or it may genuinely be a result of CTOs keeping more patients stable who would otherwise be admitted. The Mental Health Alliance (2010) concurs with this but warns that a stable life on medication does not provide any implications for the quality of patient's lives. Their report was concerned with the continued over-representation of certain BME groups; the increasing use of compulsion; and the early discharge of CTOs to free up bed space.

The Care Quality Commission (2010) provided a more detailed analysis of the CTO statistics and raised further concerns about the use of CTOs:

- 30 per cent of their sample study (208) did not have a history of repeated admissions implying that the high use of CTOs may be a result of the order being applied preventatively beyond the target group of 'revolving door' patients;

- 36 per cent of the sample did not have a statement of risk by an SOAD (Second Opinion Appointed Doctor statements record the reason for the application of the CTO);

- 35 per cent of the sample received medication above the recommended dosage and care arrangements were not always conducive to regular reviews;

- poor communication between inpatient units and the CMHT responsible for the CTO after care for example the responsible clinician applying for the CTO did not always consult with the CMHT regarding the conditions; and

- there were examples of AMHPs not consulting with anyone or limited role due to late involvement in the process.

Where do these reflections leave the approved mental health practitioner in terms of their decision-making role in CTO applications? The Care Quality Commission (2010) clearly felt that AMHPs in England and Wales play an important part in safeguarding the unjustifiable use of the order. How does an approved mental health practitioner make a distinction between justified and unjustified CTOs? The demands of balancing the legal role alongside the duty of care to the patient should be informed by knowledge and a critical understanding of the research (Campbell and Davidson 2012). But in the area of CTOs similar in many ways to the study of CRHT there are sturdy ethical debates on both sides of the evidence, leaving the interpretation open to both positive and negative impacts on the patient. Is it possible for approved mental health practitioners to challenge the applications of CTOs on the basis of a libertarian ethical approach? The discussion needs to return to the basic principles set out in the Codes of Practice and professional codes: judgements based on values; practice reflecting rights-based approaches; and challenging decisions that are oppressive and stigmatizing to minority groups. I would argue strongly for a more radical approach to CTOs particularly where the evidence about their impact is unclear; approved mental health practitioners need to consider carefully the nature and intent of CTOs before they become an automatic response to avoiding risk.

It is questionable how significant the impact of EBP has on day-to-day approved mental health practice or whether it remains a rhetorical statement. EBP could be just another trend and in the enthusiasm practitioners can jump on the bandwagon (Sheldon, 2001). However, in determining the use of least restrictive alternatives, approved mental health practitioners across all jurisdictions are regularly faced with uncertainty and risk while their decisions are based on a level of discretion and individual judgement. It could be argued that the consequence of this balancing act can lead to inconsistent decisions (Peay, 2003). Is the answer found within the territory of EBP?: I hope this chapter has warned against the danger of elevating EBP to a concept that offers certainty. Evidence at most offers support to decisions rather than determining interventions and actions, and maybe for approved mental health practitioners the importance of values and professional autonomy should drive their decisions (Webb, 2001).

Reflective Questions

1. As an approved mental health practitioner how will I keep abreast of research in order to understand the evidence?

2. When I making a decision as an approved mental health practitioner how do I reflect upon what is known?

3. How does evidence impact on my decisions as an approved mental health practitioner?

4. What does 'effective intervention' mean and how does this connect to evidence?

12

Managing Uncertainty and Developing Practice Wisdom

Jill Hemmington

Editors' Voice

Approved mental health practitioners are required to act autonomously and make independent decisions, free from the influence of others. Decisions must clearly be lawful, and they must also rest on good practice as defined by the respective Codes of Practice. It is a principal aim of this chapter to reflect on ways of making sense of practice and instilling, maintaining and advancing competence and confidence in approved mental health practice. The chapter starts with an acknowledgement that approved mental health practice is not straightforward, and uncertainty is an inherent feature of the work. The focus will be on how the practitioner navigates this, and how they are enabled to move from 'novice' towards expert with the use of critical reflection. Practice wisdom is explained and promoted. An aspiration within practice is to feel comfortable with this uncertainty and complexity and be accepting of the idea that there are no clear answers – but this does not need to lead to a sense of helplessness. Rather, an approved mental health practitioner can become more confident – and move towards this expert practice – if critical reflection underpins their overall assessment and decision making.

Schön (1987) indicated that 'practice' on the whole is characterized by complexity and confusion. He believed that

> there is a high hard ground overlooking a swamp. On the high ground, manageable problems lend themselves to the application of research-based theory and technique. In the swampy lowland, messy, confusing problems defy technical solution... in the swamp lie the problems of greatest human concern. (Schön, 1983, p. 3)

187

Elsewhere, approved mental health practice is described as 'crisis, mess and muddle' where Mental Health Act assessments often arise from and within situations where there is 'panic and confusion' (Parkinson and Thompson, 1998, p. 57). Within a context of professional practice with increasingly complex cases and competing workload priorities, it is likely that the 'swamps' will become more difficult to navigate – regardless of the extent of the practitioner's experience or technical knowledge. How, then, does the approved mental health practitioner negotiate their way through this muddle and arrive at a solution?

Approved mental health practitioners face difficult decisions at a time when the practicalities are likely to be fraught: they are for instance co-ordinating assessments, arranging for medical colleagues as part of a joint assessment and considering the need for, among others, police or ambulance personnel to attend. Simultaneously, they need a clear understanding of the statutory context, the requirements and procedures that exist as part of working within organizations and the necessary interpersonal skills to ensure sound collaborative working (Parkinson and Thompson, 1998).

Decisions that are made by approved mental health practitioners need also to be lawful, balanced and to rest on the respective Code of Practice principles, summarized in Box 12.1.

It is clear from this, and from extracting the areas of overlap from these Codes, that the approved mental health practitioner needs to have a knowledge base that is far wider than the technical aspects of the respective mental health legislation. There also needs to be: a knowledge base pertaining to mental disorder and treatment thereof (for Wales specifically 'evidence-based'); an understanding of the promotion of recovery; an ability to understand and apply the least restrictive agenda (thereby understanding the meaning of 'alternatives to admission' from a resource and theoretical point of view); an appreciation of the patient's needs, values and dignity; the ability to include and involve the patient at every step (where practitioners in Scotland are explicitly asked to provide information); having an awareness of the most efficient use of resources and an awareness of diversity, difference, culture and so on.

As this chapter progresses, and consideration is given to aspects of practice wisdom, it is clear that there is a formal anchor within these aspects of the Codes that might also be referred to as the 'knowledge base' or 'value base'. These philosophical underpinnings will hopefully be borne in mind and serve as an ongoing reference point for reflection on the explicit links to practice. It is important that approved mental health practitioners are able to understand and articulate a formal, written and defensible rationale for their practice and professional decisions.

Box 12.1   Code of Practice Principles

England

Purpose – decisions must be taken to minimize the undesirable effects of mental disorder by maximising safety and wellbeing, promoting recovery and protecting others; Least restriction – decisions must attempt to minimize restrictions on liberty; Respect – decisions must recognize and respect diverse needs, values and circumstances and consider the patient's views, wishes or feelings; Participation – patients must be involved in circumstances, planning and reviewing treatment where possible; Effectiveness, efficiency and equity – decisions must seek to use resources appropriately. (Department of Health, 2008, paras. 1.2 1.6)

Northern Ireland

People suffering from mental disorder should: be treated and cared for in a way that maintains their dignity; receive respect and consideration of their individual qualities and background (social, cultural and religious); have their needs fully taken into account, notwithstanding that resource restrictions may render it impracticable to meet them; receive necessary treatment and care with the least degree of control and segregation consistent with their own and others' safety; be discharged from constraint and control immediately the necessity is removed; be treated in a way that promotes self-determination and encourages personal responsibility where possible. (Department of Health and Social Services (Northern Ireland) 1992, para. 1.8)

Scotland

Decisions must take into account: the present and past wishes and feelings of the patient; the views of the patient's named person, carer or guardian; the importance of the patient participating as fully as possible and providing information to help with this; the range of options available; the importance of providing the maximum benefit; the need to ensure that the patient is not treated any less favourably than the way in which a person who is not a patient would be treated in a comparable situation; the patient's abilities, background and characteristics, without prejudice. (Scottish Executive, 2005c, p. 10)

Wales

Empowerment: patient well-being and safety should be at the heart of decision-making; retaining independence and promoting recovery is central; the patient should be involved in the planning and delivery of care and treatment; practitioners should pay attention to the maintenance of rights, dignity and safety. Equity – practitioners should respect diverse needs, values and circumstances of the patient as well as the views, needs and wishes of carers, and ensure effective communication takes place. Effectiveness and Efficiency – any detained person should be provided with evidence-based treatment and care for their mental disorder. (Welsh Assembly Government, 2008)

Fook and Gardner (2007, p. 3) identify the 'common issues' faced by those working in human services as including a sense of powerlessness linked to uncertainty, a fear of risk and increased complexity. They went on to highlight some organisational responses to these factors that create further stress, including: pressure to work to rules and procedures; generating paperwork; a focus on the parts rather than the whole and focus on outcomes to the exclusion of processes. The resulting issues and difficulties for practitioners can then be derived from 'the need to find ways to continually develop knowledge and practice that fit with this changing and complex context' (p. 3).

It is interesting to stop for a moment to reflect on the notion of 'uncertainty'. Significantly, perhaps, there are strong indications that human beings have a psychological aversion to uncertainty, for example cancer patients experiencing a paradoxical sense of relief upon being given a diagnosis that a tumour is malignant, following the uncertainty of the wait (Flory and Lang, 2011). It is the 'not knowing', in terms of the outcome, that is the most stress-inducing aspect. Managing uncertainty, for example how it is communicated and expressed and how it affects patient confidence and anxiety levels, continues to be the subject of research (Ogden et al., 2002; Politi et al., 2010).

In parallel, chaos (or complexity) theory has been applied to many aspects of psychology and lately counselling. In this context the term 'chaos' is used to describe the psychological experience of encountering material that is outside the bounds of an 'order' one is accustomed to (for example Butz, 1997). Chaos theory has its roots in the fields of physics and mathematics. It derives from the late nineteenth- and early twentieth-century scientist Poincare who demonstrated that simple systems can produce behaviours that are complex, unexpected and unpredictable (thereby challenging the dominant Newtonian logic). Later Lorenz, a meteorologist, wrote of the 'butterfly effect' whereby small changes could significantly change an end result or emerging pattern. The butterfly can flap its wings and create a hurricane in another part of the world (Lorenz, 1963). Similarly, an apparently minor event (a word, glance or facial expression) may well change the dynamic and outcome of an assessment scenario. Chaos and complexity theory is also interpreted in a way that illustrates consistent interaction with the environment, whereby what people do or say on a Friday evening will not necessarily be the same, given an identical factual situation, as on a Monday morning (Peay, 2003, p. 163). It is helpful to note that the broader context of Peay's analysis was to look at joint decision making (between Approved Social Workers and doctors) within a Mental Health Act (1983) assessment scenario in England. A familiar finding was that joint decision making did not equate with consistent decision making. In fact, the processes and outcomes were described as 'messy...[but] they reflected the complexity of the real world' (Peay, 2003, p. 167).

Non-linear dynamics (or 'chaology') challenge the existing understanding of universal laws and truths, and recognize 'the innate characteristics of change, variation, unpredictability and difference in the behaviour of systems' (Arrigo and Williams, 1999, p. 191). Yet the Western medical model (which underpins contemporary mental health care) is based on traditional rational and linear thought processes. Essentially, there is a view that ultimately we will be able to predict outcomes and thereby learn how we can manage the unknown (Bussolari and Goodell, 2009). From Darwin's seminal work *The Origin of the Species* (1976) there have been concerted efforts to identify patterns of order and stability, and an understanding that all living organisms will respond to predictable rules. Bussolari and Goodell (2009) also assert that psychiatry is 'firmly rooted in rationalism and reductionism' and that it rests on the

> intelligible, orderly nature of the world and in the mind's ability to discern this order; it asserts that reason, not experience, is the best guide for belief and action. (Bussolari and Goodell, 2009, p. 98)

There is clearly a tendency to take a logical, linear approach to a world that is, in fact, largely non-linear (Butz, 1995). Yet mental health professionals continue to work within this linear framework, for example, in the way they reduce mental disorders to a collection of outwardly observable symptoms (Wiggins and Schwartz, 1999, p. 6).

Chaos or complexity theory parts with traditional, modernist, linear cause-effect views with their aspirations of prediction and control. It has resonance with postmodernist ideas of non-linear 'causality, spontaneity and chance' (Arrigo and Williams, 1999, p. 179). Postmodern thinking rests on the questioning of this linear or 'unified' thinking and moves to an acceptance that there are many varied and conflicting perspectives and no 'one truth' (Parton, 1994; Fook and Gardner, 2007, p. 31). Consider your own professional or personal challenges or disagreements with others. Do you start from distinct 'viewing points'? Could you both be doing the 'right thing'? Could *neither* of you be doing the 'right thing'? Could you or they be restricted by your/their professional background, training or value base? Do you think this could happen in approved mental health practice?

The significance of chaos or complexity theories for practice is that it is a paradigm to explain 'disorder, instability, diversity, disequilibrium, non-linear relationships (in which small efforts can trigger significant consequences), and temporality' (Blackerby, 1993, p. 8). It can be applied to a practice setting (for example counselling) with a recognition that events and lives unravel in 'unexpected and unpredictable ways' and 'both client and counsellor can let go of the illusion of control and instead face the precariousness of life experiences with compassion and an attitude of positive uncertainty' (Bussolari and Goodell, 2009, p. 100).

The very nature of approved mental health practice is that more often than not it is unplanned and predictable. Is it possible to reframe practice and address this 'illusion of control'? While it is not the same professional context, Butz (1997) compared his psychotherapy clients to artists in that 'both attempt to work out their difficulties through a creative process' (p. 127). This stimulates thinking here in relation to whether approved mental health practice is 'art or science': a theme that will be returned to in due course.

Aiming to carry forward Foucault's (1977) 'social control' thesis, Arrigo and Williams (1999) draw on chaos theory. They suggest that historically psychiatry had a narrow focus on the meaning and cause of mental illness as well as the notion of 'dangerousness'. This in turn produced 'problematic criteria for civil detention' (p. 178). They follow Foucault in taking issue with the structural aspect of the 'psycho-legal system' where there is an imperative for professionals (approved mental health practitioners among them) to understand individual or social aspects of the person as 'binary oppositions such as good–evil, reason–unreason, mentally healthy–mentally ill' (p. 198).

The individual practitioner's creation of these binary opposites can convey how they construct and understand difference or service users' identities and needs, and consequently decisions in relation to whether they include/exclude or detain/not-detain (Fook and Gardner, 2007). Fook and Gardner also reflect on the use of language and suggest that the way that we speak about things or people, what we choose to label, or not, and the power relationships we build are all relevant (Fook and Gardner, 2007, p. 32). Again, there is no 'one truth' and deconstructing language in this way allows us to see where the power lies and how our use of language allows us to support (whether consciously or not) a dominant power base. If we actively listen to approved mental health practitioners' use of language and choice of words, we learn a lot about how they use the power that is invested in them.

Taylor and White (2006) pointed out that professional workers (in this case social workers, but the same applies to approved mental health practitioners) must function in conditions of uncertainty. They observed that these workers' style was to respond with a rush to a hypothesis, for which they would then endeavour to seek out confirmatory evidence. They did not search for 'disconfirming' evidence (p. 939). The authors concluded that these workers would strive for certainty but this in turn may not lead to deciding on 'the right thing'. It was evident that this desire for certainty led them to look for aspects of situations that confirmed initial assessments, rather than to be open to reconsidering their initial findings (p. 944). General theories are often said to be applied to specific practices in a 'top-down', deductive way, rather than in an inductive 'bottom up' way (Fook and Gardner 2007, p. 25). In relation to approved mental health practice, it may be suggested that because something is lawful, it is not automatically *ethical*. In this sense, an approved mental health practitioner may be satisfied that the service user's circumstances meet the criteria for compulsory detainment (by looking 'top-down' at the law), and then search for evidence that confirms this. They could, on the other hand, base their decision making on the individual's circumstances and some of the philosophical underpinnings within the Code of Practice principles. There may be sound evidence of reasons *not* to detain and to search for alternatives to admission. Clearly, the complexity is such that there are several viewing points that can be assumed here. What is clear is that there is more to approved mental health practice than a rigid 'rule-bound', binary or legalistic approach.

Acting in a mechanistic, rule-bound way has been seen as being the mark of a 'novice', where Benner's (1984) 'novice' stage is characterized by a desire and need for rules. A 'competent' practitioner will not just see the statutory assessment scenario as a set of facts to which a series of rules must be applied but, in contrast, knowing what to do is based on mature and practised understanding. Dreyfus and Dreyfus (1986) believe that 'experts deliberate before acting, not in a calculative, problem-solving way, but by reflecting on their own intuition' (p. 170 in Orme et al., 2009). Mastery of the situation means moving on from 'formalism' (mechanistic responses) to having an ability to use interpretive evaluation strategies (Benner, 1984).

Benner (1984) addressed the importance of practice experience for nursing practice. She suggested that the practitioner shifts from the 'novice' stage when they challenge, refine or disconfirm preconceived notions and expectations. A further source of knowledge arises from the nurse's level of emotional involvement – also described as 'embodied ways of knowing' (Benner 2000). The importance of 'intuition as knowing' is also raised here.

Tyreman (2000) considers the notion of the 'expert' practitioner, believing that 'critical thinking' is a core part of this expertise. But what is meant by 'expert', or indeed 'novice', in relation to professional practice? Tyreman (2000) expands on the familiar analogy of driving a car. Having been a car driver for 30 years he believed that he understood the mechanics of driving and had a 'feel for' what was happening in practice: 'I instinctively know what to do in difficult or unusual circumstances, I know the limits of the car, I know my strengths and limitations as a driver, and on the whole I can anticipate and cope with problems' (p. 118).

Some time later, he decided to learn to ride a motorbike. Here, he found that the difficulty was not around the mechanics of controlling the bike (he found that his skill gradually developed with practise) but he had lost the 'instinctive feel' for driving that he had in a car.

> With my instructor I found myself trying to do the 'right thing', I would pause too long at roundabouts just to be sure and would ask myself what I was expected to do in situations where I would normally just act. I resorted to rules; although I was a car driver, I wasn't yet a biker. A few thousand miles on and I feel that I am becoming a biker; so what has changed? (p. 118)

He concludes from this that

> experts are people who can make effective decisions with good outcomes when confronted with a specific situation that appears not to be responsive to the usual rules of practice. They are neither frozen into inactivity by the complexity and uncertainty of the situation, nor driven to make unsuitable reflex decisions based on inappropriate professional dogma. The expert clinician must be technically competent, but also able to evaluate a complex and unique situation creatively in order to benefit the patient. (p. 118)

In this way the approved mental health practitioner must be 'technically competent' in relation to statute and the Code of Practice requirements, but they must also be in possession of some practical skills.

There is an emphasis on practical *skills* within education, training and practice, but practical *knowledge* has received significantly less exploration and analysis. A simple rationale for this fact could be the difficulties in describing, assessing and researching it. This professional 'wisdom' is a concept that can be traced back to Aristotle's (1983) notion of *phronesis* as the defining feature of the expert practitioner. Aristotle's conceptualization focused on three 'virtues of character' which included theoretical ('episteme'), practical ('phronesis') and productive intellectual activity ('techne') with professional 'expertise' seen as requiring and moving between all of them. It is interesting to note that the terms 'episteme' and 'techne' are still with us as epistemology and technology, and yet 'phronesis' is not so common – in itself an indication of what society currently values (Crowden, 2004).

'Episteme' relates to scientific, theoretical, deductive knowledge that is allied to research. 'Techne' is concerned with production. This knowledge is needed to create, and focuses on the craft and productive 'act' of the practitioner. Using a music analogy, techne describes the technical skills required to play an instrument, but it is not about the musicianship of the person (Tyreman, 2000). 'Phronesis' is practical wisdom and the (human) actions that involve choice, options, alternatives and a reflection on the outcomes and consequences arising from these actions. It is knowing how to act in a situation to realize the goals of professional practice. It does not have specific measurable goals (unlike techne) and it is able to respond to situations and challenges in accordance with the relevant profession's expectations (Tyreman, 2000). Phronesis is also about the ability to act in the 'real life' situation which involves engagement with real cases and people. By definition, then, it cannot be done theoretically nor can it be prepared since it relates to action in a new (therefore uncertain) situation (Tyreman, 2000). Crucially, it is developed with the use of reflection borne out of being vigilant to and 'seeing' the critical aspects of a situation and all its variables and nuances. It is about 'facilitating the promotion of professional values and principles which guide action' (Radden, 2002, p. 56). Finally Radden (2002) reflects on phronesis as part of a 'practical moral wisdom' where moral wisdom can be identified as 'a human psychological capacity to make sound judgements about what we should do when seeking answers to difficult moral questions' (p. 57) (see also Kondrat, 1992; Kinsella, 2010; McKie et al., 2012).

So what then of approved mental health practice? 'Expert' approved mental health practice can be said to require phronetic knowledge for those uncertain situations where there are no clear rules or instructions. Phronesis must support a practitioner with decision making and moving towards 'good practice' or the 'right thing' without being able to look to rules or facts. The 'expert' is differentiated by his or her capacity for phronesis as a 'higher order capability' where the decision to adopt a particular technical approach to a problem involves a phronetic judgement (Tyreman, 2000). It is suggested that 'clinical wisdom can be cultivated but not taught' (Haggerty and Grace, 2008). Consequently, it has been acknowledged that the development of wisdom in practitioners is best approached via the deliberate adoption of 'growth' metaphors (for example 'cultivation' or 'nurture') rather than through formal, didactic teaching approaches such as lectures and tutorials (Edmondson and Pearce, 2007). It cannot be taught as a procedure or process and must be developed as part of practical experience. It is for this reason that an essential phase of an approved mental health practitioner training programme is the practice placement experience or going out 'into the field'. Similarly, much of post-qualifying learning takes place within a practical or experiential context.

Tyreman (2000) classifies the 'expert' as the person who *is*, from the novice who (merely) *does*. This practitioner, then, will be able to competently apply necessary technical skills, for example knowledge of the law and its respective philosophical underpinnings and principles. They will also have a realistic appraisal of their own capability, strengths and weaknesses, and be able to assess the context of a problem with these capabilities to find the most appropriate outcome. The expert knows their subject and their practice, but they also *know themselves*. In this way, Tyreman (2000) argues, phronesis 'adds a necessary corrective dimension to modern Western medicine's over-emphasis on techne' (p. 121).

It is interesting to raise the empirical question 'How does the competent practitioner go about knowing 'in' practice?' (for example Kinsella, 2010). In the absence of clarity, decision making within approved mental health practice needs to have reflection at its heart. Kinsella (2010, p. 566), referring to her own 'crisis' within practice suggests that 'The language of reflective practice freed me from trying to fit myself into a narrow box that did not seem to be representative of the messiness of professional practice.' The 'system' in which she was working prioritized technical approaches, efficiency and outcomes with less emphasis on 'practical reason...relational practices...compassion...or care' (p. 566).

Dewey (1938) introduced a straightforward framework of reflection in which 'we learn by doing and realising what came of what we did' (p. 26). Accordingly, reflection is simply thinking, experiencing feelings, thinking about those feelings, imagining alternatives and learning by considering experiences and what might be different had things happened differently. Reflective *practice* is not just about these cognitive and affective processes, but about *doing*.

The work of Schön (1983; 1987) is hugely influential. It is 30 years since he referred to 'a crisis of knowledge in the professions' (1983, p. 12). He compared the 'reflective paradigm' with the traditional scientific paradigm where knowledge was seen simply in terms of 'technical rationality'. Here, practitioners were instrumental problem solvers, and they did this by applying theory and technique that was derived from systematic scientific knowledge – an approach known as research-based practice (more recently as evidence-based practice) (Rolfe et al., 2011). However, this approach is frequently unsatisfactory since it fails to account for practical competence in unpredictable or uncertain situations. Schön attempted to 'search instead for an epistemology of practice implicit in the artistic, intuitive processes which some practitioners do bring to situations of uncertainty, instability, uniqueness and value conflict' (1983, p. 49).

His alternative approach to professional knowledge contains different *types* of professional knowledge: knowing 'that' (facts or theories) and knowing 'how' (the application of facts or theories). 'Reflection in action' is therefore needed to convert 'facts' into useable knowledge (Kinsella, 2010, p. 567). We need 'technical rationality' (rules) and professional artistry (reflection in action). The 'crisis' for professionals is in part because theory or rules ('espoused theory') are very different for practitioners than the theory or assumptions ('theory in use') that are part of their everyday practice. This can be because 'rules' are often limited to specific or defined situations and might not be known when the situation has changed (Fook and Gardner, 2007, p. 24). Critical reflection is about drawing these aspects closer together.

Schön (1983) proposed a refreshing theory that considers the knowledge arising from reflection in and on practice *itself*. Here the practitioner is an agent or 'experient' where he or she 'shapes' the situation and becomes part of it (Kinsella, 2010, p. 568). It is useful here to consider this conception of 'professional knowledge', or 'knowledge for practice' as it is generated in the *midst* of practice. In building this, Schön acknowledged the influence of Dewey (1938; 1958), a philosopher of education. Dewey's (1958) focus was on the relationship of artistry to work (and practice) where

> The intelligent mechanic engaged in his job, interested in doing well and find-ing satisfaction in his handiwork, caring for his materials and tools with genuine affection is artistically engaged. (p. 5)

Inspired by this, Schön went on to develop his notion of professional prac-tice as 'artistic engagement'. He considered this 'professional artistry' of practitioners, believing that it was under-valued. He saw the competence that some practitioners would demonstrate within unique, uncertain and conflicted situations of practice and viewed this as a product of 'profes-sional artistry' (Kinsella, 2010, p. 569). A crucial aspect of this reflective approach (and the framework for critical reflection) is that some aspects of practice, traditionally not valued, become key. Intuition and artistry become the focus for better understanding of how practitioners function and 'enact practice theory' (Fook and Gardner, 2007, p. 25). In opposition to the scientific, 'technical-rational' paradigms, with a focus on observable phenomena, this approach values personal experience and interpretation. In this way,

> The traditional distinctions between 'knowing and doing', 'values and facts', 'sub-jectivity and objectivity', 'art and science' are blurred. What becomes important is a holistic understanding of the complexity of experience, and the sorts of knowl-edge that support relevant practice in complex and unpredictable situations. (Fook and Gardner, 2007, p. 26)

Schön (1987) also recognized that different individual practitioners, disci-plines, professions and policy makers bring different 'frames' to the same scenarios. Here, our work is not simply to solve problems but also to actually present them (Kinsella, 2006).

> With their different ways of framing the situation, they tend to pay attention to different sets of facts, see the same facts in different ways and make judgements of effectiveness based on different kind of criteria. If they wish nevertheless to come to agreement, they must try to get inside each other's points of view. They must try to discover what models and appreciations lead each of them to focus

preferentially on one set of facts or criteria, make their tacit cognitive strategies explicit to themselves, and find out how each one understand the other's framing of the situation. Their ability to come to substantive agreement will depend on their capacity for frame reflection. (Schön, 1987, p. 218)

Peay's (2003) work indicated that there are many factors that an individual will bring to a decision-making situation, including their professional or discipline-specific expertise, but also variations on this. She questions for example what experience of the type of case the practitioner has had previously, and with what outcome? (p. 18). An approved mental health practitioner will arrive at this role with an established profession (for example nurse, social worker, occupational therapist or psychologist) that will have its own code or philosophical influence. A further layer is added through the assimilation of approved mental health practice, with its own value base and set of principles. We also have inherent human tendencies towards bias that we may not even be aware of. Rutter and Brown (2012) summarize some examples of cognitive and behavioural biases that illustrate our core beliefs, preconceptions and assumptions:

- Anchoring effect: the tendency to rely too heavily or 'anchor' on one trait or piece of information when making decisions;

- Bandwagon effect: the tendency to do or believe things because others do;

- Confirmation bias: the tendency to search for and interpret information in a way that confirms one's preconceptions;

- Hindsight bias: distorts our judgement about the predictability of an adverse outcome. When we look backwards it seems clear which assessments or actions were critical in leading to that outcome and we overestimate how visible the signs of danger were;

- Outcome bias – tendency to judge a decision by its eventual outcome rather than the quality of the decision at the time it was made;

- Pseudo-certainty effect – tendency to make risk-averse choices if the expected outcome is positive, but make risk-seeking choices to avoid negative outcomes. (p. 6)

As the authors suggest, reflecting on these natural biases allows us to realize how easily we form flawed arguments. Consider briefly whether you succumb to a confirmation bias in relation to particular diagnoses – Borderline Personality Disorder, for example, is sufficiently controversial to attract such a bias (Raven, 2009). Reflection 'in' practice means being vigilant to those aspects that, consciously or unconsciously, guide us as 'a matter of principle'.

Reflection in and on practice can be supported by several different formal and practical frameworks (for example Kolb, 1984; Gibbs, 1988; Johns, 2002). The decision to not review these here is deliberate. This is in part because they can easily be sourced, but also out of recognition that there is for some practitioners undertaking post-qualifying training, as well as practitioners-in-training, a sense of 'reflection fatigue' that is, arguably, a consequence of assessment requirements becoming overly structured and formulaic such that they may be actually restricting thinking (Coward, 2011, p. 883). The intention here, therefore, is not to be prescriptive but instead to look at knowledge acquisition, professional development and the process of enlightenment more broadly.

In order to effectively reflect on practice, a practitioner will need to have the capacity for 'critical thinking'. Key aspects of this, defined by Brookfield (1987), are: 'identifying and challenging assumptions' which involves probing and questioning our thought processes as well as our moral position, beliefs, values, stereotypes and prejudices; 'exploring and imagining alternatives, (p. 15); 'understanding the importance of context', where individuals develop 'contextual awareness' and realize that their values and beliefs are socially and culturally transmitted (p. 16) and 'engaging in reflective scepticism' which is the ability to consider alternatives to a programmed way of thinking (p. 21). The detailed principles within the Codes of Practice have relevance here. Much of this detail was about respecting diversity, anti-oppressive practice, avoiding prejudicial assumptions – all of which require some self-awareness. We are required to 'imagine alternatives' – and this does not necessarily mean at the superficial level of resources as there is an increasing need for creativity as part of approved mental health practice. Understanding the cultural context is crucial (see Taylor and Hemmington, Chapter 7, this volume) as is a consideration of the requisite 'social perspective' and how to convey this within approved mental health practice decision making. Decisions must be defensible, transparent and articulated within reports and case notes in a way that demonstrates knowledge, awareness and an appropriate value base.

As critical thinking is established, the process of critical reflection will be enabled. As indicated earlier, there is more than one way to approach critical reflection. For illustration, below are some 'questions to aid critical reflection' that are taken from Fook and Gardner's (2007) established and effective method. These are intended by the authors to be by way of illustration as, clearly, all experiences will be different and owned by the individual practitioner. What is important, however, is that questions must be asked in a way that allows the practitioner to reflect for themselves, rather than have meanings or values imposed on them.

Reflective practice questions:

● What does my account of my critical incident imply about, for example, my basic ideals or values, my beliefs about power, my view of myself and other people, and what I believe about professionalism?

● Are there any gaps or contradictions between what I say and do and what is implied by what I do?

Reflexive questions may be as follows:

● How did I influence the situation through: my presence, my actions, my pre-conceptions or assumptions, other people's perceptions of me, my physical well-being on the day?

● How have the tools I used to understand the situation affected what I say?

● How might I have acted differently if there was something different about the situation (for example the other person was of a different gender, I was older, I was in a different role)? What does this say about my own biases and preconceptions?

Postmodern/deconstructive questions:

● What words or language patterns have I used? What do these indicate about the way I am constructing the situation?

● What perspectives are missing from my account?

● What binaries, or 'either-or, forced choice' categories have I constructed?

● How have I constructed myself, or my professional role, in relation to other people?

Critical questions:

● What assumptions are implicit in my account and where do they come from?

● How do my personal experiences and beliefs from my social context interact with this situation?

● What functions (particularly powerful functions) do my beliefs hold?

The response to the 'first stage' questions are then mined further in a second stage.

This is clearly an accessible method that can form part of a formal supervision session, a focused peer supervision group with colleagues, a debriefing following a difficult statutory assessment or embedded in ongoing practice. Other practitioners make use of journals, stories or diaries (Bolton, 2011) formal Critical Incident Analysis (CIA) which is used within nursing (for example Minghella and Benson, 1995), social work (Lister and Crisp, 2007), and approved mental health practice programmes (including the authors' own). McBrien (2007), for example, uses Critical Incident Analysis to reflect on his work as a triage nurse in an Accident and Emergency department. The process allows him to reflect on how he depersonalizes a patient with psychological pain, how he takes a passive role, how he does not satisfactorily (in his own view) challenge a medical colleague and enables him to recognize that he has become 'socialized' into the culture of prioritizing waiting times and rapid triage. He acknowledges feelings of 'guilt' and 'shame' and concludes that this process assisted ultimately with his awareness of self (p. 131).

Evident here also are skills of critical *reasoning* which are indicative of personal integrity, the ability to be aware of and manage the emotional content of the work and the ability to convey a knowledgeable position within an anti-oppressive and anti-discriminatory framework (Jones, 2009). Within this context, to be 'critical' means that the practitioner is careful that they do not:

- unintentionally misuse their power;

- misunderstand key issues of discrimination and oppression; or

- fail to recognize significant events and minimize the need to take action

In turn, they *do:*

- step back and reflect on their practice and that of others;

- recognize the potential for discrimination and oppression; and

- consider a wide range of influential factors and take informed action where there is actual or potential risk. (Jones, 2009, p. 2)

Critical reflection is also seen to be a process and theory for 'unearthing individually held social assumptions in order to make changes in the social world' (Fook and Gardner, 2007, p. 14). Here, we understand the individual in their social context, and 'focus on the level at which the individual and society interact' (p. 15). This point has very clear resonance with approved mental health practice and it brings to life some of the themes pertaining to the use of resources (including ourselves as practitioners) and involving service users in planning and addressing alternatives to admission. An essential part of this for practitioners is the 'unsettling [of] assumptions to bring about social changes' (p. 16), by which they mean a 'shaking up' of our own assumptions in order to better understand ourselves and motivate learning.

This entails having an awareness of our own value base, as well as integrating the values and principles that are enshrined in statute and the relevant Codes of Practice so that our decisions are assimilated with this.

Approved mental health practice and its broader networks within psychiatry have a unique setting with distinctive areas of ethical and policy dilemmas. These are covered thoroughly elsewhere, but include frequent ethical dilemmas relating to informed consent and capacity, self-harm, compulsory detention and treatment, and treatment refusal (Radden, 2002). Radden suggests that this necessitates a 'professional ethics' within psychiatry with its unique place as a 'social and medical practice'. There are distinctive features which include the relationship or 'therapeutic alliance' between professional and patient, whereby 'the relationship is a treatment tool, analogous to the surgeon's scalpel' (Luhrmann, 2000). Secondly, Radden makes reference to 'certain characteristics' of the psychiatric patient, which include vulnerability to exploitation, dependence and inherent inequality. It is recognized that this may have resonance with any client in any professional relationship, but within a mental health setting these are marked since the vulnerability is potentially compounded by the patients' 'diminished judgement' as well as the stigma and controversy associated with a particular mental health condition (that in itself is conceptually controversial). Adding to this is the inherent power imbalance within the nature of the approved mental health practice that renders an individual vulnerable.

A 'psychiatric ethics' for Radden is a 'concern with the values, ideals and distinctive prescriptions instilled through professional education and other informal kinds of professional acculturation' (p. 52). A significant part of this is the individual practitioner's own background (professional and personal); their own value base, as well as the relevant code of practice, which itself will be based on certain values and principles. As Radden points out,

> Decision making is made more difficult by whether there are fundamental philosophical and practical disagreements (for example around what sort of thing mental illness is and how to understand it) (p. 53).

It is recognized here that no one profession has a monopoly on values. There are distinct approved mental health practitioner 'values', which rest on a social (or non-medical) perspective and are articulated through the Codes' principles. 'Values-based practice' will support balanced decision making when 'complex and conflicting values are in play' (Fulford et al., 2011, p. 145), and arguably a shared value base found within Code of Practice principles could support this. It is recognized, however, that these principles must always be interpreted and applied by individuals making situational judgements and so we return to the development of practice knowledge to allow us to embed this as wisely as our level of professional development or 'expertise' allows.

To conclude, critical reflection has been understood to offer 'both theory and processes to enable [the] making and remaking of knowledge to happen' (Fook and Gardner, 2007, p. 10). Here, it is seen as being a model for professional learning and development. Outcomes of critically reflective practice have included increased self-awareness (Tsang, 2003); better awareness of connectedness with colleagues (Maich et al., 2000); changes in thinking or practice (Fook and Gardner, 2007; a 'professional awakening' (Maich et al., 2000); a greater tolerance of ambiguity (Grant, 2001); and a feeling of emancipation and greater sense of control (Fook and Napier, 2000; Johns, 2002.) Habermas' (1974) model of critical reflection suggests that the emancipatory approach encourages 'self-knowledge' in relation to the social and institutional forces of control and an improved sense of how to transcend these (Rolfe et al., 2011, p. 37). Given some of the organizational requirements, difficulties and resource setbacks, the idea of emancipation is an attractive one. It is important as an approved mental health practitioner to be mindful of the organizational context. There is clear evidence that the culture of some organizations is more supportive and encouraging of critical reflection than others (particularly where there is a focus on task-completion and outcomes) (Reynolds and Vince in Fook and Gardner, 2007, p. 53) and there are clear links to clinical supervision here.

What is seen to be important is the creation of an atmosphere and attitude of openness and receptiveness to reflection in practice. Often, this links with what some therapists call an 'aha' or 'ouch' experience, defined as 'a shift of perception at a deep level that generates a feeling of growth or a new understanding' (Fook and Gardner, 2007, p. 136).

Discussions around 'practice knowledge' or 'wisdom' are well established, where Aristotle delivered a philosophical basis for 'reclaiming the practical' (Kondrat, 1992). This would seem to be a crucial way forward, given that much of approved mental health practice exists within an uncertain framework. Chaos or complexity approaches lend themselves well to the viewpoint or stance taken by an approved mental health practitioner. To extend a metaphor suggested by Kondrat (1992), it is suggested that the most appropriate one for understanding the nature of approved mental health practice is the hologram, given that there is an emerging recognition or discovery of the multidimensional structure, shape and significance of a problem. We view a variety of images from a range of reference points and combine them into our image or formulation of the problem. Or, more simply, it is a way of 'standing back and seeing the issues from a different perspective' (Fook and Gardner, 2007, p. 10). This viewpoint, along with an elevated or 'higher order' practice expertise, may allow the approved mental health practitioner to find a pathway to advance clearly and confidently through the swamp.

Reflective Questions

1. What factors contribute to the perceptions of chaos, mess and muddle?

2. How do you break down theoretical, technical and practical knowledge and apply them to approved mental health practice?

3. In a crisis, how does an approved mental health practitioner understand and make sense of all the differing viewpoints?

4. Can you locate your own professional development from novice to expert? How did you measure this? What would be different if you were an expert?

Conclusion: Old Values, New Problems?

Jill Hemmington, Philip O'Hare and Sarah Matthews

This endnote reflects on the changing nature of approved mental health practice from an organizational and political perspective, and considers its legacy in terms of the value base and the psychosocial orientation to practice. It views the changing organizational landscape through this lens and evaluates the impact of some of the issues raised within this book.

Approved mental health practice across the United Kingdom jurisdictions has similarity in terms of the legal, bureaucratic function and the philosophical and moral orientation. A query was raised by Matthews in Chapter 1 in relation to whether approved mental health practice simply meant a legal, bureaucratic, mechanistic process that has a set purpose and outcome. What is very clear, however, and in fact what constituted a clear motivation for compiling this book is the evidence that there is far more to the approved mental health practitioner's function, repertoire and imagination than simply the technical application of the law. Whether it is considered to be 'art or science', bureaucratic or therapeutic, approved mental health practice is certainly complex and unpredictable. Many salient themes arise from individual authors in this book. A number of problems are still being approached from the perspective of the traditional or old value base. This is not insurmountable, but it takes creativity to understand what the problem is and appreciate where the new landscape, in terms of the social policy imperative and the rationing of resources, leaves approved mental health practice.

Services and resources

Consider for example the general principles of each of the UK Codes of Practice relating to least restriction or the effective and equitable meeting of need. There can be a relatively straightforward interpretation of these principles if, for instance, an individual meets the criteria for detention and their home circumstances are chaotic, with a high level of carer burden or on the other hand no support at all for the individual. Typical practice may in such circumstances justify an in-patient admission since this outcome is arguably less oppressive and unethical than the person remaining at home in distressing circumstances.

As we have seen however decisions are not always straightforward and polarized. There are new problems and paradoxes arising from restrictions on resources and hospital bed closures which inevitably impact on approved mental health practice decision making. The Care Quality Commission (2012) recently reported that AMHPs in England recognized that their decision making was becoming increasingly influenced by the lack of availability of beds. Could this mean that approved mental health practitioners defer their decision making until beds become available or, paradoxically be more likely to detain to secure the bed? The Care Quality Commission were also concerned about the lack of resources available as an alternative to compulsory admission.

Consider also the scenario where the in-patient hospital bed is 80 miles away and the carer has no means of transport, and the service user is not familiar with this particular environment – an increasingly common area of concern (Schizophrenia Commission, 2012). As well as the impact on the patient, this situation begins to test the position of a Nearest Relative in terms of their rights and agreement with the decision to detain. Would their objection to admission on these grounds be reasonable? Arguably this objection is also supported by Human Rights legislation and their right to family life. Should an approved mental health practitioner agree with Nearest Relative, or take steps to displace? This dilemma has resonance with rural issues, discussed in Chapter 8, where isolation and the proximity of services, both in-patient and community, affect decision making.

As discussed in Chapter 6 there are also anxieties about the pressures on approved mental health practice in the face of cuts in services, training budgets, increases in workloads and the impact of bed closures (Hudson and Webber, 2012; McNicoll, 2013). This is not a new problem; a similar picture was presented during the review of the Mental Health Act in England and Wales (Evans et al., 2006). These recurring themes should raise questions about the value and recognition placed on the role of approved mental health practitioners beyond their legal mandate. What is the impact of a service or a practitioner operating under pressure? How are outcomes affected by a stressed and depleted workforce?

In addition, approved mental health practitioners are facing increasingly poor quality services in some areas. In 2008, the Mental Health Act Commission reported that the busy acute wards 'appear to be tougher and scarier places than we saw a decade ago' (Mental Health Act Commission, 2008, p. 8). There are continuing concerns about acceptable standards in psychiatric units where patients, usually women, often feel unsafe (Care Quality Commission, 2009; Mental Welfare Commission in Scotland, 2010).

The Care Quality Commission has also found that unnecessary and excessive restrictions are imposed on detained patients (Care Quality Commission, 2010) and 'cultures may persist where control and containment are prioritised over the treatment and support of individuals' (Care Quality Commission, 2012, p. 5).

How does the approved mental health practitioner reconcile decision making that creates additional distress and isolation to the service user and their family? The competing imperatives for a practitioner include an ethical, value-based position sometimes in opposition to an organizational focus on risk management. Will practitioners think that the balance between creativity and the management of risk is compromised in favour of a more defensive and oppressive default position? The challenge is for approved mental health practitioners to develop skills and confidence to be able to navigate their way through this in a way that meets with the fundamental values of the role.

Policy implications

Approved mental health practice will also be informed by the prevailing social policy orientation. For example the Recovery agenda can still have relevance to approved mental health practice despite the fact that intervention is usually within a context of short-term assessment without prolonged follow up. It is argued that the *values* of Recovery could empower those subject to compulsion (Social Care Institute for Excellence and Royal College of Psychiatrists, 2007). The language that an approved mental health practitioner chooses to use can be within the spirit of hope and recovery. Practice is essentially about understanding the lived experience of the service user, which is no less important than the legislative and policy context. Bartlett and Sandland (2003, p. 41) suggest that 'even naming individuals as mentally disordered is an exercise of power, since it changes their perception of themselves, and the perception of them by other people'. The power of language cannot be underestimated, and is something about which an approved mental health practitioner must have an ongoing awareness.

Recovery in itself is a contested term, however, in that the commonly held view is that it rests fundamentally on a service user's self-determination. Such self-direction may not sit easily with approved mental health practice and the ever-present need to make a decision that might include the loss of liberty. There remain a number of barriers to the implementation of Recovery (Davidson et al, 2006) and there is increasing evidence that mental health practitioners struggle to operationalize the concept of Recovery within a crisis situation (O'Hare et al., 2013). Arguably, by definition, an approved mental health practitioner has become involved in order to make decisions on behalf of the service user which may not always be viewed as being within a Recovery context. Recent figures from the Care Quality Commission (2012) showing an increase in the number of people subject to detention on admission and the increasing widespread use of Community (Compulsory) Treatment Orders are perhaps further evidence of a dissonance between the rhetoric of a model that promotes service user choice and one that is safety and risk conscious. Certainly, a further conundrum for approved mental health practice is that it has the potential to reinforce the service-user critique of Recovery: that it is a model that is defined by, and imposed by, professionals and speaks rather less to the subjective service user experience (Pilgrim, 2008).

Decision making and independent judgement

A justification for compulsory detainment (or social control, depending on your perspective), is found within the concept of *parens patriae* or 'parent of the nation', where the state may interfere with the individual's right to liberty and in turn their ability to decide for themselves (Geller et al., 2006). It is perhaps more comfortable, as an approved mental health practitioner, to default to a justification that a decision to detain is a protective one. Tew (2005) reflects on different modes of power with an appreciation of this care versus control dilemma. He states that 'protective power' could be said to approach 'difference' in a non-abusive way. This 'protective power' may be 'deployed to shield [service users] from potential abuse, exploitation or exclusion' (p. 79). Yet he goes on to state that:

> the issue of how it feels to be (supposedly) protected for one's own safety is a very real issue for those subject to compulsion under the Mental Health Act. Research indicates that it may only be a minority who, reflecting on their experience, would see it as something that *felt* protective. (p. 80)

Throughout this book, there is evidence that there are new problems. For an approved mental health practitioner the focus is on how to interpret and analyse appropriately and avoid any illusion that there can be certainty. The increasing complexity of the role in terms of resources, legislative interfaces, globalization and organizational culture clashes can only compound this uncertainty. Looking for certainty through evidence, legislation or ethical reasoning will not lead to definitive resolutions. The new problems discussed throughout the book highlight the multilayered, non-linear nature of approved mental health practice decision making. Peay (2003, p. 169) reflects just this;

the machinery for resolving issues appears much less developed than that we apply to the comparatively straightforward binary decision entailed in other areas of legal decision-making.

Yet what is important here is to distinguish between uncertainty as threatening or disempowering (which inevitably leads to greater anxiety) and uncertainty which can *embrace* the fundamental independence of the role of the approved mental health practitioner and to see the opportunities for creativity. It is strongly suggested that an awareness of these problems brings about a responsibility to engage with the complexity and uncertainty, and it also *permits* decision making that is rightly informed by the many variables. Considerable variability in terms of how professionals arrived at their decisions and how they arrived at different ones even given the same information reinforces this (Peay, 2003).

There is evidence to suggest that self-efficacy, or the 'belief in one's own capacity to organize and carry out action to produce an outcome' (Bandura, 1997) is closely related to work performance and effectiveness. Similarly, a practitioner's 'locus of control' which relates to their attribution of life's determiners to either internal or self-directed actions, or dimensions of externality, for example chance happenings, or actions of 'powerful others' (Levenson, 1981) has an impact. Individuals with an internal locus of control are seen as more likely to approach stressful situations with a problem-solving, proactive focus and to adapt to problems. However, those with an external locus of control are more likely to 'succumb to the effects of stress' (Koeske and Kirk, 1995). In this way confident, competent individuals frame their approved mental health practice in a way that accepts uncertainty and make decisions that rest on their collective awareness of the many variables – the professional balancing act.

So, within approved mental health practice and among individual practitioners there are multiple realities, all of which may be equally valid, and all of which have a significant effect on each other. By accepting this there is potential for a move toward a conceptual reframing of approved mental health practice and in turn balancing the associated stressful and emotional aspects with something that is rather more restorative. Skilful and effective practitioners will be able to locate where they are within this balance. With a technical knowledge of the law, an awareness of their own, and the professional value base, an ability to hear service users' stories and appreciate their diversity and an ability to reflect critically on the many practical and philosophical issues, it is likely that practice will move in the direction of the expert practitioner. It is these themes that make up this current edition and to which future ones must return.

Bibliography

Abbott, A. (1983). Professional ethics. *American Journal of Sociology*, 88, 855–85.

Adler, J. (2012). Living into the story: Agency and coherence in a longitudinal study of narrative identity development and mental health over the course of psychotherapy. *Journal of Personality and Social Psychology*, 102(2), 367–89.

Airoldi, M., Morton, A., Smith, J. and Bevan, G. (2011). *Healthcare prioritisation at the local level: A socio-technical approach*. Working Paper No. 7. London: London School of Economics.

Allen, C. (2002). Policy. *Mental Health Practice*, 6, 2.

American Psychiatric Association (2000). *Diagnostic and statistical manual of mental disorders 4th edn*. Washington: American Psychiatric Association.

American Psychiatric Association (2012) *Recent Updates for Proposed Revisions to DSM5*. Accessed 10 October 2013 at: http://www.dsm5.org/Pages/RecentUpdates.aspx

American Psychiatric Association (2013) *Diagnostic and statistical manual of mental disorders: DSM V. 5th edn*. Washington: American Psychiatric Association.

Anderson, J., Sapey, B. and Spandler, H. (2012). *Distress and disability? Debates and alliances*. Lancaster University: Centre for Disability Research.

Aristotle (1983). *The ethics of Aristotle – the Nicomachean ethics*. Harmondsworth: Penguin.

Arrigo, B.A. and Williams C.R. (1999). Chaos theory and the social control thesis: A post-Foucauldian analysis of mental illness and involuntary civil confinement. *Social Justice*, 26(1), 177–207.

Atkinson, J.M., Lorgelly, P., Reilly, J. and Stewart, A. (2007). *The early impact of the administration of new compulsory powers under the Mental Health (Care and Treatment) (Scotland) Act 2003*. Edinburgh: Scottish Executive.

Atkinson, J., Reilly, J., Garner, H.C., and Patterson, C. (2005). *Review of literature relating to mental health legislation*. Edinburgh: Scottish Executive Social Research.

Bakshtanovskii, V. and Sogomonov, I. (2007). Professional ethics. *Sociological Research*, 46, 75–95.

Bamford Review of Mental Health and Learning Disability (Northern Ireland) (2007). *A comprehensive legislative framework*. Belfast: Department of Health, Social Services and Public Safety.

Bandura, A. (1997). Self-efficacy: Toward a unifying theory of behavioural change. *Psychological Review*, 84, 191–215.

Banks, S. (2005). *Ethics, accountability and the social professions*. Basingstoke: Palgrave Macmillan.

Barber, P., Brown, R. and Martin, D. (2012). *Mental health law in England and Wales. A guide for mental health professionals*, 2nd edn. Exeter: Learning Matters.

Barker, V., Taylor, M., Kader, I., Stewart, K. and Le Fevre, P. (2011). Impact of crisis resolution and home treatment services on user experience and admission to psychiatric hospital. *The Psychiatrist*, 35, 106–10.

Barnes, H. (2011). Does mental illness have a place alongside social and recovery models of mental health in service users' lived experiences? Issues and implications for mental health education. *The Journal of Mental Health Training, Education and Practice*, 6, 65–75.

Barnes, M., Bowl, R. and Fisher, M. (1990). *Sectioned: Social services and the 1983 Mental Health Act*. London: Routledge.

Barry, M., Doherty, A., Sixsmith, J. and Kelleher, C.C. (2000). A community needs assessment for rural mental health promotion. *Health Education Research*, 15(3), 293–304.

Bartlett, P. and Sandland, R. (2003). *Mental health law: Policy and practice,* 2nd edn. Oxford: Oxford University Press.

Bartlett, P. and Sandland, R. (2007). *Mental health law: Policy and practice,* 3rd edn. Oxford: Oxford University Press.

Bayer, R. (1987). *Homosexuality and American psychiatry: The politics of diagnosis*. New Jersey: Princeton University Press.

Bean, P. (1980). *Compulsory admissions to mental hospital*. London: John Wiley and Sons.

Bean, P. (1986). *Mental disorder and legal control*. Cambridge: Cambridge University Press.

Beck, U. (1992). *Risk society: Towards a new modernity*. London, Sage.

Benner, P. (1984). *From novice to expert: Excellence and power in clinical nursing practice*. London: Addison-Wesley.

Benner, P. (2000). The roles of embodiment, emotion and life-world for rationality and agency in nursing practice. *Nursing Philosophy*, 1(1), 5–19.

Bentall, R. (1993). Deconstructing the concept of 'schizophrenia'. *Journal of Mental Health*, 2, 223–38.

Bentall, R. (2004). *Madness Explained*. London: Penguin.

Bentall, R. (2011). The social origins of psychosis. Conference presentation, *Soteria conference: Alternatives within and beyond psychiatry,*11 November 2011, Derby Conference Centre.

Berrios, G.E. and Hauser, R. (1998). The early developments of Kraeplin's ideas on classification: A conceptual history. *Psychological Medicine*, 18, 813–21.

Berzins, K.M. and Atkinson, J.M. (2009). Service users' and carers' views of the Named Person provisions under the Mental Health (Care and Treatment). (Scotland). Act 2003. *Journal of Mental Health*, 18(3), 207–15.

Bion, W.R. (1962). *Learning from experience*. London: Heinemann.

Bisman, C. (2003). Social work values: The moral core of the profession. *British Journal of Social Work*, 34, 9–13.

Blackerby, R. (1993). *Applications of chaos theory to psychological models*. Austin: Performance Strategies.

Blackstock, K.L., Innes, A., Cox, S., Smith, A. and Mason, A. (2006). Living with dementia in rural and remote Scotland: Diverse experiences of people with dementia and their carers. *Journal of Rural Studies*, 22(2), 161–76.

Blake, M. (2001). 'Distributive justice, state coercion and autonomy. *Philosophy & Public Affairs*, 30, 257–96.

Bloch, S. and Green, S. (2006). An ethical framework for psychiatry. *British Journal of Psychiatry*, 188, 7–12.

Bogg, D. (2008). *The integration of mental health social work and the NHS*. Exeter: Learning Matters.

Bogg, D. (2010a). *Mental health and personalisation: Themes and issues in recovery-based mental health care and support*. Brighton: Pavilion.

Bogg, D. (2010b). *Values and ethics in mental health practice*. Exeter: Learning Matters.

Bogg, D. (2012). Defending the social model of mental health care against medical dominance. *Community Care*, 13 December.

Bolton, G. (2011). *Reflective practice writing and professional development*. London: Sage.

Borovečki, A., Orešković, S. and Have, H.T. (2005). Ethics and the structures of health care in the European countries in transition: Hospital ethics committees in Croatia. *British Medical Journal*, 331, 227–9.

Boseley, S. (2012). Psychologists fear US manual will widen mental illness diagnosis. *The Guardian*, 9 February.

Bourdieu, P. (1977). *Outline of a theory of practice*. Cambridge: Cambridge University Press.

Bower, M. (2002). Editorial. *Journal of Social Work Practice*, 16(2), 93–8.

Bowers, L., Clark, N. and Callaghan, P. (2003). Multidisciplinary reflections on assessment for compulsory admission: The views of Approved Social Workers, General Practitioners, Ambulance Crews, Police, Community Psychiatric Nurses and Psychiatrists. *British Journal of Social Work*, 33, 961–8.

Bowlby, J. (1998). *Attachment and loss, Volume 2: Separation, anxiety and anger*. London: Pimlico.

Boyle, M. (1990). *Schizophrenia: A scientific delusion?* London: Routledge.

Boys, J. (2007). *Tackling stress in rural communities*. Accessed 14 April 2013 at: http://archive.defra.gov.uk/rural/documents/living/tackling-stress0106.pdf

Bracken, P. and Thomas, P. (2006). *Postpsychiatry: Mental health in a postmodern world*. Oxford: Oxford University Press.

Bramwell, R., Harrington, F. and Harris, J. (2000). Deafness – disability or linguistic minority? *British Journal of Midwifery*, 8(4), 222–4.

Bressington, D.T., Wells, H. and Graham, M. (2011). A concept mapping exploration of social workers' and mental health nurses' understanding of the role of the approved mental health professional. *Nurse Education Today*, 31(6), 564–70.

British Association of Social Workers (1977). *Mental health crisis services – a new philosophy: Report of the evidence of the British Association of Social Workers on the consultative document 'Review of the Mental Health Act 1959' and the White Paper 'Better services for the mentally ill' (Cmnd.6233)*. Birmingham: British Association of Social Workers.

British Association of Social Workers (2005). *Memorandum from the British Association of Social Workers*. Accessed 15 April 2013 at: http://www.publications.parliament.uk/pa/jt200405/jtselect/jtment/79/50126p02.htm

British Medical Association (2005). *Healthcare in a rural setting*. London: British Medical Association.

Britton, F., Campbell, J., Hamilton, B., Hughes, P., Manktelow, R. and Wilson, G. (1999). *A study of approved social work in Northern Ireland*. Belfast: DHSS (NI).

Bronfenbrenner, U. (1979). *The ecology of human development*. Cambridge MA: Harvard University Press.

Brookfield, S. (1987). *Developing critical thinkers: Challenging adults to explore alternative ways of thinking and acting*. San Fransisco: Jossey-Bass.

Brophy, L. and Savy, P. (2011). Broadening the evidence base of mental health policy and practice. *Health Sociology Review*, 20(2), 229–35.

Brown, R. (2002). The changing role of the approved social worker. *Journal of Mental Health Law*, 392–399.

Brown, W. and Kandirikirira, N. (2007). *Recovering mental health in Scotland: Report on narrative investigation of mental health recovery*. Glasgow: Scottish Recovery Network.

Burman, E (2004). From difference to intersectionality: Challenges and resources. *European Journal of Psychotherapy, Counselling, and Health*, 6, 293–308.

Burns, T. and Dawson, J. (2009). Community treatment orders: How ethical without experimental evidence. *Psychological Medicine*, 1583–6.

Burns, T., Rugkåsa, J., Molodynski, A., Dawson, J., Yeeles, K., Vazquez-Montes, M., Voysey, M., Sinclair, J. and Priebe, S. (2013). Community treatment orders for patients with psychosis (OCTET): A randomised controlled trial. *The Lancet*, 25 March.

Burrows, E. (1998). 'Alienists' wives: The unusual case of Mrs John Conolly. *History of Psychiatry*, 9(35), 291–301.

Bussolari, C. and Goodell, J. (2009). Chaos theory as a model for life transitions counselling: Nonlinear dynamics and life's changes. *Journal of Counselling and Development*, 87(1), 98–107.

Butler, G. (1998). Clinical formulation, in A. Bellack and M. Hersen (eds), *Comprehensive Clinical Psychology, Vol. 6*. Oxford: Pergamon.

Butler, J. (1993). *Excitable speech: A politics of the performative*. London: Routledge.

Butz, M. (1995). Chaos theory, philosophically old, scientifically new. *Counseling and Values*, 39(2), 1–16.

Butz, M. (1997). *Chaos and cmplexity: Implications for psychological theory and practice*. Washington, DC: Taylor and Francis.

Cairney, P. (2009). The 'British policy style' and mental health: Beyond the headlines. *Journal of Social Policy*, 38(4), 671–88.

Calton, T. and Spandler, H. (2009). Minimal-medication approaches to treating schizophrenia. *Advances in Psychiatric Treatment*, 15(3), 209–17.

Campbell, J. (2010). Deciding to detain: The use of Compulsory Mental Health Law by UK social workers. *British Journal of Social Work*, 1(1), 328–34.

Campbell, J. and Davidson, G. (2012). *Post-qualifying mental health: Social work practice*. London: Sage.

Campbell, J. and McCrystal, P. (2005). Mental health social work and the troubles in Northern Ireland – a study of practitioner experiences. *Journal of Social Work*, 5(2), 173–90.

Campbell, J., Wilson, G., Britton, F., Hamilton, B., Hughes, P. and Manktelow, R. (2001). The management and supervision of Approved Social Workers: Aspects of law, policy and practice. *Journal of Social Welfare and Family Law*, 23(2), 155–72.

Campinha-Bacote, J. (2011). Coming to know cultural competence: An evolutionary process. *International Journal for Human Caring*, 15(3), 42–8.

Care Quality Commission (2009). *Patient survey report 2009: Mental health acute inpatient mental health services*. London: Care Quality Commission.

Care Quality Commission (2010). *Monitoring the use of the Mental Health Act in 2009/10: The Care Quality Commission's first report on the exercise of its functions in keeping under review the operation of the Mental Health Act 1983*. London: Care Quality Commission.

Care Quality Commission (2012). *Monitoring the Mental Health Act in 2011/12*. London: Care Quality Commission.

Care Services Improvement Partnership (2007). *A positive outlook: A good practice toolkit to improve discharge from in-patient mental health care*. York: Care Services Improvement Partnership.

Castel, F., Castel, R. and Lovell. A. (1979). The psychiatrization of difference. *International Journal of Law and Psychiatry*, 2(2), 235–47.

Churchill, R., Owen, G., Hotopf, M. and Sigh, S. (2007). *International experiences of using community treatment*. London: Department of Health and Institute of Psychiatry, King's College London.

Clare, A. (1999). Psychiatry's future: Psychological medicine or biological psychiatry? *Journal of Mental Health*, 8(2), 109–11.

Cooper, D. (1978). *The language of madness*. London: Allen Lane.

Coppock, V. and Dunn, B. (2010). *Understanding social work practice in mental health*. London: Sage.

Coward, M. (2011). Does the use of reflective models restrict critical thinking and therefore learning in nurse education? What have we done?' *Nurse Education Today*, 883–6.

Crawford, K. and Mathews, I. (2011). *Evidence-based practice in social work*. Exeter: Learning Matters.

Crenshaw, K (1989). Demarginalizing the intersection of race and sex: A Black feminist critique of antidiscrimination doctrine, feminist theory and antiracist politics. *University of Chicago Legal Forum*, 139, 139–67.

Cresswell, M. (2008). Szasz and his interlocutors: Reconsidering Thomas Szasz's 'myth of mental illness' thesis. *Journal for the Theory of Social Behaviour*, 38(1), 23–44.

Cresswell, M. and Spandler, H. (2009). Psychopolitics: Peter Sedgwick's legacy for mental health movements. *Social Theory and Health*, 7(2), 129–47.

Crowden, A. (2004). The debate continues: Unique ethics for psychiatry. *Australian and New Zealand Journal of Psychiatry*, 38, 111–14.

Cummins, I. (2010). Distant voices, still lives: Reflections on the impact of media reporting on the cases of Christopher Clunis and Ben Silcock. *Ethnicity and Inequalities in Health and Social Care*, 3(4), 18–29.

Dadlani, M., Overtree, C and Perry-Jenkins, M. (2012). Culture at the center: A reformulation of diagnostic assessment. *Professional Psychology: Research and Practice*, 43(3), 175–182.

Dale, E. (2010). Is supervised community treatment ethically justifiable? *Journal of Medical Ethics*, 36, 271–4.

Darwin, C. (1976). *The origin of species*. New York: Random House.

Davidson, L. (2009). Nearest Relative consultation and the avoidant Approved Mental Health Professional. *Journal of Mental Health Law*, Spring, 70–80.

Davidson, G. and Campbell, J. (2010). An audit of assessment and reporting by ASWs. *British Journal of Social Work*, 40(5), 1609–27.

Davidson, G., McCallion, M. and Potter, M. (2003). *Connecting mental health and human rights*. Belfast: Northern Ireland Human Rights Commission.

Davidson, L., O'Connell, M., Tondora, J. Styron, T. and Kangas, K. (2006). The top ten concerns about recovery encountered in mental health system transformation. *Psychiatric Services*, 57, 640–5.

Davis, R. and Gordon, J. (eds) (2011). *Social work and the law in Scotland*. Basingstoke: Palgrave Macmillan

Daw, R. (2009). *Mental Health Act needs more monitoring as use of compulsory powers rises, says Alliance*. Accessed 5 April 2013 at: http://www.mentalhealthalliance.org.uk/news/practanniversary.html

Dawson, A., Ferguson, I., Mackay, K., Maxwell, M. (2009). *An assessment of the operation of the Named Person role and its interaction with other forms of patient representation*. Edinburgh: Scottish Executive Social Research.

Dawson, J. (2005). *Community treatment orders: International comparisons*. Dunedin, New Zealand: University of Otago.

Dawson, J. (2007). Concepts of liberty in mental health law. Inaugural Professorial Lecture, Faculty of Law. Dunedin, New Zealand: University of Otago.

Denmark, J. (1994). *Deafness and mental health*. London: Kingsley.

Department of Constitutional Affairs (1997). *Who decides?* Cm 3803. London: The Stationery Office.

Department of Constitutional Affairs (1999). *Making decisions*, Cm 4465. London: The Stationery Office.

Department of Constitutional Affairs (2004). *Government response to the Draft Mental Incapacity Bill Committee on the Draft Mental Incapacity Bill Committee Report*. London: Department of Constitutional Affairs.

Department of Constitutional Affairs (2007). *Mental Capacity Act 2005: Code of Practice*. London: The Stationery Office.

Department for Environment, Food and Rural Affairs (2005). *Rural and urban definitions*. Accessed 28 March 2012 at: http://webarchive.nationalarchives.gov.uk/20110215111010/http://archive.defra.gov.uk/evidence/statistics/rural/rural-definition.htm

Department for Environment, Food and Rural Affairs (2012). *Countryside issues*. Accessed 28 March 2012 at: http://www.defra.gov.uk/rural/countryside

Department of Health (1994). *Introduction of supervision registers for mentally ill people from 1 April 1994*, HSG (94). 5. London: Department of Health.

Department of Health (1995). *Disability Discrimination Act 1983*. London: The Stationary Office.

Department of Health (1998a). *Modernising social services: Promoting independence, improving protection, raising standards*. London: The Stationery Office.

Department of Health (1998b). *Modernising social services: Safe, sound and supportive*. London: The Stationery Office.

Department of Health (1999a). *The report of the expert committee: Review of the Mental Health Act 1983*, Cm 4480. London: Department of Health.

Department of Health (1999b). *Reform of the Mental Health Act 1983*. London: Department of Health.

Department of Health (1999c). *National service framework for mental health*. London: The Stationery Office.

Department of Health (2000a). *Managing dangerous people with severe and dangerous personality disorder*. London: Department of Health.

Department of Health (2000b). *Shaping the new Mental Health Act: Key messages from the Department of Health research programme*. London: Department of Health.

Department of Health (2000c). *The National Health service plan: A plan for investment, a plan for reform*. London: HM Stationery Office.

Department of Health (2002). *Draft Mental Health Bill*, Cm 5538. London: Department of Health.

Department Of Health (2004a). *The ten essential shared capabilities: A framework for the whole of the mental health workforce*. London: HM Stationery Office.

Department of Health (2004b). *Draft Mental Health Bill, Cm 6305-1*. London: Department of Health.

Department of Health (2005a). *The Government response to the report of the Joint Committee on the draft Mental Health Bill*, Cm 6624. London: Department of Health.

Department of Health (2005b). *Select Committee on Health 4th Report*. London: The Stationery Office.

Department of Health (2006). *Next steps for the Mental Health Bill*, Press Release. London: Department of Health.

Department of Health (2007a). *New ways of working for everyone – A best practice implementation guide*. London: Department of Health.

Department of Health (2007b). *Mental health: New ways of working for everyone: Developing and sustaining a capable flexible workforce*. Department of Health Progress Report. London: Stationery Office.

Department of Health (2008). *Code of practice: Mental Health Act 1983*. London: The Stationery Office.

Department of Health (2009). *Putting people first: A shared vision and commitment to the transformation of adult social care*. London: The Stationery Office.

Department of Health/National Mental Health Development Unit (2009). *Delivering race equality in mental health care*. London: Department of Health.

Department of Health (2010). *The Equality Act*. London: The Stationary Office.

Department of Health and Home Office (1999). *Managing dangerous people with severe personality disorder*. London: Department of Health and Home Office.

Department of Health and Home Office (2000). *Reforming the Mental Health Act Part I: The new legal framework and Part II: High-risk patients*, Cm 5016. London: Department of Health and Home Office.

Department of Health and Social Security (1976). *Consultative document, A review of the Mental Health Act 1959*. London: HM Stationery Office.

Department of Health and Social Security (1978). *Review of the Mental Health Act 1959* (the White Paper). London: HM Stationery Office.

Department of Health and Social Services (Northern Ireland) (1992). *Mental Health (Northern Ireland). Order 1986 Code of practice.* Belfast: HM Stationery Office.

Department of Health, Social Services and Public Safety (Northern Ireland). (2010). *Mental Capacity (Health, Welfare and Finance) Bill. Equality impact assessment.* Belfast: Department of Health, Social Services and Public Safety.

Department of Health and Social Services and Public Safety (NI). (2007). *The Bamford review of mental health and learning disability: A comprehensive legislative framework, consultation report.* Belfast: Department of Health and Social Services and Public Safety.

Department of Health and the Welsh Office (1993). *Code of practice: Mental Health Act 1983.* London: The Stationery Office.

Department of Health and the Welsh Office (1999). Code of practice to the Mental Health Act 1983 (revised 1999). London: The Stationary Office.

Dewey, J. (1938). *Experience and education.* New York: Macmillan.

Dewey, J. (1958). *Art as experience.* New York: Capricorn Books.

Dobson, F. (1998). *Frank Dobson outlines third way for mental health.* Press Release. London: Department of Health.

Dodd, S. and Epstein, I. (2012). *Practice-based research in social work: A guide for reluctant researchers.* London: Routledge.

Double, D. (1990). What would Adolf Meyer have thought about the neo-Kraepelinian approach? *Psychiatric Bulletin,* 14, 472–4.

Double, D. (2006). *Critical psychiatry: The limits of madness.* Basingstoke: Palgrave.

Douglas, M. (1994). *Risk and blame: Essays in cultural theory.* London: Routledge.

Dreyfus, H. and Dreyfus, S. (1986). *Mind over machine: The power of human intuition and expertise in the era of the computer.* New York: Free Press.

Du Feu, M. (2010). Mental health and deafness. *Irish Psychiatrist,* 11(1), 35.

Du Feu, M. and Ferguson, K. (2003). Sensory impairment and mental health. *The British Journal of Psychiatry,* 9, 95–103.

Duggan, M. and Foster, J. (2002). *Modernising the social model in mental health: A discussion paper.* London: Social Perspectives Network.

Dunn, J. and Fahey, T.A. (1990). Police admissions to a psychiatric hospital: Demographic and clinical differences between ethnic groups. *British Journal of Psychiatry,* 156, 379–83.

Dwyer, S. (2011). Walking the tightrope of a mental health assessment. *Journal of Social Work Practice,* 26(3), 341–53.

Edmondson, R. and Pearce, J. (2007). The practice of health care: Wisdom as a model. *Medical Health Care and Philosophy,* 10(3), 233–44.

Ellis, C. and Flaherty, M.C. (1992). *Investigating subjectivity: Research on lived experience.* California: Sage.

Emanuel, L. (2000). Ethics and the structures of healthcare. *Cambridge Quarterly of Healthcare Ethics,* 9, 151–68.

Emerson, R.M. and Pollner, M. (1976). Dirty work designations: Their features and consequences in a psychiatric setting. *Social Problems,* 23(3), 243–54.

Engel, G.L. (1980). The clinical application of the biopsychosocial model. *American Journal of Psychiatry,* 137, 535–44.

Eraut, M. (1994). *Developing professional knowledge and competence*. London: Routledge Farmer.

Erikson, E.H (1968). *Identity: Youth and crisis*. New York, Norton.

Erikson, E. (1974). *Dimensions of a new identity*. New York: Norton.

Erikson, E. and Newton, H. (1973). *In search of common ground*. New York: Norton.

Evans, S., Huxley, P., Gately, C., Webber, M., Mears, A., Pajak, S., Medina, J., Kendall, T. and Katona, C. (2006). Mental health burnout and job satisfaction among mental health social workers in England and Wales. *The British Journal of Psychiatry*, 188(1), 75–80.

Ferguson, H. (2010). Walks, home visits and atmospheres: Risks and the everyday practices and mobilities of social work and child protection. *British Journal of Social Work*, 24, 121–38.

Fincham, B., Langer, S., Scourfield, J. and Shiner, M. (2011). *Understanding suicide: A sociological autopsy*. Basingstoke: Palgrave Macmillan.

Fisher, M., Newton, C. and Sainsbury, E. (1984). *Mental health social work observed*. London: Allen and Unwin.

Flory, N.A. and Lang, E.V. (2011). Distress in the radiology waiting room. *Radiology*, 260, 166–273.

Fook, J. and Napier, J. (2000). From dilemma to breakthrough: Retheorising social work, in L.F. Napier (ed). *Breakthroughs in practice: Social workers theorise critical moments*. London: Whiting and Birch.

Fook, J.A. and Gardner, F. (2007). *Practising critical reflection: A resource handbook*. Maidenhead: Open University Press.

Ford, G.G. (2013). *Ethical reasoning in the mental health professions*. Florida: CRC Press LLC.

Foucault, M. (1977). *Discipline and punish: The birth of the prison*. New York: Vintage Books.

Francis, R. (2006). *Report of the independent inquiry into the care and treatment of Michael Stone*. Kent County Council and Kent Probation Area: South East Coast Strategic Health Authority.

Freeman, J.K. (2005). A practical guide to communicating with residents with deafness. *Nursing Homes Long Term Management*, 54(4), 56–8.

Frese, F.J. and Davis, W.W. (1997). The consumer-survivor movement, recovery and consumer professionals. *Professional psychology: Research and practice*, 28, 243–5.

Fulford, K.C., Caroll, H. and Peile, E. (2011). Values-based practice: Linking science with people. *Journal of Contemporary Psychotherapy*, 41, 145–56.

Fulop, N.J. (1995). Involuntary outpatient civil commitment: What can Britain learn from the US? *International Journal of Law & Psychiatry*, 18, 291–303.

Furminger, E. and Webber, M. (2009). The effect of crisis resolution and home treatment on assessments under the Mental Health Act 1983: An increased workload for Approved Social Workers? *British Journal of Social Work*, 39, 901–17.

Gambrill, E.D. (2006). *Social work a critical thinkers guide*. Oxford: Open University Press.

Geller, J., Fisher, W., Grudzinskas, A., Clayfield, J. and Lawlor, T. (2006). Involuntary outpatient treatment as 'deinstitutionalized coercion': The net-widening concerns. *International Journal of Law and Psychiatry*, 29(6), 551–62.

Geller, J., Fisher, W. and McDermeit, M. (1995). A national survey of mobile crisis services and their evaluation. *Psychiatric Services*, 4, 893–7.

General Social Care Council (2002). *The national occupational standards for social work.* Leeds: TOPSS.

General Social Care Council (2010). *Specialist standards and requirements for post-qualifying social work education and training: Social work in mental health services.* London: General Social Care Council.

General Social Care Council (2012). *GSCC targeted inspections of Approved Mental Health Professional (AMHP) courses in England (2011–2012).* Rugby: General Social Care Council.

Gibbs, G. (1988). *Learning by doing: A guide to teaching and learning methods.* Oxford: Oxford Further Education Unit, Oxford Polytechnic.

Gilbert, P. (2010). *The value of everything: Social work and its importance in mental health,* 2nd edn. Lyme Regis: Russell House.

Gillard, S., Adams, K., Edwards, C., Lucock, M., Miller, S., Simons, L., Turner, K., White, R., White, S., and the Self Care in Mental Health Research Team (2012). Informing the development of services supporting self-care for severe, long term mental health conditions: A mixed method study of community based mental health initiatives in England. *BMC Health Services Research*, 12, 189.

Gledhill, K. (2007). Community treatment orders. *Journal of Mental Health*, 16, 149–69.

Glover, G., Arts, G. and Suresh-Babu, K. (2006). Crisis resolution/home treatment teams and psychiatric admission rates in England. *British Journal of Psychiatry*, 189, 441–5.

Goldie, N. (1977). The division of labour amongst mental health professionals – a negotiated or imposed order?, in M. Stacey and M. Reid (eds), *Health and the division of labour.* London: Croom Helm.

Gordon, J. (2004). *A cross-comparison of the Adults with Incapacity (Scotland). Act 2000 and the Mental Health (Care and Treatment). (Scotland). Act 2003.* Edinburgh: The Scottish Executive.

Gostin, L. (1975). *A human condition Volume I: The Mental Health Act from 1959 to 1975: observations, analysis and proposals for reform.* London: MIND.

Gostin, L. (1986). *Institutions observed.* London: Kings Fund.

Gould, M, (2011). Mental health patients complain of 'zombification'. Excessive use of forced detention and coerced treatment by the NHS means patients have little control over their treatment. *The Guardian*, 15 March.

Gould, N. (2006). An inclusive approach to knowledge for mental health social work practice and policy. *British Journal of Social Work*, 36, 109–25.

Graham, J. and Martin, M. (2001). *Ballantynes' deafness.* London: Whurr Publishers.

Grant, P. (2001). The power of uncertainty: Reflections of pre-service literacy tutors. *Reflective Practice*, 2(2), 238–48.

Gregor, C. (1999). *An overlooked stakeholder? The views of the Nearest Relative on the Mental Health Act assessment.* Anglia Polytechnic University and Suffolk Social Services.

Gregor, C. (2010). Unconscious aspects of statutory mental health work: Emotional labour and the Approved Mental Health Professional. *Journal of Social Work Practice*, 24, 429–43.

Gregory, S. and Hartley, G.M. (1991). *Constructing deafness*. Milton Keynes: Open University Press.

Griffiths, R. (1988). *Community care: Agenda for action*. London: HMSO.

Guze, S. (1989). Biological psychiatry: Is there any other kind? *Psychological Medicine*, 19, 315–23.

Habermas, J. (1974). *Theory and practice*. London: Heinemann.

Haggerty, L. and Grace, P. (2008). Clinical wisdom: The essential foundation of 'good' nursing care. *Journal of Professional Nursing*, 24(4), 235–40.

Hargie, O. and Dickson, D. (2004). *Skilled interpersonal communication*, 4th edn. London: Routledge.

Hargreaves, R. (2000). 'A mere transporter' – the legal role of the Approved Social Worker. *Journal of Mental Health Law*, November, 135–46.

Hargreaves, R. (2007). The Mental Health Bill 2006 – a social work perspective. *Journal of Mental Health Law*, 85, 84–96.

Harper, D. and Moss, D. (2003). A different kind of chemistry? Rethinking formulation. *Clinical Psychology*, 25, 6–10.

Harper, D. and Spellman, D. (2006). Social constructionist formulation: Telling a different story, in L. Johnstone and R. Dallos (eds), *Formulation in psychology and psychotherapy*. London: Routledge.

Harriss, L. and Hawton, K. (2011). Deliberate self-harm in rural and urban regions: A comparative study of prevalence and patient characteristics. *Social Science and Medicine*, 73(2), 274–81.

Harteloh, P.P. (2003). Quality systems in health care: A sociotechnical approach. *Health Policy*, 64, 391–8.

Hatfield, B. (2008). Powers to detain under mental health legislation in England and the role of the approved social worker: An analysis of patterns and trends under the 1983 Mental Health Act in six local authorities. *British Journal of Social Work*, 38(8), 1553–71.

Hatfield, B. and Antcliffe, V. (2001). Detention under the Mental Health Act: Balancing rights, risks and needs for services. *Journal of Social Welfare and Family Law*, 23(2), 135–53.

Hatfield, B. and Robinshaw, P. (1994). The use of compulsory powers by approved social workers in five local authorities: Some trends. *Journal of Mental Health*, 3(3), 339.

Hatfield, B., Huxley, P. and Mohamad, H. (1997). Social factors and compulsory detention of psychiatric patients in the UK. *International Journal of Law and Psychiatry*, 20, 389–97.

Hatfield, B, Mohamad, H. and Huxley, P. (1992). The 1983 Mental Health Act in five local authorities: A study of the practice of approved social workers. *International Journal of Social Psychiatry*, 38, 189–207.

Haynes, R. (1990). After 1983: Approved social workers' perception of their changing role in emergency psychiatric assessments. *Practice: Social Work in Action*, 4(3), 184.

Health and Care Professions Council (2013). *Approval criteria for approved mental health professional programmes*. London: Health and Care Professions Council.

Health and Social Care Information Centre (2011). *In-patients formally detained in hospitals under the Mental Health Act, 1983 – and patients subject to supervised community treatment, Annual figures, England 2010/11*. Accessed 5 April 2013 at: https://catalogue.ic.nhs.uk/publications/mental-health/legislation/inp-det-m-h-a-1983-sup-com-eng-10-11/inp-det-m-h-a-1983-sup-com-eng-10-11-rep.pdf

Heffernan, M. (2011). *Wilful blindness*. London: Simon and Schuster.

Henderson, A. (2001). Emotional labour and nursing: An under-appreciated aspect of caring work. *Nursing Inquiry*, 8(2), 130–8.

Henderson, D.K. and Gillespie, R.D. (1927). *A textbook of psychiatry*. Oxford: Oxford University Press.

Herman, J. (1992). *Trauma and recovery: The aftermath of violence-from domestic abuse to political terror*. New York: Basic Books.

HM Government (2011). *No health without mental health: A cross-government mental health outcomes strategy for people of all ages*. London: Department of Health.

HM Government (2012). *Caring for our future: Reforming care and support*. London: The Stationary Office.

Hewitt, D. (2009). *The Nearest Relative handbook,* 2nd edn. London: Jessica Kingsley.

Hewitt, D. (2010). The nearest relative: Losing the right to concur. *Journal of Adult Protection*, 12(3), 35–9.

Higgins, P. (1980). *Outsiders in a hearing world*. London: Sage.

Hoare, C. (2013). Three missing dimensions in contemporary studies of identity: The unconscious, negative attributes, and society. *Journal of Theoretical and Philosophical Psychology*, 33(1), 56–67.

Hochschild, A. R. (1983). *The managed heart: Commercialization of human feeling*. Berkley and Los Angeles: University of California Press.

Hoff, P. (1995). Kraepelin, in G. Berrios and R. Porter (eds), *A history of clinical psychiatry*. London: Athlone Press.

Hoggett, B. (1996). *Mental health law,* 4th edn. London: Sweet and Maxwell.

Horne, R., Weinman, J., Barber, N., Elliot, R. and Moran, M. (2005). *Concordance, adherence and compliance in medicine taking, Report for the National Co-ordinating Centre for NHS Service Delivery and Organisational R and D*. London: NCCSDO.

Hoult, J., Reynolds, I., Charbonneau-Powis, M., Weekes, P. and Briggs, J. (1983). Psychiatric hospital versus community treatment: The results of a randomised trial. *The Australian and New Zealand Journal of Psychiatry*, 17(2), 160–7.

Hudson, J. and Webber, M. (2012). *The national AMHP survey 2012: Final report*. London: Kings Fund.

Hunter, M. (2009). We're sharing values now. *Community Care*, 6 August.

Hurley, J. and Linsley, P. (2006). Proposed changes to the Mental Health Act of England and Wales: Research indicating future educational and training needs for mental health nurses. *Journal of Psychiatric and Mental Health Nursing*, 13, 48–54.

Hurley, J. and Linsley, P. (2007). Expanding roles within mental health legislation; An opportunity for professional growth or a missed opportunity? *Journal of Psychiatric and Mental Health Nursing*, 14(6), 535–41.

Huxley, P. and Kerfoot, M. (1994). A survey of approved social work in England and Wales. *British Journal of Social Work*, 24(3), 311–24.

Huxley, P., Evans, S., Webber, M. and Gately, C. (2005). Staff shortages in the mental health workforce: The case of the disappearing approved social worker. *Health and Social Care in the Community*, 13(6), 504–13.

Jackson, C. (2009). Approved mental health practitioner: taking on the challenge of the role. *Mental Health Practice*, 12(8), 22–5.

Jacobs, R. and Barrenho, E. (2011). Impact of crisis resolution and home treatment teams on psychiatric admissions in England. *The British Journal of Psychiatry*, 199, 71–6.

James, N. (1992). Care = organisation + physical labour + emotional labour. *Sociology of Health and Illness*, 14(4), 488–509.

Jenner, F.A., Monterio, A., Zagalo-Cardoso, J.A. and Cunha-Oliveria, J.A. (1993). *Schizophrenia: A disease or some ways of being human?* Sheffield: Academic Press.

Johansson, I.M., and Lundman, B. (2002). Patients' experience of involuntary psychiatric care: Good opportunities and great losses. *Journal of Psychiatric and Mental Health Nursing*, 9, 639–47.

Johns, C. (2002). *Guided reflection*. Oxford: Blackwell Science.

Johnson, S. (2013). Can we reverse the rising tide of compulsory admissions? *The Lancet* [Early Online Publication, 26 March].

Johnson, S., Nolan, F., Hoult, J., White, I., Bebbington, P., Sandor, A., et al. (2005). Outcomes of crises before and after introduction of a crisis resolution team. *The British Journal of Psychiatry*, 187, 68–75.

Johnstone, L. (2000). *Users and abusers of psychiatry: A critical look at psychiatric practice*, 2nd edn. London: Routledge.

Johnstone, L. and Dallos, R. (2006). *Formulation in psychology and psychotherapy: Making sense of people's problems*. London: Routledge.

Joint Committee on the Draft Mental Health Bill (2005a). *Draft Mental Health Bill: Session 2004–05*, HL Paper 79-I HC 95-I. London: The Stationery Office.

Joint Committee on the Draft Mental Health Bill (2005b). *Mental Health Bill needs radical overhaul*, Press release. London: Parliament.

Joint Committee on the Draft Mental Health Bill (2005c). *Oral and written evidence*. London: The Stationery Office.

Joint Parliamentary Committee on the Draft Mental Incapacity Bill (2003). Draft Mental Incapacity Bill: 1, HL 189-I, HC 1083-I. London: The Stationery Office.

Jones, I., Ahmed, N., Catty, J., McLaren, S., Rose, D., Wykes, T. and Burns, T. for the Echo Group (2009). Illness careers and continuity of care in mental health services: A qualitative study of service users and carers. *Social Science and Medicine*, 69, 632–9.

Jones, K. (1955). *Lunacy, law, and conscience, 1744–1845: The social history of the care of the insane*. London: Routledge and Paul.

Jones, K. (1972). *A history of the mental health services*. London: Routledge and Kegan Paul.

Jones, R. (2011). *Mental health act manual*, 14th edn. London: Sweet and Maxwell.

Jones, S. (1998). Mental health case note: Identification of nearest relative. *Legal Action*, January.

Jones, S. (2009). *Critical learning for social work students*. Exeter: Learning Matters.

Joy, C., Adams, C. and Rice, K. (2006). Crisis intervention for people with severe mental illnesses. *Cochrane Database of Systematic Reviews*, 4. Art. No. CD001087.

Jutel, A. (2009). Sociology of diagnosis: A preliminary review. *Sociology Health Illness*, 31, 278–99.

Kane, E. (2002). The policy perspective: What evidence is influential?, in S. Priebe and M. Slade (eds), *Evidence in mental health care*. London: Routledge.

Keenan, T. (2010). *The support and protection of adults with mental disorder at risk in Scotland*. Scotland: lulu.com.

Keenan, T. (2011). *Crossing the acts: The support and protection of adults at risk with mental disorder across the Scottish legislative frameworks*. Edinburgh: BASW/ Venture Press.

Keeping, C. (2008). Emotional engagement in social work: Best practice and relationships in mental health, in K. Jones, B. Cooper and H. Ferguson (eds), *Best practice in social work: Critical perspectives*. Basingstoke: Palgrave Macmillan.

Kelly, G.A. (1955). *The psychology of personal constructs. Vols 1 & 2*. New York: W.W. Norton.

Kelly, J. and Horder, W. (2001). The how and the why: Competences and holistic practice. *Social Work Education*, 1(6), 689–99.

Kendall, R. and Jabelensky, A. (2003). Distinguishing between the validity and utility of psychiatric diagnoses. *American Journal of Psychiatry*, 160(1), 4–12.

Kent County Council (2005). *Memorandum from Kent County Council (DMH 217)*. Accessed 15 April 2013 at: http://www.publications.parliament.uk/pa/jt200405/jtselect/jtment/79/50112p09.htm

Keown, P., Weich, S., Bhui, K. and Scott, J. (2011). Association between provision of mental illness beds and rate of involuntary admissions in the NHS in England 1988–2008: Ecological study. *British Medical Journal*, doi: 343:d3736.

Killeen, J. and Myers, F. (2004). *The Adults with Incapacity (Scotland). Act 2000: Learning from experience*. Edinburgh: Scottish Executive.

Kingdon, D. and Young, A.H. (2007). Research into putative biological mechanisms of mental disorders has been of no value to clinical psychiatry. *British Journal of Psychiatry*, 191, 285–90.

Kinney, M. (2009). Being assessed under the 1983 Mental Health Act: Can it ever be ethical? *Ethics and Social Welfare*, 3, 329–36.

Kinsella, E. (2006). Constructivist underpinnings in Schön's theory of reflective practice. *Reflective Practice*, 7(3), 277–86.

Kinsella, E. (2010). The art of reflective practice in health and social care: Reflections on the legacy of Donald Schön. *Reflective Practice*, 11(4), 565–75.

Kisely, S. and Campbell, L.A. (2007). Does compulsory or supervised community treatment reduce 'revolving door' care? Legislation is inconsistent with recent evidence. *The British Journal of Psychiatry*, 191, 373–4.

Kisely, S.R., Campbell, L.A. and Preston, N.J. (2005). Compulsory community and involuntary outpatient treatment for people with severe mental disorders. *Cochrane Database Syst Rev 3* [Online], CD004408.

Knight, P.A. and Swanwick, R.A. (1999). *The care and education of a deaf child: A book for parents*. Clevedon: Multilingual Matters Ltd.

Knight, T. (2009). *Beyond belief: Alternative ways of working with delusions, obsessions and unusual experiences*. Berlin: Peter Lehmann Publishing.

Koeske, K. and Kirk, S.A. (1995). Direct and buffering effects of internal locus of control among mental health professionals. *Journal of Social Service Research*, 20(3/4), 1–28.

Kolb, D. (1984). *Experiential learning: Experience as the source of learning and development.* New Jersey: Prentice-Hall.

Kondrat, M. (1992). Reclaiming the practical: Formal and substantive rationality in social work practice. *Social Service Review*, 237–255.

Kraepelin, E. (1883). *Compendium der Psychiatrie.* Leipzig: Abel.

Laing, J. (2012). The Mental Health Act: Exploring the role of nurses. *British Journal of Nursing*, 21(4), 234–8.

Laing, R.D. (1960). *The divided self.* Harmondsworth: Penguin.

Laing, R.D. (1967). *The politics of experience and the bird of paradise.* Harmondsworth: Penguin.

Laing, R.D. and Esterson, A. (1964). *Sanity, madness and the family.* London: Penguin.

Langan, J. (1999). Assessing risk in mental health, in P. Parsloe (ed.), *Assessing risk in social care and social work.* London: Jessica Kingsley.

Law Commission (1995). *Mental incapacity*, Law Com No 231. London: The Stationery Office.

Lawton-Smith, S., Dawson, J. and Burns, T. (2008). Community treatment orders are not a good thing. *The British Journal of Psychiatry*, 193, 96–100.

LeFrançois, B.A. and Diamond, S.L. (Forthcoming). *Diagnosis and abjection: The case of psychiatrised children.*

Levenson, H. (1981). Differentiating among internality, powerful others, and chance, in H.M. Lefcourt (ed.), *Research with the locus of control construct, Vol. 1.* New York: Academic Press.

Lister, P. and Crisp, B. (2007). Critical incident analysis: A practice learning tool for students and practitioners. *Practice*, 19(1), 47–60.

Lloyd-Evans, B., Slade, M., Jagielska, D. and Johnson, S. (2009). Residential alternatives to acute psychiatric hospital admission: Systematic review. *British Journal of Psychiatry*, 195, 109–17.

Lobley, M. (2005). Exploring the dark side: Stress in rural Britain. *Journal of the Royal Agricultural Society of England*, 166, 3–10.

Lobley, M., Johnson, G., Reed, M., Winter, M. and Little, J. (2004). *Rural stress review final report.* Exeter: University of Exeter.

Local Authority Circular (1986). *Mental Health Act 1983 – Approved Social Workers.* LAC (1986). 15.

Lolas, F. (2006). Ethics in psychiatry: A framework. *World Psychiatry*, 5, 185–7.

Lorenz, E. (1963). Deterministic non-periodic flow. *Journal of the Atmospheric Sciences*, 20, 130–40.

Loschen, E.L. (1973). Psychiatry and religion: A variable history. *Journal of Religion and Health*, 13, 137–41.

Luhrmann, T. (2000). *Of two minds: The growing disorder in American psychiatry*, New York: Knopf.

Lupton, D. (2000). *Risk.* London: Routledge.

Lyons, D. (2008). New mental health legislation in Scotland. *Advances in Psychiatric Treatment*, 14, 89–97.

MacDermott Committee (1981). *Northern Ireland review committee on mental health legislation.* Belfast: HM Stationery Office.

MacDonald, G. and Sheldon, B. (1992). Contemporary studies of the effectiveness of social work. *British Journal of Social Work*, 22, 615–43.

Mackay, K. (2009). The Scottish adult support and protection legal framework. *The Journal of Adult Protection*, 10(4), 25–36.

Mackay, K. (2012). A parting of the ways? The diverging nature of mental health social work in the light of the new Acts in Scotland, and in England and Wales. *Journal of Social Work*, 12(2), 179–93.

Mahalingam, T., Balan, S. and Haritatos, J. (2008). Engendering immigrant psychology; An intersectionality perspective. *Sex Roles*, 59, 326–36.

Maich, N., Brown, B. and Royle, J. (2000). 'Becoming' through reflection and professional portfolios: The voice of growth in nurses. *Reflective Practice*, 1(3), 309–24.

Makoe, M.Q. (2006). South African distance students' accounts of learning in sociocultural context: A habitus analysis. *Race Ethnicity and Education*, 9(4), 361–80.

Mall, R.A. (2000). The concept of intercultural philosophy. Accessed 15 April 2013 at: http://them.polylog.org/1/fmr-en.htm

Manktelow, R. (1999). The 1986 Mental Health (NI). Order and approved social work in Northern Ireland: Time for change. *Practice*, 11(1), 23–34.

Manktelow, R., Hughes, P., Britton, F., Campbell, J., Hamilton, B. and Wilson, G. (2002). The experience and practice of approved social workers in Northern Ireland. *British Journal of Social Work*, 32, 443–61.

Marschark, M. (1997). *Psychological development of deaf children*. Oxford: Oxford University Press.

Maschi, T. and Youdin, R. (eds) (2011). *Social worker as researcher: Integrating research with advocacy*. Boston: Pearson Publishing.

Matthews, S. (2011). The changing role of social workers in developing contexts for mental health professionals, in J. Seden, S. Matthews, M. McCormick and A. Morgan (eds), *Professional development in social work: Complex issues in practice*. London: Routledge.

Mazelis, R. (2006). What's in a name? *The Cutting Edge*, issue 66, 2–6.

McAdams, D., Reynolds, J., Lewis, M., Patten, A and Bowman, P (2001). When bad things turn good and good things turn bad: Sequences of redemption and contamination in life narrative and their relation to psychosocial adaptation in midlife adults and in students. *Personality and Social Psychology Bulletin*, 27, 474–85.

McBrien, B. (2007). Learning from practice – Reflections on a critical incident. *Accident and Emergency Nursing*, 15, 128–33.

McCabe, A. and Park, J. (1998). Foreword, in J. Campbell and R. Manktelow (eds), *Mental health social work in Northern Ireland: Comparative issues in policy and practice*. Farnham: Ashgate.

McCollam, A., McLean, J., Gordon, J. and Moodie, K. (2003). *Mental health officer services: Structures and supports*. Edinburgh: Scottish Executive.

McCoy, K. (1993). *Perspectives on integration*. Belfast: Department of Health and Social Services (NI). / SSI.

McCrae, N., Murray, J., Huxley, P. and Evans, S. (2004). Prospects for mental health social work: A qualitative study of attitudes of service managers and academic staff. *Journal of Mental Health*, 13(3), 305–18.

McDonald, A. and Heath, B. (2008). Developing services for people with dementia; Findings from research in a rural area. *Quality in Ageing*, 9(4), 9–18.

McGrath, M. and Oyebode, F. (2002). Qualitative analysis of recommendations in 79 inquiries after homicide committed by persons with mental illness. *Journal of Mental Law*, December, 262–82.

McKeown, M. and Stowell-Smith, M. (2001). Big, black and dangerous? The vexed question of race in forensic care, in G. Landsberg and A. Smiley (eds), *Forensic mental health: Working with offenders with mental illness*. Kingston: Civic Research Institute.

McKeown, M. and Stowell-Smith, M. (2006). The comforts of evil: Dangerous personalities in high security hospitals and the horror film, in T. Mason (ed), *Forensic psychiatry: Influences of evil*. New Jersey: Humana Press.

McKie, A., Baguley, F., Guthrie, C, Jackson, C., Kirkpatrick, P. and Laing, A. (2012). Exploring clinical wisdom in nursing education. *Nursing Ethics*, 19(2), 252–67.

McManus, J.J. and Thomson L. (2005). *Mental health and Scots law in practice*. Edinburgh: W Green.

McNicoll, A. (2013). AMHP numbers fall at two fifths of councils despite rising demand for support. *Community Care*, 26 March.

Mental Health Act Commission (1991). *The Mental Health Act Commission 4th biennial report 1989–1991*. London: The Stationery Office.

Mental Health Act Commission (1999). *Mental Health Act Commission 8th biennial report 1997–1999*. London: The Stationery Office.

Mental Health Act Commission (2008). *Risk, rights and recovery. 12th biennial report 2005–2007*. London: The Stationery Office.

Mental Health Act Commission (2009). *Coercion and consent: Monitoring the Mental Health Act 1983: 13th biennial report: 2007–2009*. London: The Stationery Office.

Mental Health Alliance (2005). *Mental Health Alliance submission to the Joint Scrutiny Committee on the Draft Mental Health Bill*. London: Mental Health Alliance.

Mental Health Alliance (2007). *The Mental Health Act 2007: The final report*. London: Mental Health Alliance.

Mental Health Alliance (2010a). *Briefing paper 1: Deprivation of liberty safeguards: An initial review of implementation*. London: Mental Health Alliance.

Mental Health Alliance (2010b). *Briefing paper 2: Supervised community treatment*. London: Mental Health Alliance.

Mental Health Alliance (2012). Nearest Relative: House of Lords Committee Stage briefing. Accessed 20 May 2012 at: http://www.mentalhealthalliance.org.uk/policy/documents/LordsCtteeStage_NearestRelative_Briefing.pdf

Mental Health Commission for Northern Ireland (2002). *Annual reports, 1993 to 2002*. Belfast: Mental Health Commission for Northern Ireland.

Mental Welfare Commission for Scotland (1999). *Annual Report 1998-9*, (Edinburgh: Mental Welfare Commission).

Mental Welfare Commission for Scotland (2010). *Individual care and treatment in adult acute psychiatric wards*. Edinburgh: Mental Welfare Commission.

Meyer, A. (1952). *The collected works of Adolf Meyer*. New York: Basic Books.

Miller, J. and McClelland, L. (2006). Social inequalities formulation: Mad, bad and dangerous to know, in L. Johnstone and R. Dallos (eds), *Formulation in psychology and psychotherapy: Making sense of people's problems.* London, New York: Routledge.

Milner, J. and O'Byrne, P. (2009). *Assessment in social work,* 3rd edn. Basingstoke: Palgrave Macmillan.

MIND (2010). About the survivor user movement. Accessed16 October 2013 at: http://www.mind.org.uk/campaigns_and_issues/report_and_resources/814_about_the_national_survivor_user_network

Minghella, E. and Benson, A. (1995). Developing reflective practice in mental health nursing through critical incident analysis. *Journal of Advanced Nursing,* 21, 205–13.

Ministry of Justice (2008). *Mental Capacity Act 2005: Deprivation of liberty safeguards.* London: The Stationery Office.

Mischon, J., Spensky, T., Lindsey, M. and Cook, S. (2000). *Report of the independent inquiry team into the care and treatment of Daniel Joseph.* London: Lambeth Southwark and Lewisham Health Authority.

Moncrieff, J. (2009). *The myth of the chemical cure: A critique of psychiatric drug treatment.* Basingstoke: Palgrave.

Moncrieff, J. and Crawford, M. (2001). British psychiatry in the 20th century: Observations from a psychiatric journal. *Social Science and Medicine,* 53(3), 349–56.

Mooney, G., Sweeney, T. and Law, A. (2006). Introduction: Social care, health and welfare in the devolved Scotland, in G. Mooney, T. Sweeney and A. Law (eds), *Social care, health and welfare in contemporary Scotland.* Paisley: Kynoch and Blayney.

Morago, P. (2010). Dissemination and implementation of evidence-based practice in the social services: A UK survey. *Journal of Evidence Based Social Work,* 7, 452–65.

Morgan, S. (2007a). *Are crisis resolution and home treatment services seeing the patients they are supposed to see?* London: National Audit Office.

Morgan, S. (2007b). Working with risk. *Mental Health Today,* 36–37.

Muijen, M., Marks, I., Connolly, J. and Audini, B. (1992). Home-based care and standard hospital care for patients with severe mental illness: A randomised controlled trial. *British Medical Journal,* 304, 749–54.

Mullen, R., Dawson, J. and Gibbs, A. (2006). Dilemmas for clinicians in use of community treatment orders. *International Journal of Law and Psychiatry,* 29, 535–50.

Munro, E. (2002). The role of theory in social work research: A further contribution to the debate. *Journal of Social Work Education,* 38(3), 461–70.

Myers, F. (1999). Social workers as mental health officers: Different hats, different roles in mental health and social work, in M. Ulas and A. Connor (eds), *Research highlights in social work.* London: Jessica Kingsley.

Nathan, J. and Webber, M. (2010). Mental health social work and the bureau-medicalisation of mental health care: Identity in a changing world. *Journal of Social Work Practice,* 24(1), 15–28.

National Audit Office (2007). *Helping people through mental health crisis: The role of crisis resolution and home treatment services.* London: The Stationery Office.

National Institute for Mental Health in England (2007). *New ways of working for everyone: A best practice implementation guide.* London: Department of Health.

National Institute for Mental Health England (2009). New roles early implementer site project: A report for the NIMHE national workforce and national legislation programmes. National Institute for Mental Health England.

Nelson-Jones, R (2006). *Theory and practice of counselling and therapy*. London: Sage.

Nelson-Jones, R. (2008). *Basic counselling skills: A helper's manual*. London: Sage.

Nevo, I. and Slonim-Nevo, V. (2011). The myth of evidence-based practice: Towards evidence-informed practice. *British Journal of Social Work*, 41, 1167–97.

Newell, R. and Gournay, K. (2011). *Mental health nursing: An evidence based approach*. 2nd edn. London: Elsevier.

Nicholson, L. (2011). *Understanding rural mental health*, Royal College of Psychiatrists. Accessed 28 March 2012 at: http://www.psychiatrycpd.co.uk/learningmodules/ruralmentalhealthpart1.aspx

Norfolk, Suffolk and Cambridgeshire Strategic Health Authority (2003). *Independent inquiry into the death of David Bennett*. Cambridge: Norfolk, Suffolk and Cambridgeshire Strategic Health Authority.

Northern Ireland Association for Mental Health (NIAMH). (2004). *Counting the cost: The economic and social costs of mental illness in Northern Ireland*. Belfast: NIAMH Publications/ Sainsbury Centre for Mental Health.

Northern Ireland Review Committee on Mental Health Legislation (1981). *Report of Northern Ireland Review Committee on Mental Health Legislation (The MacDermott Report)*. Belfast: HMSO.

Northern Ireland Social Care Council (2002). *Promoting research and evidence-based practice. From rhetoric to reality* Belfast: Northern Ireland Social Care Council.

O'Brien, A.J., McKenna, B.G. and Kydd, R.R. (2009). Compulsory community mental health treatment: Literature review. *International Journal of Nursing Studies*, 46, 1245–55.

Octet (2012). Oxford community treatment order evaluation [online]. Accessed 5 April 2013 at http://www.psych.ox.ac.uk/research/social-psychiatry-group/current-trials/octet

Ogden, J.F., Fuks, K., Gardner, M., Johnson, S., McLean, M., Martin, P. and Shah, R. (2002). Doctors expressions of uncertainty and patient confidence. *Patient Education and Counselling*, 48(2), 171–6.

O'Hare, P., Davidson, G., Maas-Lowit, M. and Campbell, J. (2013). Mental health law: A comparison of social work practice across three jurisdictions. *Journal of Mental Health Training*, 8(4).

Olsen, R.M. (1984). *Social work and mental health: A guide for the approved social worker*. London: Tavistock.

Orme, J.M., MacIntyre, G., Green Lister, P., Cavanagh, K., Crisp, B., Hussein, S., Manthorpe, J., Moriarty, J., Sharpe, E. and Stevens, M. (2009). What (a) difference a degree makes: The evaluation of the new social work degree in England. *British Journal of Social Work*, 39, 161–78.

Orme, J. and Shemmings, D. (2010). *Developing research based social work practice*. Basingstoke: Palgrave.

Padden, C. and Humphries, T. (1988). *Deaf in America — Voices from a culture*. London: Harvard University Press.

Padden, C. and Humphries, T. (2005). *Inside deaf culture*. London: Harvard University Press.

Park, W. (2012). Creative suicidal anxiety: Self-diagnosis of chaos. *Asylum*, 19(1): 24–5.

Parker, I., Georgaca, E., Harper, D., McLaughlin, T. and Stowell-Smith, M. (1995). *Deconstructing psychopathology*. London: Sage.

Parker, J. (1994). Approved social work and older people with dementia. *Elders: The Journal of Care and Practice*, 3(3), 15–27.

Parker, J. (2010). Approved social worker to approved mental health professional: Evaluating the impact of changes within education and training. *Journal of Mental Health Training, Education and Practice*, 5(1), 19–26.

Parkinson, C.A. and Thompson, P. (1998). Uncertainties, mysteries, doubts and approved social worker training. *Journal of Social Work Practice*, 12(1), 57–64.

Parr, H., Philo, C. and Burns, N. (2004). Social geographies of rural mental health: Experiencing inclusions and exclusions. *Transactions of the Institute of British Geographers*, 29, 401–19.

Parton, N. (1994). Problematics of government, (post).modernity and social work. *British Journal of Social Work*, 24, 9–32.

Patrick, H. (2006). *Mental health, incapacity and the law in Scotland*. Edinburgh: Tottel Publishing.

Payne, M (2006). *What is professional social work?* 2nd edn. Bristol: Policy Press.

Peay, J. (2003). *Decisions and dilemmas; Working with mental health law*. Oxford: Hart Publishing.

Peplau, H (1997). Peplau's theory of interpersonal relations. *Nursing Science Quarterly*, 10, 162–7.

Percy Commission (1957). *Report of the Committee on the law relating to mental illness and mental deficiency 1954–57*. London: HMSO.

Petr, C.G. (2009). *Multidimensional evidence-based practice: Synthesizing knowledge, research, and values*. London: Routledge.

Pilgrim, D. (2000). Psychiatric diagnosis: More questions than answers. *The Psychologist*, 13, 302–5.

Pilgrim, D. (2002). The bio psychosocial model in Anglo-American psychiatry: Past, present and future? *Journal of Mental Health*, 11(6), 585–94.

Pilgrim, D. (2005). *Key concepts in mental health*. London: Sage.

Pilgrim, D. (2007a). New 'mental health' legislation for England and Wales: Some aspects of consensus and conflict. *Journal of Social Policy*, 36(1), 79–95.

Pilgrim, D. (2007b). The survival of psychiatric diagnosis. *Social Science and Medicine*, 65(3), 536–44.

Pilgrim, D. (2008). Recovery and current mental health policy. *Chronic Illness*, 4(4), 295–304.

Pilgrim, D. (2009). *Key concepts in mental health*, 2nd edn. London: Sage.

Pilgrim, D. (2011). The hegemony of cognitive-behaviour therapy in modern mental health care. *Health Sociology review*, 20(2), 120–32.

Pilgrim, D. (2012a). The British welfare state and mental health problems: The continuing relevance of the work of Claus Offe. *Sociology of Health and Illness*, 34(7), 1070–84.

Pilgrim, D. (2012b). Final lessons from the Mental Health Act Commission for England and Wales: The limits of legalism-plus-safeguards. *Journal of Social Policy*, 41(1), 61–81.

Pilgrim, D. and Bentall, R. (1999). The medicalisation of misery: A critical realist analysis of the concept of depression. *Journal of Mental Health*, 8(3), 261–74.

Pilgrim, D. and Rogers, A. (2010). *Sociology of mental health and illness*. Buckinghamshire: Open University Press.

Pilgrim, D. and Tomasini, F. (2012). On being unreasonable in modern society: Are mental health problems special? *Disability and Society*, 27(5), 631–46.

Pilgrim, D. and Waldron, L. (1998). User involvement in mental health service development: How far can it go? *Journal of Mental Health*, 11(1), 95–104.

Pinker, S. (2007). *The stuff of thought*. London: Penguin.

Politi, M.C., Clark, M., Ombao, H., Dizon, D. and Elwyn, G. (2010). Communicating uncertainty can lead to less decision satisfaction: A necessary cost of involving patients in shared decision making? *Health Expectations*, 14(1), 84–91.

Porter, R. (1987). *A social history of madness: Stories of the insane*. London: Weidenfeld and Nicholson.

Porter, R. (2003). *Madness: A brief history*. Oxford: Oxford University Press.

Prior, P.M. (1992). The approved social worker – reflections on origins. *British Journal of Social Work*, 22, 105–19.

Prior, P. (1998). Mental health policy in Northern Ireland, in J. Campbell and R. Manktelow (eds), *Mental health social work in Northern Ireland: Comparative issues in policy and practice*. England: Ashgate.

Proctor, G. (2007). Disordered boundaries? A critique of 'borderline personality disorder', in H. Spandler and S. Warner (eds), *Beyond fear and control: Working with young people and self-harm*. Ross-on-Wye: PCCS Books.

Proctor, G. and Shaw, C. (2004). Borderline personality disorder under the microscope. *Asylum*, 14(3), 6–7.

Pugh, R. (2000). *Rural social work*. Lyme Regis: Russell House Publishing Ltd.

Pugh, R. (2007). Dual relationships: Personal and professional boundaries in rural social work. *British Journal of Social Work*, 37(8), 1405–23.

Pugh, R. (2009). Social work and rural mental health in rural areas. *Rural Society*, 19(4), 283–5.

Pugh, R., Scharf, T., Williams, C. and Roberts, D. (2007). *Obstacles to using and providing rural social care*. London: Social Care Institute for Excellence.

Quirk, A., Lelliott, P., Audini, B. and Buston, K., (1999). *'Performing the Act': A qualitative study of the process of mental health act assessments*. London: Department of Health.

Quirk, A., Lelliott, P., Audini, B. and Buston, K. (2000). *A qualitative study of the process of Mental Health Act assessments*. College Research Unit: Royal College of Psychiatrists.

Quirk, A., Lelliott, P., Audini, B. and Buston, K. (2003). Non clinical and extra-legal influences on decisions about compulsory admission to psychiatric hospital. *Journal of Mental Health*, 12(2), 119.

Radden, J. (2002). Notes towards a professional ethics for psychiatry. *Australian and New Zealand Journal of Psychiatry*, 36, 52–9.

Raftery, J. (1996). The decline of the asylum or poverty of concept?, in D. Tomlinson and J. Carrier (eds), *Asylum in the community*. London: Routledge.

Rapaport, J. (2003). The ghost of the Nearest Relative under the Mental Health Act 1983 – past, present and future. *Journal of Mental Health Law*, August, 51–65.

Rapaport, J. (2004). A matter of principle: The Nearest Relative under the Mental Health Act 1983 and proposals for legislative reform. *Journal of Social Welfare & Family Law*, 26(4), 377–96.

Rapaport, J. (2006). New roles in mental health: The creation of the approved mental health practitioner. *Journal of Integrated Care*, 14(5), 37–46.

Rapaport, J. (2012). *Reflections on 'A relative affair': The Nearest Relative under the Mental Health Act 1983*. London: King's College Social Care Workforce Research Unit.

Rapaport, J. and Manthorpe, J. (2008). Family matters: Developments concerning the role of the nearest relative and social worker under mental health law in England and Wales. *British Journal of Social Work*, 38, 1115–31.

Raven, C. (2009). Borderline personality disorder: Still a diagnosis of exclusion? *Mental Health Today*, 26–31.

Read, J., Haslam, N., Sayce, L. and Davies, E. (2006a). Prejudice and schizophrenia: A review of the 'mental illness is an illness like any other approach'. *Acta Psychiatrica Scandinavica*, 114(5), 303–18.

Read, J., Mosher, L. and Bentall, R. (2004). *Models of madness: Psychological, social and biological approaches to schizophrenia*. London: Routledge.

Read, J., Rudegeair, T. and Farrelly, S. (2006b). The relationship between child abuse and psychosis. Public opinion, evidence, pathways and implications, in W. Larkin and A. Morrison (eds), *Trauma and psychosis: New directions for theory and therapy*. London: Routledge.

Reeve, D. (2012). Psycho-emotional disablism in the lives of people experiencing mental distress, in J. Anderson, B. Sapey and H. Spandler (eds), *Distress and disability? Debates and alliances*. Lancaster University: Centre for Disability Research.

Regulation and Quality Improvement Authority (2012). Personal correspondence received on 3 March 2012 to confirm the relative proportion of applications by Nearest Relatives and Approved Social Workers under the Mental Health (Northern Ireland). Order 1986.

Repper, J. and Perkins, R. (2006). *Social inclusion and recovery: A model for mental health practice*. United Kingdom: Bailliere Tindall.

Rethink (2010). *NHS reform 2010: Making it work for mental health*. London: Rethink.

Ridley, J., Hunter, S. and Rosengard, A. (2010). Partners in care? Views and experiences of carers from a cohort study of the early implementation of the Mental Health (Care and Treatment). (Scotland). Act 2003. *Health and Social Care in the Community*, 18(5), 474–82.

Ridley, J., Rosengard, A., Hunter, S. and Little, S. (2009). *Experiences of the early implementation of the Mental Health (Care and Treatment). (Scotland). Act 2003: A cohort study*. Edinburgh: Scottish Government.

Ritchie, J., Dick, R. and Lingham, R. (1994). *The report of the inquiry into the care and treatment of Christopher Clunis*. London: The Stationery Office.

Roberts, C., Peay, J. and Eastman, N. (2002). Mental health professionals' attitudes towards legal compulsion in England and Wales: Report of a national survey. *International Journal of Forensic Mental Health*, 1(1), 69–80.

Robertson, M. and Walter, G. (2007). 'Overview of psychiatric ethics: Professional ethics and psychiatry. *Australasian Psychiatry*, 15, 201–6.

Robins, J. (1986). *Fools and the mad – A history of the Insane in Ireland*. Dublin: Institute of Public Administration.

Rolfe, G., Jasper, M. and Freshwater, D. (2011). *Critical reflection in practice: Generating knowledge for care*, Basingstoke: Palgrave Macmillan.

Romme, M. and Escher, A. (1989). Hearing voices. *Schizophrenia Bulletin*, 15(2), 209–16.

Romme, M. and Escher, A. (2005). Trauma and hearing voices, in W. Larkin and A. Morrison (eds), *Trauma and psychosis: New directions for theory and therapy*. London: Routledge.

Romme, M. and Morris, M. (2007). The harmful concept of schizophrenia. *Mental Health Nursing*, 27(2), 7–11.

Romme, M., Escher, A. and Dillon, J. (2008). *Recovery with voices*. London: MIND.

Rogers, A. (1993). Coercion and voluntary admissions: An examination of psychiatric patients' views. *Behavioral Sciences and the Law*, 11, 259–67.

Rogers, A. and Pilgrim, D. (2003). *Mental health and inequality*. Basingstoke: Palgrave Macmillan.

Rogers, C. (1957). The necessary and sufficient conditions of therapeutic personality change. *Journal of Consulting Psychology*, 21, 95–103.

Rogers, C.R. (1986). Reflection of feelings. *Person-Centered Review*, 1(4), 375–7.

Rogers, C.R. (2004). *On becoming a person*. London: Constable and Company.

Rolfe, G., Jasper, M. and Freshwater, D. (2011). *Critical reflection in practice: Generating knowledge for care*. Basingstoke: Palgrave Macmillan.

Rose, D. (2004). Telling different stories: User involvement in mental health research. *Research,. Policy and Practice*, 22(2), 1–8.

Rose, D., Ford, R, Lindley, P., Gawith, L. and the KCW Mental Health Monitoring Users' Group (1998). *In our experience. User focused monitoring of mental health services*. London: The Sainsbury Centre for Mental Health.

Rose, N. (1989). *Governing the soul: The shaping of the private self*. London, Routledge.

Royal College of Psychiatrists (2011). *Standards on the use of section 136 of the Mental Health Act 1983 (England & Wales)*. London: Royal College of Psychiatrists.

Royal Pharmaceutical Society of Great Britain (1997). *From compliance to concordance: Achieving shared goals in medicine taking*. London: Royal Pharmaceutical Society.

Ruch, G., Turney, D. and Ward, A. (2011). *Relationship based social work: Getting to the heart of practice*. London: Jessica Kingsley.

Rushmer, R. and Hallam, A. (2004). *Mental health law in Scotland: Mental health law research programme. Analysis of responses to consultations*. Edinburgh: Scottish Executive.

Rutter, L. and Brown, K. (2012). *Critical thinking and professional judgement for social work*, 3rd edn. Exeter: Learning Matters.

Sackett, D., Rosenburg, W., Muir Gray, J., Haynes, R. and Richardson, W. (1996). Evidence based medicine: What it is and what it isn't. *British Medical Journal*, 312, 71–2.

Sainsbury Centre for Mental Health (2006). *Crisis resolution and home treatment: A practical guide*. London: The Sainsbury Centre for Mental Health.

Sapey, B. (2013). Compounding the trauma: The coercive treatment of voice hearers. *European Journal of Social Work*, 1, 1–16.

Sapey, B. and Bullimore, P. (forthcoming). Listening to voice hearers. *British Journal of Social Work*.

Schizophrenia Commission (2012). *Abandoned illness: A report from the Schizophrenia Commission*. London: Rethink Mental Illness.

Schön, D. (1983). *The reflective practitioner*. Farnham: Ashgate.

Schön, D. (1987). *Educating the reflective practitioner: Toward a new design for teaching and learning in the professions*. London: Wiley.

Scottish Executive (2001). *The Millan Committee: New directions. Report on the review of the Mental Health (Scotland). Act 1984*. Edinburgh: Scottish Executive.

Scottish Executive (2003a). *Improving health in Scotland – The challenge*. Edinburgh: The Stationery Office.

Scottish Executive (2003b). *The framework for social work education in Scotland*. Edinburgh: The Stationery Office.

Scottish Executive (2005a). *Standards for mental health officer services provided by local authorities in partnership with health*. Edinburgh, Scottish Executive. Accessed 2 February 2012 at http://www.scotland.gov.uk/Resource/Doc/924/0011888.pdf.

Scottish Executive (2005b). *The new mental health act: A guide to named person*. Edinburgh: Scottish Executive.

Scottish Executive (2005c). *Mental Health (Care and Treatment). (Scotland). Act 1983 Code of Practice, Vol. 1*. Edinburgh: Scottish Executive.

Scottish Executive Social Research (2005). *Mental health law research: Update and agenda 2005–2007*. Edinburgh: Scottish Executive.

Scottish Government (2011). Mental Health Officers Survey, Scotland, 2010–11. Accessed 12 January 2012 at: http://www.scotland.gov.uk/Resource/Doc/352635/0118631.pdf

Scottish Law Commission (1995). *Report on incapable adults*. Edinburgh: Scottish Executive.

Scottish Office (1998). *Press release: Donald Dewar*, 3 November 1998.

Scottish Recovery Network (2007). *Routes to recovery: Collected wisdom from the SRN narrative research project*. Glasgow: Scottish Recovery Network (www.Scottishrecovery.net).

Scottish Social Services Council (2007). *Introduction to the standards and practice competences to achieve the Mental Health Officer Award (MHOA)*. Accessed 2 February 2012 at: http://ewd.sssc.uk.com/component/option,com_docman/Itemid,486/gid,930/task,doc_details

Scourfield, J., Fincham, B. and Langer, S. (2010). Sociological autopsy: An integrated method for the study of suicide in men. *Social Science and Medicine*, 74(4), 466–73.

Scull, A. (1979). *Museums of madness: The social organisation of insanity in the nineteenth century*. London: Allen Lane.

Seden, J. (2005). *Counselling skills in social work practice*. Maidenhead: Open University Press.

Sedgwick, P. (1987). *Psychopolitics*. London: Pluto Press.

Segal, J. (2004). *Melanie Klein*, 2nd edn. London: Sage.

Seng, J., Lopez, W., Sperlich, M., Hamama, L. and Meldrum, C. (2012). Marginalized identities, discrimination burden, and mental health: Empirical exploration of an interpersonal-level approach to modeling intersectionality. *Social Science and Medicine*, 75, 2437–45.

Shaw, C. and Proctor, G (2004). Women at the margins: A feminist critique of borderline personality disorder. *Asylum*, 14(3), 8–10.

Sheldon, B. (2001). The validity of evidence-based practice: A reply to Stephen Webb. *British Journal of Social Work*, 31, 801–9.

Sheldon, B. and Chilvers, R. (2000). *Evidence-based social care: A study of prospects and problems*. Lyme Regis: Russell House Publishing.

Shepherd, D. (1996). *Learning the lessons*. London: Zito Trust.

Sheppard, M. (1990). *Mental health: The role of the approved social worker*. Sheffield: JUSSR.

Sheppard, M. (1993). Theory for approved social work: The use of the compulsory admissions assessment schedule. *British Journal of Social Work*, 23, 231–57.

Shulman, L. (1999). *The skills of helping individuals, families, groups and communities*. Illinois: F.E. Peacock.

Simon, B. (1999). *A place in the world: Self and social categorisation*. Oxford: Blackwell Publishers.

Simmons, P. and Hoar, A. (2001). Section 136 use in the London borough of Haringey. *Medical Science & the Law*, 41, 342–8.

Singh, G. (2012). *Curriculum guide – Diversity and oppression*. London: The College of Social Work.

Singh, P. (2010). Encouraging intercultural communication using an action research approach. *Systemic Practice and Action Research*, 23(4), 341–52.

Smith, R. (1991). *A study of mental health officer work in Scotland*. Stirling: Social Work Research Centre.

Social Care Institute for Excellence (2003). *Using evidence from diverse research designs*. London: Social Care Institute for Excellence.

Social Care Institute for Excellence and Royal College of Psychiatrists (2007). *A common purpose: Recovery in mental health services*. London: Social Care Institute for Excellence.

Social Service Inspectorate (2001). *Detained: Social Services Inspectorate inspections of compulsory mental health admissions CI (2001). 1*. London: Department of Health.

Spandler, H. (1996). *Who's hurting who? Young people, self harm and suicide 42nd Street, Manchester*, 2nd edn. Gloucester: Handsell Publications.

Spandler, H. (2012). Setting the scene, in J. Anderson, B. Sapey and H. Spandler (eds), *Distress and disability? Debates and alliances*. Lancaster University: Centre for Disability Research.

Spandler, H. and Calton, T. (2009). Psychosis and human rights: Conflicts in mental health policy and practice. *Social Policy & Society*, 8(2), 245–56.

Spandler, H. and Warner, S. (2007). *Beyond fear and control: Working with young people and self-harm.* Ross-on-Wye: PCCS Books.

Spandler, J. (2010). Mental illness or self-interpretation? *Asylum*, 17(4), 15–16.

Spencer-Lane, T (2011). The Nearest Relative and Nominated Person: A tale of parliamentary shenanigans. *Journal of Mental Health Law*, Spring, 48–60.

Springford, D. (1997). Cochlear implants: The head on collision between medical technology and the right to be deaf. *Canadian Medical Association Journal*, 157(7), 929–32.

Stastny, P. and Lehmann, P. (2007). *Alternatives beyond psychiatry.* Shrewsbury: Peter Lehmann Publishing.

Stein, L. and Test, M. (1980). Alternatives to mental hospital: A conceptual model, treatment program and clinical evaluation. *Archives of General Psychiatry*, 37, 392–7.

Stephan, C.W. and Stephan, W.G. (2000). The measurement of racial and ethnic identity. *International Journal of Intercultural Relations*, 24, 541–52.

Stowell-Smith, M. and McKeown, M. (1999). Race, psychopathy and the self: A discourse analytic study. *British Journal of Medical Psychology*, 72(4), 459–70.

Summerskill, E. (1959). Commons sitting 26 January 1959, Hansard 5th Series (Commons), 598, 736.

Szasz, T. (1960). The myth of mental illness: Foundations of a theory of personal conduct. *American Psychologist*, 15, 113–18.

Szasz, T.S. (1961). The use of naming and the origin of the myth of mental illness. *American Psychologist*, 16, 59–65.

Szasz, T. (1991). *Ideology and insanity: Essays on the psychiatric dehumanization of man.* New York: Syracuse University Press.

Szmukler, G. and Appelbaum, P. (2001). Treatment pressures, coercion and compulsion, in G. Thornicroft and G. Szmukler (eds), *Textbook of community psychiatry.* Oxford: Oxford University Press.

Taylor, C. and White, S. (2006). Knowledge and reasoning in social work: Educating for humane judgement. *British Journal of Social Work*, 36, 937–54.

Tew, J. (2005). *Social perspectives in mental health: Developing social models to understand and work with mental distress.* London: Jessica Kingsley.

Tew, J. (2011). *Social approaches to mental distress.* Basingstoke: Palgrave Macmillan.

Tew, J. and Anderson, J. (2004). The mental health dimension in the new social work degree: Starting a debate. *Social Work Education*, 23(2), 231–40.

The College of Social Work (2012). *Professional capabilities framework.* Accessed 4 April 2013 at: http://www.tcsw.org.uk/pcf.aspx

Thoits, P. (1985). Self-labelling processes in mental illness: The role of emotional deviance. *American Journal of Sociology*, 91, 221–49.

Thomas, P. (1997). *Dialectics of schizophrenia.* London: Free Association Books.

Thompson, N. (2001). *Anti-discriminatory practice*, 3rd edn. Basingstoke: Palgrave.

Thompson, P. (1997). Approved social work and psychotherapy. *Practice: Social Work in Action*, 9(2), 35–46.

Thornicroft, G., Farrelly, S., Szmuckler, G., Birchwood, M., Waheed, W., Flach, C., et al. (2013). Clinical outcomes of joint crisis plans to reduce compulsory treatment for people with psychosis: A randomised controlled trial. *The Lancet* [Online Edition 26 March 2013].

Tierney, A. (2011). Asperger's syndrome and schizophrenia: Exploring the overlap between the two diagnoses. *Asylum*, 18(2), 22–5.

Timimi, S. (2011). *No more psychiatric labels*. Accessed 25 May 2012 at: http://www. criticalpsychiatry.net/?p=527

Timimi, S. (2013). No more psychiatric labels: Campaign to abolish psychiatric diagnostic systems such as ICD and DSM (CAPSID). *Self and Society*, 40(4), 6–14.

Tosh, J. (2011a). The medicalisation of rape? A discursive analysis of 'Paraphilic coercive disorder' and the psychiatrization of sexuality. *Psychology of Women Section Review*, 13(2), 2–12.

Tosh, J. (2011b). 'Zuck Off!' A commentary on the protest against Ken Zucker and his 'treatment' of childhood gender identity disorder. *Psychology of Women Section Review*, 13(1), 10–16.

Trevithick, P. (2012). *Social work skills: A practice handbook*, 3rd edn. Buckingham: Open University Press.

Tsang, K. (2003). Journaling from internship to practice teaching. *Reflective Practice*, 4(2), 222–40.

Turbett, C. (2009). Tensions in the delivery of social work services in rural and remote Scotland. *British Journal of Social Work*, 39(3), 506–21.

Turner, M. and Beresford, P. (2005). *User controlled research. Its meanings and potential. Report summary, Shaping our lives and the Centre for Citizen Participation*. Hampshire: INVOLVE.

Turner, T., Ness, M.N. and Imison, C.T. (1992). Mentally disordered persons found in public places. *Psychological Medicine*, 22, 765–74.

Tyreman, S. (2000). Promoting critical thinking in health care: Phronesis and criticality. *Medicine, Healthcare and Philosophy, 3*, 117–24.

Tyrer, P., Gordon, F., Nourmand, S., Lawrence, M., Curran, C., Southgate, D., et al. (2010). Controlled comparison of two crisis resolution and home treatment teams. *Psychiatrist*, 34, 50–4.

Ulas, M. and Connor, A. (eds) (1999). *Mental health and social work: Research highlights in social work*. London: Jessica Kingsley.

Ulas, M., Myers, F. and Whyte, B. (1994). *The role of the mental health officer*. Edinburgh: HM Stationery Office.

Unsworth, C. (1979). The balance of medicine, law and social work in mental health legislation, 1889–1959, in N. Parry, M. Rustin and C. Satyamurti (eds), *Social work, welfare and the state*. London: Edward Arnold.

Unsworth, C. (1987). *The politics of mental health legislation*. Oxford: Clarendon Press.

Voronka, J. (2010). Making bipolar Britney: Proliferating psychiatric diagnoses through tabloid media. *Radical Psychology*, 7(2).

Walker, J. and Crawford, K. (2010). *Social work and human development*, 3rd edn. Exeter: Learning Matters.

Walter, I., Nutley, S., Percy-Smith, J., McNeish, D. and Frost, S. (2004). *Improving the use of research in social care practice: SCIE knowledge review 07*. London: SCIE.

Walton, P. (2000a). Reforming the Mental Health Act 1983: An approved social work perspective. *Journal of Social Welfare and Family Law*, 22(4), 401–14.

Walton, P. (2000b). Psychiatric hospital care: The case of the more things change, the more they remain the same. *Journal of Mental Health*, 9(1), 77–88.

Ward, J., Cody, J., Schaal, M. and Mohammadreza, H. (2012). The empathy enigma: An empirical study of decline in empathy among undergraduate nursing students. *Journal of Professional Nursing*, 28(1), 34–40.

Warner, S. (2009). *Understanding the effects of child sexual abuse: Feminist revolutions in theory, research and practice. Women and psychology series*. London: Routledge.

Warner, S. (2010). What's going on? Getting stuck with borderline personality disorder. Accessed May 2012 at: http://www.cabl.co.uk/dr-sam-warner.php

Warner, S. and Wilkins, T. (2003). Diagnosing distress and reproducing disorder: Women, child sexual abuse and 'borderline personality disorder, in P. Reavey and S. Warner (eds), *New feminist stories of childhood sexual abuse*. London: Routledge.

Watts, D. and Morgan, G. (1994). Malignant alienation: Dangers for patients who are hard to like. *British Journal of Psychiatry*, 164, 11–15.

Webb, S. (2001). Some considerations on the validity of evidence based practice in social work. *British Journal of Social Work*, 31, 57–79.

Webber, M. (2011). *Evidence based policy and practice in mental health social work*, 2nd edn. Exeter: Learning Matters.

Welsh Assembly Government (2008). *Mental Health Act 1983 Code of Practice for Wales*. Cardiff: Welsh Assembly Government.

Welsh Assembly Government (2010). *The Mental Health (Wales) Measure*. Accessed 5 April 2013 at: http://www.legislation.gov.uk/mwa/2010/7/pdfs/mwa_20100007_en.pdf

Westermeyer, J. and Kroll, J. (1978). Violence and mental illness in peasant society: Characteristics of violent behaviours and 'folk use' of restraints. *British Journal of Psychiatry*, 133(6), 529–41.

Wiggins, O.A. and Schwartz, M.A. (1999). The crisis of present day psychiatry: The loss of the personal. *Psychiatric Times*, 2–8.

Wilson, G. and Daly, M. (2007). Shaping the future of mental health policy and legislation in Northern Ireland: The impact of service user and professional social work discourses. *British Journal of Social Work*, 37, 423–39.

Wilson, G., Hamilton, B., Britton, F., Campbell, J., Hughes, P. and Manktelow, R. (2005). Approved social worker training in Northern Ireland: Using research to examine competence-based learning and influence policy change. *Social Work Education*, 24(7), 721–36.

Wilson, G. and Kirwan, G. (2007). Mental health social work in Northern Ireland and the Republic of Ireland: Challenges and opportunities for developing practice. *European Journal of Social Work*, 10(2), 175–91.

Winnicott, D. (1964). *The child, the family and the outside world*. Harmondsworth: Penguin.

World Health Organization (2010). *International statistical classification of diseases and related health problems: 10th revision*. Geneva: World Health Organization.

Worrell. J. (2001). *The encyclopaedia of gender, Vol. 1*. San Diego: Academic Press.

Yianni, C. (2009). Aces high: My control trumps your care. *Ethics and Social Welfare*, 3, 337–43.

Zayas, L., Drake, B. and Jonson-Reid, M. (2011). Overrating or dismissing the value of evidence-based practice: Consequences for clinical practice. *Clinical Social Work Journal*, 39, 400–5.

Zigmond, T. (2002). The Royal College of Psychiatrists response to the Draft Mental Health Bill. *Journal of Mental Health Law*, 8, 376.

Zigmond, T. (2008). Changing mental health legislation in the UK. *Advances in Psychiatric Treatment*, 14, 81–3.

Zucker, K. (2006). Gender identity disorder, in D. Wolfe and E. Mash (eds), *Behavioural and emotional disorders in adolescents*. London: Guildford Press.

Index